JOURNAL FOR THE STUDY OF THE NEW TESTAMENT SUPPLEMENT SERIES
134

Executive Editor
Stanley E. Porter

Sheffield Academic Press

Striking New Images

Roman Imperial Coinage
and the New Testament World

Larry J. Kreitzer

Journal for the Study of the New Testament
Supplement Series 134

For Diana, Loretta, Doris, Beverly and Julie

Published by Sheffield Academic Press Ltd
Mansion House
19 Kingfield Road
Sheffield S11 9AS
England

Printed on acid-free paper in Great Britain
by Bookcraft Ltd
Midsomer Norton, Bath

British Library Cataloguing in Publication Data

A catalogue record for this book is available
from the British Library

ISBN 1-85075-623-6

CONTENTS

Part I
PROPAGANDA IN THE JULIO-CLAUDIAN AGE

Part II
THE WORLD OF PAUL THE APOSTLE

Part III
THE TRAVELS OF HADRIAN

PREFACE

Coin collecting has been a hobby of mine since I was a teenager. I can remember reading the story in Mk 12.14-17 concerning the question of taxation and wondering what sort of coin was brought to Jesus that occasioned such a cryptic response from him, 'Render to Caesar the things that are Caesar's, and render to God the things that are God's.' What began as an innocent curiosity has grown into an ardent passion.

I have been particularly interested in how the study of Roman numismatics can contribute to our understanding of the New Testament and its world. The various chapters presented here attempt to address this matter. Some of the material in this volume has been published in various scholarly journals over the years. Included are:

'The Diplomatic Triumph of Augustus', *Sacra Moneta* (1987), pp. 10-17.

'A Numismatic Clue to Acts 19.23-41', *JSNT* 30 (1987), pp. 59-70.

'Hadrian and the Nero Redivivus Myth', *ZNW* 79 (1988), pp. 92-115.

'The Personification of Judaea: Illustrations of the Hadrian Travel Sestertii', *ZNW* 80 (1989), pp. 278-79.

'Nero's Rome: Images of the City on Imperial Coinage', *EvQ* 61 (1989), pp. 301-309.

'Sibylline Oracles 8, the Roman Imperial Adventus Coinage of Hadrian and the Apocalypse of John', *JSP* 4 (1989), pp. 69-85.

'Apotheosis of the Roman Emperor', *BA* 53 (1990), pp. 210-217.

In each instance the study has been enlarged and adapted so as to conform to the aims of the volume as a whole. I would like to thank the editors of the various journals for allowing me to use the material in this new form.

Regent's Park College, Oxford
Michaelmas 1995

LIST OF FIGURES

Chapter 6

ABBREVIATIONS

AB	Anchor Bible
ABD	D.N. Freedman (ed.), *Anchor Bible Dictionary*
AJA	*American Journal of Archaeology*
AJP	*American Journal of Philology*
ANRW	*Aufstieg und Niedergang der römischen Welt*
BA	*Biblical Archaeologist*
BASOR	*Bulletin of the American Schools of Oriental Research*
BIES	*Bulletin of the Israel Exploration Society*
BIJS	*Bulletin of the Institute of Jewish Studies*
BJRL	*Bulletin of the John Rylands Library of the University of Manchester*
BJS	Brown Judaic Studies
BZNW	Beihefte zur *ZNW*
CAH	S.A. Cook *et al.* (eds.), *Cambridge Ancient History*
CJ	*Classical Journal*
CP	*Classical Philology*
CQ	*Classical Quarterly*
CR	*Classical Review*
CREBM	H. Mattingly *et al.* (eds.), *Coins of the Roman Empire in the British Museum*
CRR	E.A. Sydenham, *The Coinage of the Roman Republic*
EncJud	*Encyclopaedia Judaica*
EvQ	*Evangelical Quarterly*
HR	*History of Religions*
HSCP	*Harvard Studies in Classical Philology*
HTR	*Harvard Theological Review*
IBD	F.F. Bruce *et al.* (eds.), *The Illustrated Bible Dictionary*
IDB	G.A. Buttrick (ed.), *Interpreter's Dictionary of the Bible*
IEJ	*Israel Exploration Journal*
INB	*Israel Numismatic Bulletin*
INJ	*Israel Numismatic Journal*
Int	*Interpretation*
JAC	*Jahrbuch für Antike und Christentum*
JAOS	*Journal of the American Oriental Society*
JB	Jerusalem Bible
JBL	*Journal of Biblical Literature*
JBPC	J.B. Phillip's Commentaries

JHS	*Journal of Hellenistic Studies*
JJS	*Journal of Jewish Studies*
JPOS	*Journal of the Palestine Oriental Society*
JQR	*Jewish Quarterly Review*
JRH	*Journal of Religious History*
JRS	*Journal of Roman Studies*
JSJ	*Journal for the Study of Judaism*
JSNT	*Journal for the Study of the New Testament*
JSNTSup	*Journal for the Study of the New Testament*, Supplement Series
JSP	*Journal for the Study of the Pseudepigrapha*
JTS	*Journal of Theological Studies*
LCL	Loeb Classical Library
LH	*Life of Hadrian*
NEB	*New English Bible*
NC	*The Numismatic Chronicle*
NCB	New Century Bible
NICNT	New International Commentary on the New Testament
NIDNTT	C. Brown (ed.), *The New International Dictionary of New Testament Theology*
NovT	*Novum Testamentum*
NovTSup	*Novum Testamentum*, Supplements
NTS	*New Testament Studies*
OTP	J. Charlesworth (ed.), *Old Testament Pseudepigrapha*
P P	*Past and Present*
PBA	*Proceedings of the British Academy*
PEQ	*Palestine Exploration Quarterly*
PRS	*Perspectives in Religious Studies*
RIC	H. Mattingly *et al.* (eds.), *Roman Imperial Coinage*
RM	*Rassegna Monetaria*
RSV	Revised Standard Version
SAC	Studies in Antiquity and Christianity
SBLDS	SBL Dissertation Series
ST	*Studia Theologica*
TB	*Tyndale Bulletin*
TPAPA	*Transactions and Proceedings of the American Philological Association*
TDNT	G. Kittel and G. Friedrich (eds.), *Theological Dictionary of the New Testament*
TTod	*Theology Today*
VC	*Vigiliae Christianae*
WBC	Word Biblical Commentary
WUNT	Wissenschaftliche Untersuchungen zum Neuen Testament
YCS	*Yale Classical Studies*
ZNW	*Zeitschrift für die neutestamentliche Wissenschaft*
ZPE	*Zeitschrift für Papyrologie und Epigraphik*

Numismatic Abbreviations

The following abbreviations appear frequently in the descriptions of the Roman Imperial coins discussed.

AVG	AVGVSTVS. This was the Imperial title from 27 BCE onwards and was adopted by all ruling Emperors.
CAES	CAESAR. This was a common title for the reigning Emperor or his designated heirs.
CLAVD	The name CLAVDIVS.
COS	CONSUL. The consul was one of the two main magistrates for the Roman state and the Emperor frequently served in this capacity. Consulships lasted for a year and they were generally numbered; this means that the title becomes one of the most important means of dating coins.
DOMIT	The name DOMITIAN.
F	FILIUS. This title is used to assert a claim of family relationship (i.e. sonship). Usually it is included as a way of associating the person issuing the coin with an illustrious or deified predecessor.
GER (or GERM or GERMAN)	GERMANICVS. This title declares that its bearer was recognized to have achieved some military victory over the peoples of Germania. To a certain degree it was also a hereditary title and was passed on from one successful military commander to his heir.
IMP	IMPERATOR. This title is used almost exclusively for the Roman Emperor or his heirs.
P M	PONTIFEX MAXIMVS. This title declares the Emperor as the supreme head of the Roman religion.
P P	PATER PATRIAE. This is an honorific title and declares the Emperor to be the 'Father of the Country'.
S C	SENATVS CONSVLTVM. This means that the coin bearing this inscription has been issued as a decree of the Roman Senate.
S P Q R	SENATVS POPVLVSQUE ROMANVS. This is a standard abbreviation for the 'Senate and People of Rome'.
T	The name TITVS.
TI	The name TIBERIVS.
TR P	TRIBVNICIA POTESTAS. This title refers to the tribunicial power accorded the Emperor and reflects his position as the civil head of state. Such authority was renewed annually and successive holdings were generally numbered which means that the title is one of the most important means of dating coins.
VESP	The name VESPASIANVS.

INTRODUCTION

There is something magical about examining an artifact of the past at close range which makes history come to life, and helps to bridge the 2000 year gap between the New Testament age and our own. When one holds in one's hand an example of the tribute denarius (Figure 1), mentioned in the story of Jesus' confrontation with the religious authorities in Mk 12.13-17, for example, an immediate connection between Jesus' day and ours is established. Could it even be that this very coin was the one that Jesus' challengers held in their hand? Or, when examining at close hand an example of a shekel from the Phoenician cities of Tyre or Sidon (Figure 2), or a tetradrachma from Antioch on the Orontes (Figure 3), or a didrachma of Rhodes (Figure 4), or a silver tetradrachma of the cities of Ephesus (Figure 5) or Amphipolis (Figure 6), or a tetradrachma of Alexander the Great or one of the Ptolemaic or Seleucid kings who followed him (Figure 7a, b, c), one is tantalized by the prospect that these coins may indeed have formed part of the thirty pieces of silver for which Jesus was betrayed by Judas.[1] Our appreciation and understanding of the story of the widow's mite, recorded in Mk 12.41-44 and Lk. 21.1-4, is greatly enhanced when we are able to inspect one of the bronze leptons indicated in the story. The size and weight of the coin, the fact that it was made of bronze and was thus rather insignificant when compared to the larger silver and gold denominations which prevailed, make the irony of Jesus' statement about the widow's sacrifice in the story all the more powerful. These small coins, issued

---

1. The references to τὰ ἀργύρια in Mt. 26.15 and 27.3, 5, 9 are generally taken to mean large silver coins from the larger Hellenistic world of Palestine. These six coin types are often cited as being examples of the kind of coins indicated in the New Testament. See E.T. Newell, *Royal Greek Portrait Coins* (Racine, WI: Whitman, 1937); R.S. Yeoman, *Moneys of the Bible* (Racine, Wisconsin: Whitman, 1961), pp. 25-27; E.T. Newell, *Standard Ptolemaic Silver* (New York: Sanford J. Durst, 1981); I. Carradice, *Ancient Greek Portrait Coins* (London: British Museum Publications, 1978). Most scholars accept that Matthew has the curious passage from Zech. 11.12-13 in mind when he relates this part of the Passion story.

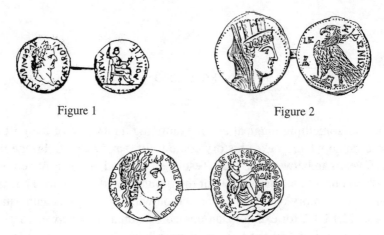

Figure 1   Figure 2

Figure 3

under the authority of the Roman procurator of the province, also demonstrate a tantalizing coincidence of people and dates. For instance, one issue struck under Pontius Pilate (appointed procurator by Tiberius from 26–36 CE) brings together the Roman inquisitor of Jesus and the probable year of Jesus' crucifixion. The reverse of the coin (Figure 8) gives us a view of a sacred vessel surrounded by the inscription

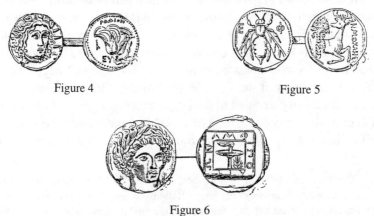

Figure 4   Figure 5

Figure 6

TIBEPIOY KAICAPOC LIS; the last three letters date the coin to year 16 of Tiberius's reign, 29–30 CE.[2]

2.   D.R. Sear, *Greek Imperial Coins and their Values: The Local Coinages of the Roman Empire* (London: Seaby, 1982), p. 553, lists this coin as 5622.

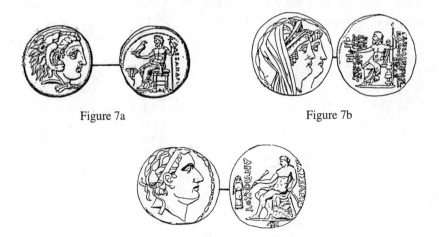

Figure 7a   Figure 7b

Figure 7c

Other fascinating connections between history and coins also abound. Who will not find their imaginations running away with them when viewing one of the sestertia minted under the Emperor Titus which depicts on its reverse the famous Colosseum in Rome (Figure 9), legendary site of the martyrdom of so many early Christians and constantly associated in our minds with gladiatorial contests? Coins minted by Jewish authorities as part of their rebellion against Rome in 66–70 CE

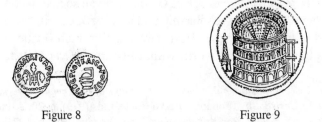

Figure 8   Figure 9

stand as one of the most intriguing sources of history available to us. Thus silver shekels and half shekels proudly proclaiming in Hebrew script the importance of 'Jerusalem the Holy', while presenting sacred images of a chalice and a pomegranate (Figure 10a, b), offer much insight into the mindset of many Jewish nationalists within the rebellion. Similarly, silver tetradrachma issued during the Second Jewish Revolt of 132–135 CE provide us with one of the few available representations

of the screen of the Tabernacle and the Ark of the Covenant within the
Temple of Jerusalem (Figure 11).[3]

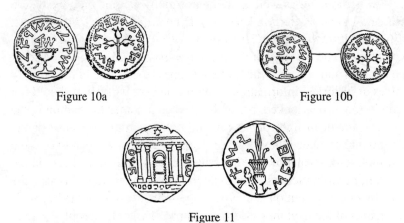

Figure 10a   Figure 10b

Figure 11

In short, on a purely impressionistic level ancient coins can make quite
an impact upon us. Moreover, there is also a serious side to numismatics
which needs to be addressed. The scientific value of numismatic
evidence as a means to enlarging one's understanding of and appreciation for the ancient world is generally acknowledged, at least in theory.[4]
Yet it is remarkable how rarely this particular avenue is explored with
any degree of enthusiasm by New Testament scholars; in the main the
field has been abandoned either to classicists or numismatic specialists.
As R. Oster put it, 'Any vestige of Graeco-Roman society is a desidera-
tum for New Testament scholarship and numismatics remains a largely
untapped source.'[5] Oster uses the helpful image of 'numismatic windows'
onto the New Testament world within his article; yet how few New

3.   H. Rosenau, *Vision of the Temple: The Image of the Temple of Jerusalem in
Judaism and Christianity* (London: Oresko Books Ltd, 1979), p. 20, discusses the
coin. Also see Y. Yadin, *Bar-Kokhba* (New York: Random House, 1971), pp. 25-
27, for a discussion and some colour photographs of the relevant coins.

4.   M. Grant, *Roman History from Coins* (Cambridge: Cambridge University
Press, 1968) addresses the matter. The debate among classicists and historians about
the value of numismatic evidence has at times been quite fierce. For more on this
subject see C.H.V. Sutherland, *Ancient Numismatics: A Brief Introduction* (New
York: American Numismatic Society, 1958), and A.H.M. Jones, 'Numismatics and
History', in R.A.G. Carson and C.H.V. Sutherland (eds.), *Essays in Roman Coinage
Presented to Harold Mattingly* (Oxford: Oxford University Press, 1956), pp. 13-33.

5.   'Numismatic Windows into the Social World of Early Christianity: A
Methodological Inquiry', *JBL* 101 (1982), p. 218.

Testament specialists ever bother to look through the windows to see what lies beyond! Most of the available handbooks and introductions to the New Testament, as well as the major multi-volume dictionaries on the market such as the *Interpreter's Dictionary of the Bible* (1962, 1976), the *Illustrated Bible Dictionary* (1980), the *Encyclopedia of the Bible* (1988), and the *Anchor Bible Dictionary* (1992), include a discussion of coins and coinage within them. Coins stand as one of the primary sources of historical information about the ancient world and should not be neglected or overlooked, particularly when it comes to examining the New Testament in light of its contemporary setting.[6] Because of the inscriptional evidence they provide, coins have always been one of the most important means by which archaeological finds have been dated. However, numismatics can contribute in several other ways. Perhaps the most obvious contribution is to provide portraits of some of the key political figures of the day; they afford a glimpse of what the people we read about in the pages of the New Testament actually looked like. The Roman Emperors, including Augustus, Tiberius, Claudius, Nero, Vespasian, Titus and Domitian, whose powerful presence sets the historical scene for the rise of Christianity, can all be seen in officially sanctioned portraits. Beyond that, fascinating portraits of such Jewish leaders as Herod Philip II (mentioned in Lk. 3.1), Agrippa I (mentioned in Acts 12.1-3; 12.21-23) and Herod Agrippa II (mentioned in Acts 25.13; 26.2, 28) can also be readily viewed on ancient coins. A good example is the small bronze coin of Herod Agrippa I (37–44 CE) which has on its obverse a bust portrait of the king surrounded by the inscription ΒΑCΙΛΕΥC ΜΕΓΑC ΑΓΡΙΠΠΑC ΦΙΛΟΚΑΙCΑΡ. The reverse of the coin shows an image of Fortuna standing to the left and holding a cornucopia in her left hand and balancing a rudder with an extended right hand. The inscription ΚΑΙCΑΡΙΑ Η ΠΡΟC ΤΩ CΕΒΑCΤΩ ΛΙΜΕΝΙ (a reconstructed reading meaning 'Caesarea near the port of Augustus') surrounds the scene (Figure 12).[7] Similarly, Herod Agrippa II (56–95 CE) minted a small bronze coin in 66 CE which has a bust of the king on the obverse

---

6. J.W. Betylon, 'Numismatics and Archeology', *BA* 48 (1985), pp. 162-65, offers a general introduction to the value of numismatics in archaeological research. M. Crawford, 'Numismatics', in *idem* (ed.), *Sources for Ancient History* (Cambridge: Cambridge University Press), pp. 185-233, discusses some of the methodological questions raised by using coins within a study of ancient history.

7. Y. Meshorer, *Jewish Coins of the Second Temple Period* (Tel Aviv: Am Hassefer & Massada, 1967), lists this coin as 90.

surrounded by the inscription ΒΑΣΙΛΕΩΣ ΑΓΡΙΠΠΟΥ. The reverse of this coin shows an anchor with the letters L and I on either side giving a date of the King's tenth year of rule for the coin (Figure 13).[8]

Figure 12   Figure 13

We can also enlarge our understanding of the complex political situation which existed in Judaea during the Second Temple period through the coins issued by major players on the scene. Thus we can detect something of the tensions surrounding the rule of Herod the Great (37–4 BCE) through the attempt to justify his appointment as a vassal of his Roman masters and present himself as a legitimate ruler of the Jewish people within his coins. As a case in point we note the bronze coins which show on their obverse a tripod surrounded by the inscription ΗΡΩΔΟΥ ΒΑΣΙΛΕΩΣ and two dating symbols on either side. The reverse shows a helmet flanked with palm branches, while a six-pointed star of David stands above it (Figure 14).[9]

Numismatic evidence can also help to shed light on important historical events which had a direct bearing on the lives of the New Testament writers and their audiences. Key events which helped shape the lives of people living in the early days of the Roman Empire frequently found their way onto the official coinage produced by the Imperial mints. Thus, coinage served as one of the primary vehicles of the communication of news and policies, in much the same way that postage stamps or official press releases on radio or TV function in the modern world. And just as postal issues or press releases reflect the views and opinions of the government issuing them, so too did Roman Imperial coins lend themselves to propaganda purposes. In this sense the Imperial mints were continually involved in striking new images, moulding and shaping public opinion in light of the political demands of the day.[10] Occasionally these

8.   Meshorer, *Jewish Coins*, p. 98. Madden, *History of Jewish Coinage and of Money in the Old and New Testament* (London: Bernard Quaritch, 1864), pp. 115-16, discusses the coin and notes its rarity.

9.   Meshorer, *Jewish Coins*, p. 37.

10. E.S. Ramage, 'Denigration of Predecessor under Claudius, Galba, and Vespasian', *Historia* 32 (1983), pp. 201-214, uses numismatic evidence to suggest

coin issues help to enlarge our understanding of the first and second centuries, enabling us to catch a glimpse of socio-political concerns which directly affected the lives of many within an emerging Christianity. Take, for example, the sestertius issued by the Imperial mint in Rome during the reign of Tiberius (14–37 CE) which alludes to a particular instance of the Emperor's generosity shown to Asia Minor. This coin (Figure 15)[11] shows on its reverse the seated figure of Tiberius, wearing a laurel wreath with his feet rested on a stool. He holds in his right hand a patera, while in his left he brandishes a long spear. The inscription surrounding the scene reads, CIVITATIBVS ASIAE RESTITVTIS, proudly proclaiming the fact that Tiberius had personally financed the restoration of several key cities in Asia Minor, including Sardis and Magnesia, following the devastating earthquake which struck the region in 17 CE. The coin is dated to 22–23 CE and the Emperor's beneficence is recorded in both Tacitus (*Annals* 2.47) and Suetonius (*Tiberius* 48.2). Clearly the coin stands as an example of Imperial propaganda, but it does nonetheless reveal something about policy towards the earthquake-prone region of Asia Minor and thus sheds light on such passages as Rev. 3.1-6 which alludes to the city's past history filled with alternating periods of triumph and disaster.

Another good example is the sestertius issued by the Emperor Nerva (96–98 CE) which proclaimed changes in the collection of the special tax on Jews instituted by Vespasian in 70 CE. This special tax of two drachma per person was levied upon the Jews following the suppression of the First Jewish Revolt, ostensibly to pay for the rebuilding of the temple of Jupiter Capitolinus in Rome.[12] The coin (Figure 16) has

that each of the three Emperors under discussion makes subtle use of coin types to downplay the achievements of his immediate predecessor and thus enhance his own position.

11. The coin type is listed in C.H.V. Sutherland, *Roman Imperial Coinage: Volume 1 (31 BC–AD 69)* (London: Spink & Son Ltd, 1984, rev. edn), p. 97, as nos. 48-50. Also see the discussion in Sutherland *Roman History and Coinage (44 BC–AD 69)* (Oxford: Clarendon Press, 1987), pp. 47-49.

12. Josephus, *War* 7.218; Suetonius, *Domitian* 12.2; Cassius Dio, *Hist.* 65.7.2; 68.1.2 and *Sib. Or.* 12.126 all relate to this matter. For fuller discussion see R. Syme, 'The Imperial Finances under Domitian, Nerva and Trajan', *JRS* 20 (1930), pp. 55-70; M.S. Ginsburg, 'Fiscus Judaicus', *JQR* 21 (1930–31), pp. 281-91; I.A.F. Bruce, 'Nerva and the Fiscus Iudaicus', *PEQ* 96 (1964), pp. 34-35; A. Carlebach, 'Rabbinic References to Fiscus Judaicus', *JQR* 66 (1975–76), pp. 57-61; L.A. Thompson, 'Domitian and the Jewish Tax', *Historia* 31 (1982), pp. 329-42; D.C.A. Schotter,

as its reverse a palm tree surrounded by the inscription FISCI IVDAICI
CALVMNIA SVBLATA with the letters S C in exergue.[13] It commemorates the suppression by Nerva of wrongful accusations against Jews in
regard to this tax. The coin stands as a testimony to the politically
sensitive nature of Jewish-Roman relations following the Jewish Revolt
and offers a tantalizing insight into the delicate situation of Judaism (and
Christianity?) as a religion holding a special position within Roman law.

Figure 14   Figure 15   Figure 16

The scientific study of numismatics can greatly enhance our understanding of the sociological and economic conditions of a given geographical area. Which coins have survived to be discovered in archaeological sites, and in what quantities, can provide important information
about the lifestyle and standard of living for the people concerned. The
number and size of coin hoards can also be quite revealing, serving as an
index into the perceptions of the populace as to the stability of the
reigning government. Generally people hoard money in times of great
stress and political instability, so that an increase of hoarding (datable by
the coins contained within the hoards) is usually taken to indicate a sense
of insecurity among the populace at large.

The essays brought together in this volume share a common theme in
that they aim to demonstrate the contribution that numismatic studies
can make to serious investigation of the New Testament and its world.
Each of the eight chapters addresses an aspect of the ancient world

'The Principate of Nerva: Some Observations on the Coin Evidence', *Historia* 32
(1983), pp. 215-26; S. Mandell, 'Who Paid the Temple Tax When the Jews Were
under Roman Rule?', *HTR* 77 (1984), pp. 223-32; and M. Goodman, 'Nerva, the
Fiscus Judaicus and Jewish Identity', *JRS* 79 (1989), pp. 40-44. C.J. Hemer, 'The
Edfu Ostraka and the Jewish Tax', *PEQ* 105 (1973), pp. 6-12, offers evidence of the
collection of the tax among Egyptian Jews.
   13. The *Oxford English Dictionary* (1989) defines 'exergue' as 'A small space
usually on the reverse of a coin or medal, below the principal device, for any minor
inscription, the date, engraver's initials, etc. Also, the inscription there inserted.'

during the time that events recounted within the New Testament either took place, or were being recorded into the documents we all take as foundational for the Christian movement. Thus we cover the period from the reign of the Roman Emperor Augustus (27 BCE–14 CE) through to the reign of Hadrian (117–38 CE), and discuss the contribution that select issues of Roman Imperial coinage can make to our understanding of the New Testament world. The eight chapters are divided into three sections. The first two focus on themes connected with the reign of the Julio-Claudian Emperors, the next three focus on aspects of the Pauline letters which may be illuminated by specific issues of Roman coinage, and the final three concentrate on coinage minted during the reign of Hadrian. More specifically, Chapter 1 is given over to a study of the image of legionary *aquilae* as a background to the saying of Jesus recorded in Mt. 24.28/Lk. 17.37. It concentrates on three incidents in Roman history; namely the battle of Actium in 31 BCE, the return of the legionary standards from the Parthians in 19 BCE during the reign of Augustus, and the return of the *aquilae* lost in the fated German campaigns of 9 CE. These episodes were among the most important in Augustus's early career and helped to establish his position within the complex political scene of the day. In particular, Augustus made much political mileage out of the Parthian incident and the coinage minted at Pergamum in connection with the event is a classic example of Imperial propaganda in operation. Chapter 2 examines the idea of the deification of the Roman Emperor as it is reflected in Roman coinage. This is a phenomenon which underwent a marked development during the reign of Augustus, with the elevation of the recently assassinated Julius Caesar serving as a catalyst. The deification, or apotheosis, of the Roman Emperor presented a major challenge to Christians who believed in the special position of Jesus Christ and is well worth examining against the backdrop of parallels from the Graeco-Roman world. Fortunately for our purposes, the idea of the apotheosis of the Roman Emperor is frequently proclaimed on Roman coins from the time of Augustus onwards, which provide much food for thought for those interested in tracing the development of christological claims within early Christianity.

Chapter 3 examines the incident described in Acts 19.23-41 where Paul encounters opposition in Ephesus from Demetrius and the guild of silversmiths who made their living in the ancient city. The challenge that Paul made to the sale and distribution of images of the goddess Artemis sparked one of the most dangerous episodes in Paul's career, if the

veiled references to his brush with death mentioned in 1 Cor. 15.32 and
2 Cor. 1.8 are anything to go by. In this study careful attention is given
to a special set of coins minted by the Emperor Claudius (41–54 CE)
and issued in commemoration of his marriage to Agrippina in 51 CE.
The coins exhibit a representation of the cultic statue of the goddess
Artemis housed in the temple of Ephesus and thus are an important
piece of evidence for the religious practices in Paul's own day. More to
the point, a proper appreciation of the social and political significance
surrounding the minting of these coins also helps us to understand the
hostile reception which Paul experienced in Ephesus.

Chapter 4 examines some of the Roman Imperial coins issued during
the reign of the Emperor Nero (54–68 CE) which depict scenes of the
city of Rome. Through these coins we can catch a glimpse of sights
which Paul himself might have seen during the period of his Roman
captivity. These coins also shed light on two interesting passages in the
Pauline letters, notably Phil. 1.13 and Col. 2.15. The passage in Philippians
speaks of the praetorian guard responsible for Paul's imprisonment,
while the passage from Colossians speaks of the victory of Christ in the
language of a Roman military triumph. Both passages invite consideration of key themes which are found in official coinage minted in Nero's
time. Chapter 5 follows up this idea of the Roman military triumph more
thoroughly and examines the passage in Col. 2.15, as well as its counter-
part in 2 Cor. 2.14-16, against the wide variety of coin types which
depict the victory of Rome over its enemies. Most striking among these
are the so-called 'Judaea Capta' reverses minted under the Flavian
Emperors Vespasian, Titus and Domitian (69–96 CE). These portray a
personification of Judaea in subjection to the triumphant Emperor and
offer a striking image of the political situation following the Roman
crushing of the First Jewish Revolt (66–70 CE).

Chapter 6 concentrates on the so-called 'Travel Sestertia' which were
produced to commemorate the wide-ranging journeys of the Emperor
Hadrian as he travelled around the various provinces and regions which
constituted the Empire of his day. Of special note for students of the
New Testament are the sestertia from Hadrian's visit to Judaea in 130
CE. Here we see an interesting development of the 'Judaea Capta'
reverses associated with the First Jewish Revolt in that Hadrian authorized the minting of several coin types which depict him as a victorious
leader standing over a subdued personification of Judaea at the conclusion of the Bar Kochba Revolt. The study also paves the way for the

next two chapters which follow through suggestions arising from the study of Hadrian's journeys and examine two inter-related theological ideas in light of them. More specifically, Chapter 7 examines the idea that Nero would return from the dead in the person of a new Emperor, the aptly-named *Nero redivivus* myth, as it becomes applied in second-century Jewish and Christian writings to Hadrian himself. Similarly, Chapter 8 examines how the idea of the arrival[14] of the Emperor in the province is reflected in such writings as the Apocalypse of John in the New Testament and the *Sibylline Oracles*. Particular attention is paid to the contribution that coins issued by the Imperial mint have to make in establishing the expectation of the parousia of the Emperor Hadrian as a backdrop for apocalyptic ideas of the second coming of Jesus Christ at the end of the world.

The study is concluded with an annotated resource list of some of the most important books and articles which discuss numismatics and its relevance for the study of the New Testament world. This bibliography should serve as a launching point for anyone wishing to pursue the relationship between numismatics and New Testament study further. The section also contains a listing of additional literature on the more specialized area of Jewish numismatics, a field in which a great deal of research has been done in the past twenty or thirty years.

There is much work that remains to be done in the field of numismatics, particularly in the area of local coin issues as opposed to those produced by the centralized Imperial mints.[15] C.J. Hemer puts the critical point thus:

> Coinage is often in fact the most illuminating key to local religion, and so to the formative ideas of the society.[16]

I. Carradice makes a similar point, stressing the coinage which comes from the eastern provinces of Rome:

> the real value of the types of coins of the Greek East is the insight into local city life which they reveal. Topography, architecture, literature and mythology, religious beliefs and practices, entertainments and celebrations

---

14. The relevant Greek term is παρουσία and the Latin is *adventus*.

15. K. Butcher, *Roman Provincial Coins: An Introduction to the Greek Imperials* (London: Seaby, 1988), provides a helpful introduction to the subject. The best catalogue of these coins is Sear, *Greek Imperial*.

16. *The Letters to the Seven Churches of Asia in their Local Setting* (JSNTSup, 11; Sheffield: Sheffield Academic Press, 1986), p. 25.

were all considered suitable subjects for illustrations because the coinage provided citizens with a vehicle on which to express their civic pride.[17]

Full details about most of the coins discussed in this book are to be found within the standard numismatic texts, such as M. Crawford's *Roman Republican Coinage*,[18] the *Roman Imperial Coinage* volumes,[19] E.A. Sydenham's *Coinage of the Roman Republic*,[20] the *Coins of the Roman Empire in the British Museum* volumes,[21] D.R. Sears's *Greek Imperial Coins and their Values: The Local Coinages of the Roman Empire*, and Y. Meshorer's *Jewish Coins of the Second Temple Period*. Generally coins are catalogued under the name of the Emperor reigning at the time they were issued and this practice is adopted here.

Most of the line drawings of coins, statues and gems contained herein are taken from F.W. Madden's *History of Jewish Coinage and of Money in the Old and New Testament*,[22] H. Cohen's *Description historique des monnaies frappées sous l'Empire Romain*,[23] the various volumes of V. Duruy's *History of Rome and the Roman People from Its Origin to the Establishment of the Christian Empire*,[24] and D.R. Sear's *Roman Coins and their Values*.[25]

17. 'The Roman Empire and Provinces', in M.J. Price (ed.), *Coins: An Illustrated Survey 650 BC to the Present Day* (London: Hamlyn, 1980), p. 101.

18. 2 vols.; Cambridge: Cambridge University Press, 1974.

19. Notably, C.H.V. Sutherland, *Volume I (31 BC—AD 69)*, and H. Mattingly and E.A. Sydenham, *Volume II: Vespasian to Hadrian*. These volumes are hereafter abbreviated as *RIC*.

20. London: Spink & Son Ltd, 1952. This book is hereafter abbreviated as *CRR*.

21. H. Mattingly (ed.), *Volume III: Nerva to Hadrian* (London: Trustees of the British Museum, 1936). This book is hereafter abbreviated as *CREBM*.

22. London: Bernard Quaritch, 1864.

23. 8 vols.; Paris: Chez M.M. Rollin & Feuardent, 1880–1892.

24. London: Kegan Paul, Trench & Co., 1885.

25. London: Seaby, 2nd rev. edn, 1974.

Part I

PROPAGANDA IN THE JULIO-CLAUDIAN AGE

Chapter 1

LEGIONARY *AQUILAE* AS MILITARY IMAGE: THE BACKGROUND TO MATTHEW 24.28/LUKE 17.37

As part of his description of the advancement of Vespasian's army into Galilee during the early stages of the First Jewish Revolt, the Jewish historian Josephus includes an interesting comment about the importance of legionary *aquilae* within the life of the military. He describes the order in which Titus's military units marched, and makes in passing a comment that serves to initiate my investigation (*War* 3.6.2):

> Then came the legates, the prefects of the cohorts and the tribunes, with an escort of picked troops. Next the ensigns surrounding the eagle (τὸν ἀετόν), which in the Roman army precedes every legion, because it is the king and the bravest of all the birds: it is regarded by them as the symbol of empire, and, whoever may be their adversaries, an omen of victory. These sacred emblems (τοῖς δὲ ʻιεροῖς) were followed by the trumpeters, and behind them came the solid column, marching six abreast.[1]

My aim in this chapter is to examine the place that the image of legionary *aquilae* had within the world of the New Testament. I shall seek to determine how widespread the symbol of the eagle was at the time, with a view to illuminating the cryptic saying of Jesus recorded in Mt. 24.28/ Lk. 17.37. In particular, I shall concentrate on three specific incidents in Roman history which focus on the legionary *aquilae*, all of which have significant coin issues associated with them. Following the examination of these three historical episodes I shall turn my attention to the Gospel saying itself.

First, I examine one of the turning points of the ancient world, the battle of Actium, and note several coin series that are associated with the two protagonists in the battle, Octavian and Mark Antony.

---

1. The person responsible for carrying the legionary emblem was known as an *aquilifer*. Artistic portrayals of this abound in Roman sculpture, including the Column of Trajan. See L. Rossi, *Trajan's Column and the Dacian Wars* (London: Thames and Hudson, 1971), pp. 80-81.

1. *The Battle of Actium and Mark Antony's Legionary Denarii of 32–31 BCE*

The victory of Octavian over Mark Antony at the battle of Actium on 2 September 31 BCE is generally acknowledged to be one of the most decisive in military history. It irreversibly altered the political scene of the time, establishing Octavian as *the* force to be reckoned with in the dying days of the Roman Republic.[2] Octavian (or *Augustus*, as he was later to style himself) proudly proclaimed his victory on the major propaganda tool at his disposal, that of coinage. For example, a set of six denarii issued c. 30 BCE proclaimed the peace brought about by the victory at Actium and associated this with the divine protection of the goddess Venus with whom Octavian had linked his cause. The six denarii are a deliberately designed set, containing interlocking themes.[3] Three of the coins have an idealized portrait of Augustus on the obverse while the reverses have representations of Venus,[4] Pax[5] and Victory,[6] each of whom carries an appropriate symbol. The other three coins have representations of Venus,[7] Pax[8] and Victory[9] on their obverses, while the reverses have the figure of Octavian in various military poses. On the Venus coin Octavian is presented in military dress, cloak flowing behind, as he advances to the left holding a spear. On the Pax coin he is again presented in military dress, raising his right hand in a gesture of greeting and carrying a spear over his shoulder. On the Victory coin he is pre-

---

2.   W.W. Tarn, 'The Battle of Actium', *JRS* 21 (1931), pp. 173-99; G.W. Richardson, 'Actium', *JRS* 27 (1937), pp. 153-64; W.W. Tarn, 'Actium: A Note', *JRS* 28 (1938), pp. 165-68. The best overall treatment of this crucial event in history remains J.M. Carter, *The Battle of Actium* (London: Hamish Hamilton, 1970). Also see E.G. Huzar, *Mark Antony* (London: Croom Helm, 1986), pp. 214-26; A. Roberts, *Mark Antony: His Life and Times* (Upton-upon-Severn: Malvern Publishing, 1988), pp. 316-28.

3.   See S. Walker and A. Burnett, *The Image of Augustus* (London: British Museum Publications, 1981), pp. 27-28. P. Zanker, *The Power of Images in the Age of Augustus* (Ann Arbor, MI: University of Michigan Press, 1988), pp. 53-57, also discusses the series which he dates prior to the battle of Actium.

4.   *RIC* Augustus 250.

5.   *RIC* Augustus 252.

6.   *RIC* Augustus 254-55.

7.   *RIC* Augustus 251.

8.   *RIC* Augustus 253.

9.   *RIC* Augustus 256.

sented in the style of Neptune, holding a long spear in his left hand and standing with his right foot on a globe of the world. All six coins carry the reverse inscription CAESAR DIVI F(ilius) in the field, announcing Octavian as the son of the Deified One, namely Julius (Figure 1a-f shows the six coins).

A host of other coins appeared in the few years following the battle of Actium, many of them produced by regional mints. The intention was to proclaim the peace that was wrought by Octavian as he began to consolidate his position following the removal of Mark Antony from the political scene. Coins became the medium upon which the victory was proclaimed and new heroes created, many of whom were to abide in the Roman mind for decades. For example, Augustus's naval commander Marcus Agrippa, so instrumental in the victory,[10] was honoured by the issue of an as by the mint at Rome during Caligula's reign (Figure 2).[11]

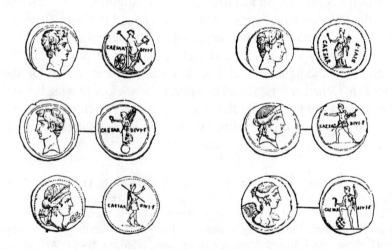

Figures 1a-f

10.   F.A. Wright, *Marcus Agrippa: Organizer of Victory* (London: George Routledge & Sons, 1937), pp. 102-127, discusses this point. He describes Agrippa as 'the first Roman who showed any perception of the importance of sea power' (p. 5).

11.   *RIC* Gaius 58; other specialists attribute this coin to the reign of Tiberius. However, the fact that Agrippa was Caligula's grandfather makes the attribution of the coin to the latter's reign more likely. See S. Jameson, 'The Date of the Asses of M. Agrippa', *NC* 6 (1966), pp. 95-124 + Plates 6-10; G.F. Carter and W.E. Metcalf, 'The Dating of the M. Agrippa Asses', *NC* 148 (1988), pp. 145-48, for a full treatment of the matter.

It has as its obverse the laureated head of Agrippa facing left, together with the surrounding inscription M(arcus) AGRIPPA L. F. COS III. The reverse of the coin has a representation of the god Neptune (quite suitable for a coin honouring a naval hero) standing and holding a trident in his left arm while his outstretched right hand holds a small dolphin. The letters S C stand in exergue. Augustus also honoured his military commander with the minting of a denarius in 12 BCE. The reverse shows a portrait of Agrippa wearing a combined mural and rostral crown, symbolic of his achievements on both land and sea. The inscription M. AGRIPPA COS TER COSSVS LENTVLVS surrounds the portrait (Figure 3).[12]

Figure 2   Figure 3

In 28 BCE the city of Ephesus began to issue a number of cistophori which celebrated the liberation of the city from Antony's influence and proclaimed Octavian as its champion. The obverse of this coin bears a portrait of Octavian facing to the right and wearing a laurel wreath. The inscription surrounding the portrait reads IMP(erator) CAESAR DIVI F(ilius) COS VI LIBERTATIS P(opuli) R(omani) VINDEX. The reverse of the coin has a representation of Pax holding a caduceus in her right hand. Behind her is a snake emerging from the *cista mystica*, the sacred chest of Dionysus, a cultic symbol long associated with the city of Ephesus. The whole scene has a laurel-wreath surround and the word PAX stands in the field (Figure 4).[13] This coin seems to be a deliberate repudiation of a very similar cistophorus issued by Mark Antony when he was still closely linked to Octavia (that is, c. 40–32 BCE, *before* Cleopatra). It presents a reverse scene of Dionysus standing on the *cista mystica* between two interlocked serpents with the words III VIR R. P. C. (for *Triumvir Rei Publicae Constituendae*) on either side. The obverse

---

12.   *RIC* Augustus 414. The moneyer C. Sulpicius Platorinus issued a similar aureus (*RIC* Augustus 409) the year before. V.A. Maxfield, *The Military Decorations of the Roman Army* (London: B.T. Batsford, 1981), pp. 67-81, discusses the various crowns awarded as military decorations.

13.   *RIC* Augustus 476.

of the coin shows the portrait busts of Antony and Octavia with the surrounding inscription M ANTONINVS IMP COS DESIG ITER ET TERT (Figure 5).[14] Similarly, in c. 28–27 BCE a series of aurei and

Figure 4   Figure 5

denarii were produced, probably by a mint in Alexandria, which carry an obverse portrait of Octavian together with the inscription CAESAR COS VI. The reverse has a representation of a crocodile and the words AEGVPTO CAPTA in the field, obviously proclaiming Octavian's capture of the province following the suicides of Mark Antony and Cleopatra in 30 BCE (Figure 6).[15]

However, there is also another important issue associated with the battle of Actium which calls for our attention. It does not come from the side of the victor, Octavian, but from the side of the vanquished, Mark Antony. In 32–31 BCE he issued a series of denarii as a means of paying his fleet and troops in the run-up to the battle of Actium.[16] The obverse of these so-called 'Legionary Denarii' depicts a Roman galley, complete with a bank of oars and a standard on the ship's prow (Figure 7). Above the galley is the inscription ANT(oninus) AVG(ur) while beneath the galley we read III VIR R.P.C. There are several different reverse types for the denarii, although they all display military standards of some sort, most including a legionary *aquila* in the centre. The various legions of Mark Antony's army are honoured by the inscriptions on the reverse; abbreviations for some twenty-three legions are extant.[17] In the main the inscriptions follow a similar pattern, with the letters LEG and the number of the legion placed on either side of the *aquila* at the base of the coin. Pride of place is given to the first legion, which bears the letters LEG PRI (for *Legionis Primae*) (Figure 8 shows the reverse for Legions

14.   *CRR* 1198.
15.   *RIC* Augustus 545.
16.   Some rare examples of aurei are also known. Details of the series as a whole can be found in Crawford, *Republican Coinage*, pp. 539-41.
17.   W.W. Tarn, 'Anthony's Legions', *CQ* 26 (1932), pp. 75-81.

Figure 6	Figure 7	Figure 8

I and IV[18]). There are also denarii representing specialist military units, including the Speculatorum Cohort and the Praetorian Cohort, which bear the inscriptions CHORTIS SPECVLATORVM and CHORTIVM PRAETORIARVM respectively around the upper edge of the coin

Figure 9	Figure 10	Figure 11

(Figure 9).[19] Three of the denarii also carry a reference to their legionary *cognomina* on the reverse, bearing the inscriptions LEG XII ANTIQVAE, LEG XVII CLASSICAE and LEG XVIII LYBICAE respectively around the top of the coin (Figure 10 is an example).[20] A denarius bearing the portraits of both Mark Antony and Queen Cleopatra on obverse and reverse respectively probably also belongs with the series. The obverse portrait of Antony shows him bare-headed and facing right with a surrounding inscription, ANTONI ARMENIA DEVICTA, and a royal tiara in the field behind his head. Meanwhile, the reverse portrait of the coin shows a bust of Cleopatra wearing a royal diadem. The surrounding inscription reads, CLEOPATRAE REGINAE FILIORVM REGVM (Figure 11).[21]

This series is one of the most extensive issues known from antiquity, with thousands of examples known and catalogued. In fact, a Mark Antony legionary denarius is one of the most easily obtainable Roman coins, and examples regularly appear in popular sales catalogues at fairly reasonable prices. One reason why the legionary denarii coins are so prevalent has to do with their composition, the fact that they do not contain as high a silver content as many other denarii from antiquity, such

18.   *CRR* 1216 and 1219.
19.   *CRR* 1214 and 1213.
20.   *CRR* 1231.
21.   *CRR* 1210.

as the coins issued under the Julio-Claudian Emperors. When official changes to the monetary system were made, such as the economic reforms under Nero in 64 CE,[22] or that of Trajan in c. 100 CE, the temptation was always to melt down denarii containing a high percentage of silver and restrike them as a mixed alloy, thereby making a tidy profit. Since the Mark Antony denarii were already of a mixed alloy this temptation was not so great. In short, the Mark Antony legionary series survived partly due to their inferior quality as silver-based coins. A consequence of this is that the denarii regularly appear in coin hoards around the Empire, from regions as far away as Britain and North Africa. In Britain alone over sixty coin hoards, dating right through to the reign of Postumus (259–268 CE), have included one or more of the Mark Antony legionary denarii within them.[23] Without doubt they are among the most long-lived coins of ancient Rome, remaining in circulation for several hundred years after they were originally produced. Such was the enduring popularity of the series that a restitution coin honouring Legion VI was issued during the reign of Marcus Aurelius (161–180 CE). It reproduces the obverse image of the Mark Antony legionary series almost exactly (the only change being that the galley faces the opposite direction) and adopts the reverse image of the *aquilae* and military standards. Around the edge of the coin reads the inscription ANTONINVS ET VERVS AVG REST. Two versions of this denarius are extant which differ slightly in the way in which they present the legionary standards and an *aquila* on the reverse (Figure 12a, b).[24] Similarly, Septimius Severus (193–211 CE) issued a denarius which has the same reverse but

22.   M.A.K. Thornton, 'Nero's New Deal', *TPAPA* 102 (1971), pp. 621-29.

23.   A.S. Robertson, 'Romano-British Coin Hoards: Their Numismatic, Archaeological and Historical Significance', in J. Casey and R. Reece (eds), *Coins and the Archaeologist* (London: Seaby, 2nd edn, 1988), pp. 13-38, discusses this. See also A.S. Robertson, 'The Circulation of Roman Coins in North Britain: The Evidence of Hoards and Site-Finds from Scotland', in R.A.G Carson and C.M. Kraay (eds.), *Scripta Nummaria Romana: Essays Presented to Humphrey Sutherland* (London: Spink & Son Ltd, 1978), pp. 186-216; R. Reece, *Coinage in Roman Britain* (London: Seaby, 1987), pp. 17, 58-59.

24.   G. Askew, *The Coinage of Roman Britain* (London: Seaby, 1967), pp. 15-16, discusses the suggestion that the two reverses are meant to honour two different legions; namely Legion VI Victrix which served in Britain in Hadrian's reign and Legion VI Ferrata which served in Syria and Judaea and was instrumental in the crushing of the Jewish Revolt.

with an altered inscription. It reads LEG XIII IG E M MV around the edge and has the words T R P COS in exergue (Figure 13).[25]

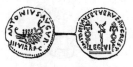 

| Figure 12a | Figure 12b | Figure 13 |

The legionary denarii types were also adopted by L. Clodius Macer, the governor of Africa, who rose up in rebellion against Nero in April of 68 CE. Clodius Macer styled himself the Propraetor of Africa and issued a small number of denarii, presumably from a mint in Carthage, which displayed a reproduction of the galley on the reverse together with the words PROPRAE(toris) AFRICAE as an inscription. The obverse of these denarii show a bust of the bare-headed Macer surrounded by the inscription L. CLODIVS MACER S C (Figure 14).[26] Other coins issued by the Imperial upstart show the legionary *aquila* between two vexillae.[27] A legionary *aquila* also appears on the reverse of some bronze coins issued by the Emperor Hadrian following the crushing of the Second Jewish Revolt in 132–135 CE and the renaming of the city of Jerusalem as Aelia Capitolina.[28] This coin shows an obverse of the Emperor Hadrian, laureated and wearing a *paludamentum*, with an inscription IMP HADRIAN. The reverse shows the aquila on a standard with the inscription COL AE CAP (for Colonia Aelia Capitolina) in the field (Figure 15). Similarly, the city of Berytus in Phoenicia (modern Beirut) issued a large bronze coin during the reign of the Emperor Hadrian (117–138 CE) which is also worth mentioning. It has on its reverse a representation of two legionary *aquilae* facing one another with the

25.　*RIC* Septimius Severus 14.

26.　*RIC* L. Clodius Macer 32-42.

27.　Two different legions are specified within the legends on these coins, Legio I Macriana and Legio III Augusta, both of which supported Macer's revolt against Nero. For a full discussion see K.V. Hewitt, 'The Coinage of L. Clodius Macer', *NC* 143 (1983), pp. 64-80 + Plates 10-13; C.H.V. Sutherland, *Roman History*, pp. 106-109.

28.　L. Kadman, *The Coins of Aelia Capitolina* (Corpus Nummorum Palaestinensium, 1; Jerusalem: Israeli Numismatic Society, 1956), pp. 57-59, discusses the legionary images on these coins.

words COL(onia) BER(ytus) between them; the whole scene is
surrounded by a laurel wreath.[29]

Figure 14   Figure 15   Figure 16

2. *The Diplomatic Triumph of Augustus and the Pergamene Cistophori of 19–18 BCE*

Within the *Res Gestae Divi Augusti* we have recorded this boast of
Augustus concerning the Parthians:

> I compelled the Parthians to restore to me the spoils and standards of
> three Roman armies and to ask supplicants for the friendship of the
> Roman people. Those standards I deposited in the innermost shrine of the
> temple of Mars the Avenger. (29.2)[30]

This brief account of Augustus's dealings with the Parthians, presented
so matter-of-factly, is but the official summary of what was in reality a
long and complicated process of diplomatic negotiation.[31] It is true to say
that the negotiated return of the captured *aquilae* of the Roman legions
by Augustus in 20 BCE was the most significant diplomatic triumph of
his long reign. At the same time, the return of the military standards
prompted the Imperial mints to strike a number of coin types given over
to proclaiming the glories of Augustus and his settlement of the question
of the Parthian eagles. A case in point are the set of seven denarii issued

29.   Sear, *Greek Imperial,* p. 114, lists this coin as 1242. The coin is 23 mm in
diameter.

30.   The translation is that of P.A. Brunt and J.M. Moore, *Res Gestae Divi
Augusti* (Oxford: Oxford University Press, 1967), p. 33. D.N. Wigtil, 'The Ideology
of the Greek "Res Gestae"', *ANRW,* II.30.1, pp. 624-38, offers some interesting
remarks about the various versions of the *Res Gestae.*

31.   See N.C. Debevoise, *A Political History of Parthia* (Chicago: University of
Chicago Press, 1938); K.-H. Ziegler, *Die Beziehungen zwischen Rom und dem
Partherreich* (Wiesbaden: Franz Steiner Verlag, 1964); A.N. Sherwin-White,
Roman Foreign Policy in the East (168 BC to AD 1) (London: Gerald Duckworth,
1984), pp. 279-90, 307-340. B. Campbell, 'War and Diplomacy: Rome and Parthia,
31 BC–AD 235', in J. Rich and G. Shipley (eds.), *War and Society in the Roman
World* (London: Routledge, 1993), pp. 213-240, contains the most recent discussion
of the matter and offers a full bibliography.

by the moneyer L. Aquillius Florus in 18 BCE. The reverse of one of these depicts a kneeling Parthian presenting a Roman legionary standard; the inscription CAESAR AVGVSTVS SIGN(is) RECEPT(is) surrounds the scene (Figure 16).[32] In the words of A.N. Sherwin-White, the return of the Parthian eagles was 'feted on coinage more than any other imperial achievement of Augustus'.[33] Among the most beautiful of these coin issues is the set of three silver cistophori issued by the mint of Pergamum in 19–18 BCE. These cistophori provide us with an opportunity to examine more closely the issue of the Parthian eagles and thereby come to understand more fully the event which occasioned their issue. Allow me to review the extant historical sources which record the incident before moving on to discuss the Pergamene cistophori themselves.

a. *The Parthian Campaigns*

I begin by focusing our attention very much earlier than the grand occasion of the return of the standards in 20 BCE. To understand the significance of their return we must appreciate the historical context of the Parthian question within Roman political and military history. We must remember that the threat of Parthian invasion of Rome was a perennial political reality long before Octavian ever rose to any degree of power or influence and continued long after his death.[34] Much of the form of Roman foreign politics was shaped by this eastern threat. With respect to the issue of the military standards themselves, the role of two of Rome's most powerful figures, Crassus and Mark Antony, and their military involvement in Parthia is crucial. It is the military defeat of the armies of these two leaders by Parthian forces, along with the humiliating loss of legionary *aquilae*, which eventually necessitates the diplomatic exchanges which we see come to fruition in 20 BCE under Augustus's guiding hand. Thus it is in the military proceedings of the generation prior to Augustus that the question of the 'Parthian Eagles' begins.

---

32.   *RIC* Augustus 304. A very similar coin from the same year was issued by the moneyer P. Petronius, Turpilianus (*RIC* Augustus 287-289).

33.   Sherwin-White, *Roman Foreign Policy*, p. 324.

34.   M.-L. Chaumont, 'L' Arménie entre Rom et l'Iran: I. De l'avènement d'Auguste à l'avènement de Dioclétian', *ANRW*, II.9.1, pp. 71-194, provides a historical survey of the issue and examines relevant numismatic evidence.

1. *Crassus and the Battle of Carrhae* (*53 BCE*). Crassus, who in 60 BCE along with Pompey and Caesar formed the 'First Triumvirate', led the first fateful military excursion into Parthia in 55 BCE. He had been elected as consul for the second time in the previous year and undertook the invasion of Parthia in an effort to match the military successes of both Pompey and Caesar.[35] Pompey had distinguished himself in several campaigns in the east as had Caesar in Gaul in the north. Crassus had already experienced some success in the part he played in crushing the slave revolt of Spartacus in 72 BCE,[36] but a victory over slaves did not carry quite the same prestige as a victory over a foreign army. Thus Crassus sought to keep pace with his fellow *triumviri* when he accepted the governorship of Syria in the spring of the year following his consulship (54 BCE). From this vantage point Crassus planned to pursue his invasion of Parthia.

The Parthian king at the time was a man named Orodes and he was fortunate to have an able military commander serving him named Surenas. Surenas was able to lure Crassus to the plains of Carrhae between the Euphrates and the Tigris rivers and there inflicted upon the ageing Crassus (he was over 60 at the time) one of the most humiliating defeats in Roman military history. Crassus had seven legions with him, totalling some 40,000–45,000 men, when he engaged Surenas and the Parthians in battle at Carrhae. Surenas conducted a brilliant campaign combining effective strategic planning with the ingenious use of famed Parthian arrows and cataphracts.[37] Quite simply, Surenas was able to subject the Roman formations to a withering hail of arrows from long distance without ever risking the bulk of his own troops in a close battle. In the end, this strategy destroyed Crassus's army. Over 10,000 men

35.   B.A. Marshall, *Crassus: A Political Biography* (Amsterdam: A.M. Hakkert, 1976), pp. 139-61, discusses the Parthian campaign.

36.   Crassus's triumph for the suppression of the slave rebellion is discussed in B. Marshall, 'Crassus' Ovation in 71 BC', *Historia* 21 (1972), pp. 669-73.

37.   Parthians were noted for their horsemanship as well as their archery skills. They were famous for firing arrows backwards while riding on a retreating horse at full gallop. This tactic is mentioned frequently by the Augustan poets. Note for instance Ovid, *Art of Love* I.209-212; *Fasti* 591-93; Horace, *Odes* I.19.11-12; II.13.17-19; Propertius, *Poems* II.10.13-14; III.4.17; III.9.54; IV.3.66; Virgil, *Georgics* III.31-32. This Parthian war tactic also lends itself in a humorous fashion to sexual double entendre. Ovid picks up the image in *Art of Love* III.245-49 in reference to one of this mistresses accidentally putting her wig on backwards. In III.785-87 the image is used in veiled reference to rear-entry sexual intercourse.

were taken prisoner and only a further 10,000 survived[38] to return to Syria under the leadership of Cassius, one of Crassus's lieutenants.[39] Crassus himself was killed in the campaign under very mysterious circumstances.[40] Most importantly for my considerations, the standards of the legions were captured by the Parthians. This was a signal disgrace to any Roman legion and was tantamount to absolute failure in the service of Rome. The loss of the *aquilae* looms large in the ancient sources which relate the story. The whole campaign is surrounded by ominous portents and impending signs of disaster,[41] many of which were later recorded as a predicted testimony to the folly of the whole campaign and the obstinacy of Crassus in pursuing the war despite advice to the contrary. Cassius Dio, for instance, relates an incident which occurred at Zeugma as the army of Cassius was crossing the Euphrates River. One of the legionary *aquilae* firmly rooted itself into the ground and anthropomorphically refused to proceed any further into Parthian territory (*Hist.* 40.18 1-2). Only by force was the eagle pulled from the ground and carried along with the rest of the fated army.

The battle of Carrhae was a disaster of such magnitude that the Roman people were profoundly shocked for years to come. The memory of such an ignominious defeat was a blot on the pages of Rome's military history. The call for revenge on the proud Parthian hordes and

38.   The two legions which survived were later part of Pompey's army marshalled against Caesar (Appian, *Civil Wars* II.49).

39.   Later one of Julius Caesar's murderers. Cassius governed Syria from 53 to 51 BCE and was responsible for inflicting quite severe blows upon the Parthian forces of the province. On this whole point, see Velleius Paterculus, *History of Rome* II.46.4; Livy, *Summaries* 108; Frontinus, *Stratagems* II.5.35; Appian, *Civil Wars* IV.59. Cicero makes frequent mention of the Parthian incursion into Syria in his letters written while he was governor of Cilicia beginning in 51 BCE. Note, for instance, the passing references in *Letters to Friends* II.10, 17; III.8; VIII.5, 6, 7, 10, 14; IX.25; XII.19; XV.1, 2, 3, 4, 9; *Letters to Atticus* V.9, 11, 14, 16, 18, 20, 21; VI.1, 2, 6; VII.1, 2, 26; VIII.11; XIII.27, 31; XIV.9.

40.   Florus, *Epitome of Roman History* I.46, relates that he was killed by being forced to drink molten gold.

41.   Some of the omens associated with the disastrous Parthian campaign of Crassus are recorded in Pliny, *Natural History* II.147; Julius Obsequens, *A Book of Prodigies* 64; Cassius Dio, *Hist.* 40.17-19; Plutarch, *Crassus* 19.3-6; Florus, *Epitome of Roman History* I.46. Crassus's military career is discussed in T.J. Cadoux, 'Marcus Crassus: A Revaluation', *Greece and Rome* 3 (1956), pp. 153-61; E.J. Parrish, 'Crassus, New Friends and Pompey's Return', *Phoenix* 27 (1973), pp. 357-80.

recovery of the symbolic legionary eagles was widespread. Appian tells us that a Parthian campaign to avenge Crassus's defeat was one of the programmes conceived by Julius Caesar shortly before his assassination in 44 BCE. [42] In fact, Caesar was murdered only four days prior to his scheduled departure on the proposed campaign. A Parthian war of vengeance also stands as a prominent motif within much of the Latin poetry of the Augustan period. Note, for instance, Ovid's comments on Gaius's appointment by his grandfather Augustus to the east as consul-designate with a view to clearing up the lingering disgrace of the loss of the eagles (*Art of Love* I.177-81):

> Now Caesar is planning to fill in the final gaps of Empire:
> > now the furthest east will be ours,
> Revenge will fall on Parthia; joy lighten the grave of Crassus,
> Redeem the standards profaned.
> By barbarian hands!

I shall have occasion to discuss this motif within the Augustan poets more fully below.

2. *Mark Antony and the Parthian War (40–36 BCE)*. The second episode of Roman military defeat at the hands of the Parthians focuses on the figure of Mark Antony. This instance is more complicated and protracted, covering a period of four years or so. It begins with the Parthian invasion of the Roman province of Syria in the early spring of 40 BCE. Antony was in Alexandria with Cleopatra at the time of the invasion and quickly headed north where he was to stay for the next four years until forced in despair to abandon the campaign against the Parthians.

The Parthian army which invaded Syria was led by Pacorus, the son of King Orodes.[43] Pacorus was ably assisted by the Roman Q. Labienus, a representative of Cassius who had gone to Parthia in an attempt to secure help for the Republican cause prior to the battle of Philippi. The Roman military presence in Syria was only two legions commanded by

---

42.   *Civil Wars* II.110-111. Also note, Plutarch, *Caesar* 58.2-5; Suetonius, *Caesar* 44.2-3 and 79.3; Cassius Dio, *Hist.* 44.15.3. On this subject, see G.B. Townsend, 'A Clue to Caesar's Unfulfilled Intentions', *Latomus* 42 (1983), pp. 601-606.

43.   The Parthians also celebrated their military victories from this invasion on commemorative coins. See B. Simonetta, 'On Some Tetradrachms of Orodes II and the Probable Issues of Pacorus I', *NC* 18 (1978), pp. 7-13.

Decidius Saxa whom Antony had appointed governor of the province. Unfortunately, from Antony's point of view, the two legions were primarily composed of troops from Cassius's old army and they quickly defected to Labienus's side, fatally crippling Saxa's defence of the province. The *aquilae* of these two legions were thus added to those lost by Crassus thirteen years before and Roman military pride was dealt another severe blow at the hands of the Parthians.

On his way to confront Pacorus and Labienus in Syria, Antony received news of the defeat from his wife Fulvia. Fulvia was a politically ambitious woman who had recently been involved in an anti-Octavian campaign along with Mark Antony's younger brother Lucius. The campaign was unsuccessful and both Lucius and Fulvia had been forced to flee Italy by a pursuing Octavian. The potential clash between Antony and Octavian was averted when Fulvia died. Her convenient removal from the scene allowed a reconciliation to be facilitated between Octavian and Antony in October of 40 BCE. The reconciliation was sealed by the marriage of Mark Antony to Octavian's half-sister Octavia around November of 40 BCE. Antony also delayed his arrival in Syria by participating in the conference at Misenum in the spring of 39 BCE along with Octavian and Sextus Pompey. Following this conference he turned his attention once again to the Parthian question.

Antony sent P. Ventidius Bassus as his legate and military commander to check the advance of Labienus and the Parthian army in Asia. Meanwhile, Antony travelled to Greece along with his new wife Octavia. It was while he was wintering in Athens that he received reports of Ventidius's successes against the Parthian forces at the Cilician Gates and Mount Amanus. Labienus was killed in these exchanges. Ventidius extended his successes over the Parthians in the battle at Gendarus in which Pacorus was also killed (Velleius Paterculus, *History of Rome* II.78.1). Having served Antony's interests well, the able Ventidius was allowed to return to Rome and celebrate a much-deserved triumph.

In 37 BCE, following the conference at Tarentum with Octavian and his controversial marriage to Cleopatra, Antony himself landed in Syria to take up command of the Parthian campaign. By this time Orodes had been assassinated by his scheming son Phraates who took over as king.[44] Antony's main campaign against Phraates in 36 BCE was ill-conceived and badly conducted in spite of the fact that he commanded a total of sixteen legions. Plutarch attributes this to Antony's infatuation with

44.   This assassination is alluded to in Ovid, *Art of Love* I.198-99.

Cleopatra (*Life of Mark Antony*, 37). Antony foolishly outdistanced his support columns by pushing deep into Parthian territory in pursuit of what he believed to be the main Parthian force. Disastrously, he allowed the vital siege engines along with two supporting legions to be destroyed by a secondary Parthian army. Once again the long-distance archers proved decisive, as they had against Crassus sixteen years previously, by raining arrow after arrow upon the surrounded Roman legionaries. This severe blow to the larger campaign was to a great degree precipitated by the flight of the protective cavalry of Artavasdes the Armenian. In any case, the *aquilae* of the two supporting legions were also added to the Parthian collection and more shame heaped upon the beleaguered Roman army. In frustration, Antony advanced and engaged the main body of Parthian troops, but with little success. Finally, with winter fast approaching and the scarcity of provisions making a continuation of the campaign next to impossible, Antony began a strategic withdrawal. Both sides suffered considerable losses during Antony's 27-day long retreat. The weary and emaciated Roman army finally reached the Mediterranean coast near Sidon where they were eventually met by Cleopatra's supply ships.[45] But the campaign had been very costly and achieved little. Antony's army suffered a loss of 22,000 infantry and 4000 cavalry, a staggering 37%! Plutarch mentions that a great percentage of these deaths were not battle-related but due to sickness and severe winter weather (*Life of Mark Antony*, 50).

Thus it is to the military defeats of Crassus in 53 BCE, of Saxa in 40 BCE and of Mark Antony in 36 BCE that the *Res Gestae* refers when it speaks of the 'spoils and standards of three Roman armies'.

b. *Augustus and the Negotiated Settlement*
Augustus's approach to the resolution of the Parthian Eagles question appears to have been a largely diplomatic one from the beginning. This is hardly surprising given the tremendous amount of consolidation which was needed following the defeat of Mark Antony at Actium in 31 BCE.

---

45.   Cleopatra's support of Antony's Parthian campaign is best understood as part of a larger Egyptian aim within the eastern half of the Empire. Antony is spoken of in col. IV of the fragmentary papyrus from Herculaneum entitled 'Carmen de Bello Actiaco' as the one who subjected the Parthians to the Egyptian realm. The words are put in the mouth of Cleopatra by the unknown author. See H.W. Benario, 'The "Carmen de Bello Actiaco" and Early Imperial Epic', *ANRW*, II.30.3, pp. 1656-62, for a reconstructed text and translation.

Further military engagement was hardly desirable for the war-weary Roman legionaries. Augustus's diplomatic position was strengthened by the fact that the son of the Parthian King Phraates, himself also named Phraates, fell into his hands through the complicity of a rival usurper to the Parthian throne by the name of Tiridates. Tiridates had kidnapped the young Phraates and offered him to Augustus.[46]

Following the appointment in 23 BCE of Agrippa as vice-regent to the east, and perhaps through his intermediary efforts,[47] requests soon reached Rome from Parthia calling for the return of both Tiridates and the young Phraates. Augustus agreed to return the Parthian king's son on the proviso that the legionary standards of the armies of Crassus and Antony, along with the surviving prisoners of war, be returned. Two years passed without any further developments. Finally, in late 21 BCE, Augustus undertook a tour of the eastern provinces. At the same time he ordered his step-son Tiberius to bring a large legionary force drawn from the armies of Macedonia and Illyrium overland into Armenia.[48] Ostensibly, this was an attempt to help to solve some problems which had been brewing in Armenia involving rival claims to the throne. However, the placement of such a large military force so near to the Parthian border undoubtedly injected fresh vigour to the stalled diplomatic negotiations over the legionary standards.

Augustus himself entered Syria in the spring of 20 BCE effectively presenting Phraates with the prospect of war on two fronts. This had the desired effect and the Parthian king quickly capitulated. On May 12 both the standards and the surviving prisoners of war were handed over to the representatives of Augustus.[49] Perhaps the most striking illustration from antiquity of this return of the Parthian eagles appears on the famous Prima Porta statue of Augustus, discovered in 1863 at the villa of Augustus's wife Livia. The breastplate of this majestic statue depicts a youthful Tiberius receiving an *aquila* from a Parthian representative.[50]

Augustus's successful resolution of the Parthian eagles question by

46.   On the intrigues of Tiridates, see Cassius Dio, *Hist.* 51.18.2-3 and 53.33.1-2.

47.   As argued by D. Magie, 'The Mission of Agrippa to the Orient in 23 BC', *CP* 3 (1908), pp. 145-52.

48.   Horace addresses several of his letters to members of Tiberius's staff who served on this expedition. See *Epistles* I.3.1-5; I.8.1-2; I.9. Also note *Res Gestae* 27.2.

49.   Horace, *Epistles* I.12.27-28, refers to this event.

50.   N. Hannestad, *Roman Art and Imperial Policy* (Aarhus: Aarhus University Press, 1986), pp. 50-56, and Zanker, *Power*, pp. 188-92 discuss the statue.

diplomatic means, albeit with the threat of military intervention, was heralded as a glowing victory. It prompted many triumphs, celebrations and commemorative building projects in Rome. It also resulted in the placement of four of Phraates's legitimate sons in protective custody in Rome, perhaps as a guarantee against further problems with the troublesome Parthians.[51]

From the time of Augustus's victory over Mark Antony at Actium in 31 BCE to the actual restoration of the standards in 20 BCE the prospect of a retributive war with Parthia became a popular cause. Several of the Augustan poets reflect a growing demand for revenge on the Parthians as a means to restore Roman military honour. Allow me briefly to examine this motif within the writings of four of these poets.

c. *The Parthian Campaign and the Augustan Poets*

Several of the major Augustan poets take up this theme of Roman revenge upon Parthia for humiliations of the past.[52] Many times this hope is allied with flattering praise of Augustus as the one who ended the civil wars which had convulsed Rome for a generation. Note for instance, Horace, *Odes* I.2.21-24, where it is proclaimed that the energy spent hitherto on civil war is better directed against the Parthians:

> Youth made few by parents' vice, shall hear
> of swords whetted for civil strife which better
> had slain fell Parthians; shall hear
> of battles fought.

This destruction of the Parthians is conceived as part of a generalized campaign of Augustus against eastern peoples. We see how the military might of Augustus was anticipated to hold sway not only over the Parthians, but over other nations as well. Note these two passages from

---

51.   The ancient sources are divided as to the reason for this placement of Phraates's children under protective custody in Rome. The issue is mentioned in the following sources: *Res Gestae* 32; Velleius Paterculus, *History of Rome* II.94.4; Suetonius, *Augustus* 21, 43; *Tiberius* 9; Cassius Dio, *Hist.* 54.8; Strabo, *Geography* 6.4.2; 16.1.28; Tacitus, *Annals* II.1; Josephus, *Ant.* 18.39-43. For further discussion of the incident see L.R. Taylor, 'M. Titius and the Syrian Command', *JRS* 26 (1936), pp. 161-73; F.E. Romer, 'Gaius Caesar's Military Diplomacy in the East', *TPAPA* 109 (1979), pp. 199-214.

52.   See H.D. Meyer, *Die Aussenpolitik des Augustus und die Augusteische Dichtung* (Kölner Historische Abhandlungen, 5; Böhlau Verlag: Köln, 1961), on this subject, especially pp. 5-9.

Horace which were published c. 23 BCE as part of his first collection of *Odes*:[53]

> Father and Guardian of the human race,
> son of Saturn, to you the Fates have given
> the care of mighty Caesar: you reign,
> and Caesar next.
> After you he rules, with equity, Earth,
> whether he leads in a just triumph
> the Parthians tamed that threaten Rome
> or else, brought low,
> the Indians and Seres of the Eastern borders:
> yours with your heavy car to shake Olympus,
> yours to launch down thunderbolts upon
> polluted groves. (I.12.49-60)

> Augustus shall be held
> an earthly God for adding to the Empire
> the Britons and redoubtable Parthians.
> Did Crassus' troops live in scandalous
> marriage to barbarians (O Senate,
> and custom perverted), grow old
> bearing arms for alien fathers-in-law;
> Did Marsians, Apulians, under a Parthian
> king, forget their sacred shields,
> the name, the toga, and immortal Vesta;
> while Jove and his city Rome were unharmed? (III.5.2-12)

Indeed, the particularly galling offence of the loss of Crassus's legionary eagles comes out in this further passage from Horace's pen:[54]

> Already twice Monaeses and Pacorus' band
> have crushed our ill-starred offensive
> and preen themselves on having added
> Roman spoils to their paltry gauds. (*Odes* III.6.9-12)

Ovid too speaks of the victorious Parthian campaign in glowing terms. Within the *Fasti* he magnifies Augustus for restoring Roman pride in arranging the return of Crassus's eagles.[55]

---

53. See also *Odes* I.21.13-16; II.9.19-22; IV.5.25-27 (published c. 13 BCE); *Centennial Hymn* 49-46 (published c. 16 BCE); *Epistles* II.1.256.

54. Compare this with *Odes* IV.15.4-7 in which the return of the eagles has already been effected. This fourth book of Horace's *Odes* appeared c. 13 BCE. Also note his *Epistles* I.18.55-58.

55. This is part of a longer section of the *Fasti* which runs from V.579-98. Also

The Parthians kept the Roman standards, the glory of war, and a foe was
the standard-bearer of the Roman eagle. That shame would have endured
till now, had not Ausonias' empire been guarded by Caesar's powerful
arms. He put an end to the old reproach, to the disgrace of a whole generation: the recovered standards knew their true owners again. (585-590)

The Parthian campaigns of Augustus even figure within the poetry of
Propertius, albeit with a characteristically anti-Augustan touch. Note, for
instance, *Poems* II.7.13-14, where Propertius is railing against the strict
marriage laws introduced by Augustus and interjects this comment
about the proposed eastern war:[56]

How could I offer sons for Parthian triumphs?
There will be no soldier from my blood.

In *Poems* III.4.1-10 we find the eastern campaign of Augustus discussed
with an explicit reference to the recovery of Crassus's legionary
standards:[57]

God Caesar ponders war against rich India,
Would cleave with his fleet the foam of pearl-bearing seas,
Men, the reward is high: farthest earth gets ready triumphs:
Tigris, Euphrates shall flow beneath your rule:
Though late, that province shall come to Ausonian rods:
Parthian trophies shall grow accustomed to Latin Jove.
Begin at once: prows proved in war, set your sails:
Armour-bearing horses, lead on in your usual office!
I sing auspicious omens. Atone for Crassus' loss!
Go, and take thought for Roman history.

However, we would be mistaken if we took this passage as an indication of Propertius's wholehearted support for the Augustan campaign.
On the contrary, in the subsequent lines he registers his lack of enthusiasm for it by being content to view any resultant triumphs and spoils
from a distance while leaning on the breast of his precious girl Cynthia
(line 15). He thus leaves us in no doubt as to whether his primary
allegiance is to military victory or romantic conquest.[58]

note VI.465-68. This work was probably written just prior to Ovid's exile in 8 CE.
    56.   One of the reasons Propertius is not very supportive of such a Parthian
campaign is that it involves warring with descendants of Roman soldiers—that is,
those who were captured in Crassus's disaster at Carrhae and subsequently married
Parthian women. On this see *Poems* II.30.7-11.
    57.   Also note the brief allusion to the Parthian war in II.27.5; II.12.3; IV.3.67.
    58.   Ovid also turns to the idea of the Roman campaign against the Parthians as

This tongue-in-cheek support of the Parthian campaign is echoed in *Poems* III.5.47-48 where Propertius declares:

> You who welcome war, bring Crassus' standards home.

Once again, the implication is that Propertius himself is not to be counted among those who welcome war. In *Poems* IV.6.79-84 the proposed Parthian campaign is presented as the logical follow-up to Augustus's victory over Mark Antony at Actium in 31 BCE. Crassus is to be avenged thereby. One of the Muses is called upon to provide inspiration for Propertius's account of this victory:

> Another [Muse] recalls the Parthian conceding defeat in a tardy truce:
> 'Let him give back her standards to Rome: soon he will give
> His own: If Augustus spares at all the Eastern quivers,
> May it be because he leaves such trophies for the boys.[59]
> If in the dark sand you feel anything, Crassus, rejoice:
> We may go across Euphrates to your grave.'

Finally, Virgil (70–19 BCE), perhaps the greatest of the Augustan poets, has the occasional reference to the proposed Parthian campaign of his hero Augustus. Note, for example, the following two passages:

> There was a sacred custom in Latium, Land of the West, which the Alban Cities continuously observed, and Rome, supreme in all the world, observes today when Romans first stir Mars to engage battle, alike if they prepare to launch war's miseries with might and main on Getae, Hyrcanians, or Arabs, or to journey to India, in the track of the dawn, and to bid the Parthians hand our standards back. (*Aeneid* VII.601-606)

> This song of the husbandry of crops and beasts
> And fruit trees I was singing while great Caesar
> Was thundering beside the deep Euphrates
> In war, victoriously for grateful peoples
> Appointing laws and setting his course for Heaven. (*Georgics* IV.558-562)

a convenient image for the battle between the sexes. There is thus a strong link between sexual conquest and military war imagery in his writing. Note, for instance, *Cures for Love* 155-59; 224-25; *Art of Love* II.175. Indeed, Ovid's most detailed account of the military triumphs celebrated by Augustus in Rome (*Art of Love* I.177-228) is set within the context of its providing an ideal opportunity to chase a new mistress. See his *Poems* II.14.21-24. L. Cahoon, 'The Bed as Battlefield: Erotic Conquest and Military Metaphor in Ovid's *Amores*', *TPAPA* 118 (1988), pp. 93-107, discusses the theme.

59.   The reference to 'the boys' in line 82 in all probability points to Drusus and Tiberius as Augustus's adopted step-sons and their role in following up his successes.

In summary, the Parthian campaign of Augustus, along with the closely associated aim of effecting the return of the captured legionary eagles, are important motifs within several of the poets of the time. I will now turn to consider another contemporary expression of the glorification of Augustus's achievements in this regard, namely the cistophori issues of Pergamum.

d. *The Pergamene Cistophori*

The set of three cistophori issued by Pergamum in 19–18 BCE provides us with a convenient means of discussing some of the celebrations associated with the diplomatic achievement of Augustus over the Parthians. The city of Pergamum was the Roman administrative capital for the province of Asia, and as such it had enjoyed very special privileges within the province. One such privilege was the right to mint commemorative gold and silver coinage in the name of the Emperor. Generally, the minting of gold and silver coins was the prerogative of the Imperial mints, such as the one in Lugdunum, which were directly under the Emperor's control. Occasionally, however, certain cities or states within the Empire were allowed to produce their own gold or silver issues, usually as an acknowledgment of faithful service to Rome or as a means of furthering Imperial interests in these localized settings. Much of the time such indigenous issues were designed for local circulation or use and their language of inscription was Greek. The cistophori[60] we are considering, on the other hand, have Latin inscriptions which serves as an indication of their semi-official status. They were in all likelihood issued as part of the extensive propaganda effort surrounding Augustus's achievements with respect to the return of the Parthian eagles.[61] It seems that this was not the first time that Pergamum was privileged to issue such a set of commemorative cistophori in Augustus's honour. There exists another set of three cistophori, dated to c. 27–26 BCE, all of which contain the title AVGVSTVS within their reverse inscription and which were probably issued to commemorate Octavian's assumption of

60.   A cistophorus was the equivalent of three Roman denarii. It weighed approximately 12 grams.

61.   C.H.V. Sutherland, *The Cistophori of Augustus* (London: Royal Numismatic Society, 1970), p. 34, suggests that as many as 1,000,000 coins were issued within the series. The whole subject of the Parthian conquest on Roman coins is briefly discussed in G.F. Hill, *Historical Roman Coins* (London: Constable and Co., 1909), pp. 138-43.

that title in 27 BCE.[62] However, it is impossible positively to assign this commemorative set to the Pergamum mint as neither their inscriptions nor their use of subject motifs clearly links them to that city.

With respect to the set of cistophori with which we are more directly concerned, we are fortunate to be in a position to date them positively and assign them as issues of the mint of Pergamum in the years 19–18 BCE. This is achieved via several clues gleaned from the coins themselves. The first and most important one is derived from the obverse inscription found in all three coins of the set. The obverse bears a portrait bust of Augustus facing right together with the inscription IMP IX TR PO V, the last letter of which dates the coin to the fifth year of his tribunicial power (Figure 17).[63] A less common inscription is IMP IX TR PO IV, which dates the coin to the previous year.[64] According to C.H.V. Sutherland, Augustus's fourth tenure of *tribunicia potestas* began on 27 June 20 BCE and his fifth tenure expired on 26 June 18 BCE.[65] This sets the absolute dating limits within which the coins must have been issued. Sutherland, on the basis of portraiture style and execution of design, restricts their issue even further to 19–18 BCE. This suggested dating is supported by the subject motifs of the reverses of the coins as a set—that is to say that two of the reverses contain clear references to the return of the Parthian Eagles to Roman hands in 20 BCE. In addition, the reverse of the third type of the set serves to link it quite clearly to the city of Pergamum. I will now examine each of the reverses in turn.

62.   These three cistophori all bear the same obverse bust portrait of Augustus. The reverses all, in one way or another, reflect Augustan themes. For instance, one of the reverses shows a seated sphinx. It is known that Augustus used the Sphinx as his regal symbol and carried a ring with a sphinx emblem as his official document seal (Suetonius, *Augustus* 50; Pliny, *Natural History* 37.4.10). Another of the three reverses bears a capricorn, the astrological sign of his birthdate (Suetonius, *Augustus* 5). The third reverse bears a bunch of corn-ears, perhaps a reminder of his defeat of Antony and Cleopatra in Egypt in 30 BCE and of his restoration of the grain-channels from there to Rome.

63.   *RIC* Augustus 505-510.

64.   One of the three types of the set, the Mars Temple reverse, has not been found with this less common inscription.

65.   *Cistophori*, p. 34. Augustus assumed the title of Imperator for the ninth time in connection with the Parthian victory. See T.D. Barnes, 'The Victories of Augustus', *JRS* 64 (1974), pp. 21-26, for a chronological study of his imperatorships.

1. *Triumphal Arch Reverse*. This reverse type (Figure 18)[66] is the most interesting of the set so far as inscriptional evidence is concerned. It contains a triumphal arch which is decorated with *aquilae* on either side and which is surmounted by a quadriga and driver. On the entablature of the arch itself is the inscription which we have noted above was common to the reverses of the set: IMP IX TR POT V. Once again the variant IMP IX TR PO IV is also known, as is the even rarer variant IMP IX TR PO V.[67] A second inscription is found within the arch which reads, in three lines, SPR SIGNIS RECEPTIS. Thus, through these two reverse inscriptions we are able not only to date the coins specifically to 19–18 BCE (the appropriate years of Augustus's tenure of *tribunicia potestas*), but also to associate them with the celebrated return of the legionary eagles to Roman hands.

Figure 17   Figure 18

What of the triumphal arch itself? What do we know of such an arch and its erection as part of the celebrations surrounding this diplomatic victory over the Parthians? We do know, for instance, that Cassius Dio, *Hist.* 54.8, discusses the incident and makes specific mention of the new buildings which were erected as part of the celebrations. In all likelihood, the triumphal arch depicted on the cistophorus is a representation of one erected by Augustus to this end. Possibly it originally stood in the Forum of Augustus. Are we able to go any further and date the time of the erection of such a triumphal arch? In order to answer this question more fully it is necessary to examine in more detail the cistophorus of the set which bears the Mars Temple reverse.

2. *Mars Temple Reverse*. This reverse type (Figure 19)[68] is in many ways the most aesthetically appealing. It depicts a circular, domed temple within which is placed a legionary vexillum. A set of four or five steps grace

66.   *RIC* Augustus 508-510.

67.   For an explanation of how these variants may have arisen, see A.M. Woodward, 'Notes on the Augustan Cistophori', *NC* 12 (1952), pp. 19-32.

68.   *RIC* Augustus 507.

the front of the temple, and a set of four columns support the domed roof. In the field of the coin is the inscription MART VLTO. The exact date of the dedication of the temple of Mars the Victor in Rome is a matter of some scholarly debate. We do know that it was vowed by Octavian before the battle of Philippi and that it was eventually con-structed in the Forum of Augustus (*Res Gestae* 21.1). But do we know exactly when it was dedicated?

Several of the ancient sources are united in presenting 12 May 2 BCE as the date of such a dedication. Ovid's *Fasti*, V.545-598, for instance, clearly associates the Parthian standards with the dedication of the temple of Mars on this date. The *Res Gestae* 22.2 concurs by placing the Ludi Martiales within the thirteenth consulship of Augustus (2 BCE). Velleius Paterculus's *History of Rome*, II.100.2, also confirms the date by reference to the dedication as taking place within the year that Augustus shared the consulship with Gallus Caninius (2 BCE). The chronological problems are highlighted by Cassius Dio who gives a rather confused account of the incident. In his *Hist.* 55.10.4 he specifically refers to the placement of the recovered military standards within the Mars Temple, and in 60.5.3 1 August is given as the day on which the temple of Mars was originally dedicated in 2 BCE and as the date on which subsequent anniversary cele-brations were held.[69] This slight discrepancy of a few months between Cassius Dio and other ancient sources might easily be absorbed were it not for the fact that in *Hist.* 54.8.3 the return of the Parthian eagles in 20 BCE is discussed with reference to their placement within the temple of Mars *at that time*. One way in which this discrepancy is handled is to suggest that the standards were placed in a temporary temple until the permanent temple of Mars was constructed some 18 years later in 2 BCE. In other words, it is suggested[70] that Cassius Dio's reference in 54.8.3 is to the date on which a formal decision to build such a temple to Mars was taken, in 20 BCE, and that it is to be distinguished from the date of the temple's official dedication which took place in 2 BCE.[71] One final

---

69.   Livy, *Summaries* 141, specifically dates the return of the Parthian eagles to 11–10 BCE.

70.   As in C.J. Simpson, 'The Date of the Dedication of the Temple of Mars Ultor', *JRS* 67 (1977), pp. 91-94.

71.   F.E. Romer, 'A Numismatic Date for the Departure of C. Caesar?', *TPAPA* 108 (1978), pp. 187-202, offers an interesting argument in support of the 2 BCE date based on the interpretation of the reverse of one particular issue of aureus (*RIC* Augustus 198-99).

puzzling fact is that within both Horace, *Odes* IV.16.6, and Propertius, *Poems* III.4.6, the recaptured Parthian eagles are associated with the temple of Jupiter on the Capitol instead of the temple of Mars. Perhaps this temple of Jupiter itself was the temporary resting place for the standards which only later became housed permanently within the temple of Mars in the Forum of Augustus.[72]

In any event, the cistophorus bearing the Mars temple reverse was certainly issued as a means of associating the return of the Parthian standards with the benevolent protectorate of Mars the Avenger over the Augustan house. Even if we cannot be absolutely certain about the exact date and place of the dedication of the temple to Mars, we are left in no doubt as to the clear message that such a reverse type communicated.

3. *Commune Temple Reverse*. This reverse type (Figure 20)[73] provides us with a most important clue for determining the provenance of the cistophori under consideration. It depicts a hexastyle temple with a series of four or five steps gracing the front of the temple entrance. There are six Corinthian columns which support the roof of the temple, the entablature of which reads ROM(a) ET AVGVST(us). In the field to the right

Figure 19   Figure 20

and left of the temple itself is the important inscription COM ASIAE. It is the combination of these two inscriptions which enables us to establish that it is a representation of the Temple of Roma and Augustus which stood in Pergamum. As mentioned above, we know that Pergamum was the Roman administrative capital of the province of Asia (the Commune Asiae which gives rise to the abbreviated inscription in the field on the reverse of the coin). We also know through Cassius Dio, *Hist.* 51.20.6-8, that in 29 BCE the city of Pergamum was allowed to erect a temple dedicated to the worship of Roma and Augustus.[74] This was a significant

72.   C.J. Simpson, 'Date', p. 93, suggests this. Also note the discussion in G.F. Hill, *Historical,* pp. 141-43.

73.   *RIC* Augustus 508.

74.   The temple is discussed within S.R.F. Price, *Rituals and Powers: The*

new move on behalf of the developing Emperor cultus of the time. Up until that time the worship of the reigning Emperor had never been directly associated with the worship of Roma itself. A precedent of a sort had been set earlier in the form of temples erected within select cities of Asia Minor for the worship of the Divine Julius. These were erected at the instigation of Augustus himself who actively promoted the Senate's acceptance of the apotheosis of Julius Caesar following his murder in 44 BCE. Augustus benefitted directly from the elevation of his adopted father, and we are certainly correct in seeing these temples to the Divine Julius as helping to pave the way for the later cult of the reigning Emperor. Nevertheless, we must not overlook the significance of the step taken by Pergamum in erecting the Temple to Roma and Augustus, nor the close relationship engendered between the Imperial throne and the provinces by such expressions of cultic worship. As G.F. Hill remarks on the importance of this development of a provincial cult,

> This provincial cult was the focus of the official religion of the provinces during the first three centuries of the Empire, and its importance cannot be exaggerated as a public expression of the relations between the provinces and Rome. Its organization was one of the most masterly achievements of Augustus.[75]

Thus it appears that we have within this reverse type an ideal example of how the city of Pergamum was allowed to publicize its own specific privileges with regard to the imperial cultus of the time. It was a mutually beneficial arrangement whereby the glories of Augustus's recent diplomatic triumph regarding the Parthian eagles was highlighted; at the same time, as the unique position of power and responsibility of the city of Pergamum itself, the seat of the provincial worship of both Roma and Augustus, is proudly asserted.

One final historical episode is worthy of brief attention. It too involves the loss of Roman legionary *aquilae* to a foreign army.

3. *The Military Disaster in Germany in 9 CE and the Triumph of Germanicus on Coinage of Caligula*

Roman military interest in Germany was longstanding. The crossing of the Rhine by Roman troops took place in 12 BCE while Augustus reigned

---

Roman Imperial Cult in Asia Minor (Cambridge: Cambridge University Press, 1984), pp. 182, 252. A similar temple was erected in Nicomedia in Bithynia.

    75.   G.F. Hill, *Historical*, p. 145.

as Emperor and was led by Nero Claudius Drusus, Augustus's stepson and the brother of the future Emperor Tiberius. Unfortunately the extremely successful Drusus died three years later, the victim of a horse-riding accident. By this time Roman troops had reached as far as the Elbe river and were well on the way to subduing the whole area. Tiberius succeeded his deceased brother as commander of the expedition and concluded it with his usual efficiency and precision, retiring from public life shortly thereafter in 6 BCE.

Tiberius next appears on the German scene some ten years later, in 4 CE when Roman troops were preparing for an expedition across the Danube. Tiberius led a portion of this expeditionary force from German soil across the Danube into the regions of Bohemia and Dacia. The military legions remaining in Germany, a much weakened force, were left under the command of one Publius Quinctilius Varus. This was to prove a fatal miscalculation, for the local German tribes rebelled in the summer of 9 CE and wiped out three Roman legions, killing Varus in the process. This so-called 'Varian disaster' was to prove one of the most embarrassing defeats of the Roman imperial army and set the tone for nearly a century afterwards; no serious attempt to reconquer the lost area was made and Roman troops were content to stay on the west bank of the Rhine. More to the point as far as this study is concerned, the three Varian legions, the 18th, the 19th and the 20th, lost their legionary *aquilae* in the rebellion.[76] Tiberius was assigned to clear up the disaster as far as possible and made some cautious forays into German territory before taking up the reins of power following the death of Augustus in 14 CE. He was succeeded by Germanicus, the son of Drusus (mentioned above), who also distinguished himself in several skirmishes in 14–16 CE. Yet, Tacitus, *Annals* 1.3, tells us that Germanicus's actions were 'designed less to extend the empire's frontiers, or achieve any lucrative purpose, than to avenge the disgrace of the army lost with Publius Quinctilius Varus'.

Nevertheless, the exploits of Germanicus were commemorated on coinage issued by his son, the Emperor Caligula (37–41 CE). One of these issues, a dupondius, is particularly suited for our consideration in that it alludes to the victories of Germanicus and the return of Varus's lost legionary eagles to Roman control. The obverse of the coin presents an image of Germanicus riding in a triumphal quadriga with the inscription

---

76. An entertaining fictional account of the events of 26 August–10 September 9 CE is found in G. Solon, *The Three Legions* (London: Constable, 1957). See also S. Eden, *Military Blunders* (New York: Friedman, 1995), pp. 12-16.

Figure 21

GERMANICVS CAESAR above; the reverse has an image of the general, in military uniform and cradling an *aquila* in his left arm, with the inscription SIGNIS RECEPT(is) DEVICTIS GERM(anis) above the standard initials S C which are in the field (Figure 21).[77]

4. *Matthew 24.28/Luke 17.37: 'Where the Carcass is, There the Eagles Will Be Gathered Together.'*

What makes the numismatic evidence presented here so fascinating for New Testament studies is the obvious association between military legions and the symbol of the *aquilae*. There seems little doubt that the image of a legionary *aquila* would have been widely known throughout the Empire and that it came to symbolize the power of the Roman military which held the Imperial state together.[78] As J. Helgeland remarks, 'Throughout the history of Rome the eagle has been identified with the destiny of the empire.'[79] Early on in his reign Augustus himself had adopted the eagle as an Imperial symbol on coinage, as a finely executed aureus from the mint of Rome illustrates. This coin was issued in c. 27 CE and shows an obverse bust of a bare-headed Augustus surrounded by the inscription CAESAR COS VI CIVIBVS SERVATIS. The reverse shows an eagle with his wings spread, clutching an oak wreath in his claws.

77.   *RIC* Gaius 57.

78.   The vision contained in 4 Ezra 11–12 uses the symbol of an eagle for the Roman Empire, with the author cleverly updating the four empire scheme of Dan. 7 to his own day. For a recent discussion of this see M.E. Stone, *Fourth Ezra* (Hermeneia; Minneapolis, MN: Fortress Press, 1990), pp. 343-71. Stone interprets the three heads of the eagle (11.1) to be the Flavian Emperors (Vespasian, Titus and Domitian) and on this basis dates the vision to the late 90's CE.

79.   'Roman Army Religion', *ANRW*, II.16.2, p. 1473. Helgeland discusses legionary *aquilae* as an illustration of how closely interwoven religion and the military were in Roman life. A number of passages dealing with legionary eagles are usefully brought together here.

Above the eagle the inscription AVGVSTVS appears flanked by two laurel branches; the letters S C stand in exergue (Figure 22).[80] The *aquila* was a striking military and political image and had been so for many years, as the numismatic evidence I have surveyed shows. Moreover, military symbols, such as that of the legionary *aquilae*, stood as real points of controversy in Jerusalem itself, as the celebrated incident wherein Herod the Great erected a large golden eagle over the entrance to the Temple indicates (see Josephus, *Ant.* 17.6.2).[81] Another incident, which is remarkably similar to this act of King Herod, occurred in 26 CE where the newly appointed procurator Pontius Pilate allowed his soldiers to enter Jerusalem under cover of darkness and offend the Jews of the city by carrying images of the Emperor among their military standards (see Josephus, *Ant.* 18.3.1; *War* 2.9.2-3).[82]

Figure 22

I turn now to the cryptic statement of Jesus recorded in Mt. 24.28/ Lk. 17.37 and seek to examine it in light of our study of the image of military symbols such as the legionary *aquilae*. Let me begin by noting some of the recent discussion of this cryptic saying of Jesus.

The Jesus Seminar panel of New Testament scholars led by Robert Funk has offered an interesting basis for discussion of the historicity of the various Gospel accounts; that is, the four canonical Gospels together with the *Gospel of Thomas*. Ultimately the aim is to try and determine what things Jesus actually said, while at the same time give some account of how the early Christians expanded and adapted and reinterpreted his words. The various Gospel sayings attributed to Jesus are sorted into four groups, ranging from the actual words of Jesus to obvious later interpretative comment (arising out of the early traditions of the church

80.   *RIC* Augustus 277.
81.   On this incident see C. Roth, 'An Ordinance against Images in Jerusalem, AD 66', *HTR* 49 (1956), pp. 169-77.
82.   C.H. Kraeling, 'The Episode of the Roman Standards at Jerusalem', *HTR* 35 (1942), pp. 263-89, discusses this. Pilate also embroiled himself in a variety of other related clashes along these lines. See P.L. Maier, 'The Episode of the Golden Roman Shields at Jerusalem', *HTR* 62 (1969), pp. 109-21.

communities, or perhaps even coming from the Gospel writer as he is engaged in the process of putting his Gospel together). To assist with the visual presentation of the results, each of the four categories of sayings is assigned a different colour (red, pink, grey, black). The effect is to present something of a modern-day red-letter edition of the sayings of Jesus, albeit this time in a much more sophisticated, multi-colour version which attempts to be sensitive to the historical problems associated with contemporary Gospel studies.

The passage under scrutiny here, the Q saying of Mt. 24.28/Lk. 17.37, is given a grey rating by the panel. This means that the saying is deemed *not* to be the words of Jesus himself, but that the ideas contained within it are thought to be close to Jesus' own. The possibility that the saying was proverbial, and that Jesus may have been quoting it, is acknowledged.[83] The exact connection that such a proverbial saying has with Matthew's or Luke's context is said by the Jesus Seminar panel to be 'unclear'.

A wide variety of interpretations of the saying have been offered, sometimes with bizarre associations between the key elements in the proverb. A prime example is L.T. Johnson who offers this remark on the saying: 'Vultures gather wherever there is carrion. The kingdom is wherever the people are gathered by God's word.'[84] M. Davies offers a much more believable interpretation, one which focuses on the theme of false prophets which runs through Matthew's Gospel. She interprets the saying to mean, 'Where the corpse [the false prophet] is, there will the vultures [unjust people] gather.'[85] Much revolves around the central imagery of the eagle/vulture and what one takes that to mean within the proverbial saying. The image of an eagle as a symbol of swift judgment is frequently found in the Old Testament, and this offers a promising way forward. One oft-cited passage illustrating this is Hab. 1.8. Here Chaldean horsemen,

83.   R.W. Funk, R.W. Hoover and the Jesus Seminar, *The Five Gospels: The Search for the Authentic* Words *of Jesus* (New York: Macmillan, 1993), p. 249 (for Mt. 24.28) and p. 368 (for Lk. 17.37). The work of the Jesus Seminar has come under considerable attack as being motivated by the American phenomenon known as political correctness. See R.B. Hays, 'The Corrected Jesus', *First Things* 43 (1994), pp. 43-48; H.C. Kee, 'A Century of Quests for the Culturally Compatible Jesus', *TTod* 51 (1995), pp. 17-28; C.H. Talbert, 'Political Correctness Invades Jesus Research: A Review Essay', *PRS* 21 (1994), pp. 245-52; B.A. Pearson, 'The Gospel according to the Jesus Seminar', *Religion* 25 (1995), pp. 317-38.

84.   *The Gospel of Luke* (Sacra Pagina, 3; Collegeville, MN: Liturgical Press, 1991), p. 267.

85.   *Matthew* (Readings; JSOT Press: Sheffield, 1993), p. 168.

Striking New Images

who are enacting God's judgment upon the nation Israel, are likened to a variety of animals including the eagle swooping down upon its prey with unexpected fury: 'Their horses are swifter than leopards, more fierce than the evening wolves; their horsemen press proudly on. Yea, their horsemen come from afar; they fly like an eagle swift to devour.' Many New Testament commentaries fail to mention the possibility of the legionary *aquila* as underlying the statement by Jesus; others simply dismiss the suggestion altogether. Thus, N. Geldenhuys suggests that Jesus' saying was 'probably a well-known Palestinian proverb',[86] but does not make any reference to the Roman military imagery as a possible basis for such a proverb, even at a secondary level. E.E. Ellis, commenting on Lk. 17.37, is more forthright and describes the reference to eagles as a 'proverbial symbol of judgment and not Roman standards conquering Jerusalem'.[87] The same sort of remarks are made about the Matthean version of the saying. For example, D. Hill comments, 'It is unlikely that *ptoma* (body) includes a reference to the crucified body of Jesus or to the city of Jerusalem sacked by Roman legions.'[88] Similarly, R.H. Gundry, commenting on Mt. 24.28, acknowledges the theoretical possibility of the military imagery, but dismisses it as a valid interpretation when he says,

86. *Commentary on the Gospel of Luke* (NICNT; Grand Rapids, MI: Eerdmanns, 1979), p. 442. A. Maclaren, *Expositions of Holy Scripture: The Gospel according to Saint Matthew (Chapters XVIII–XXVIII)* (London: Hodder & Stoughton, 1906), p. 159, disagrees and describes the verse as a grim parable in which the Roman eagles are 'God's scavengers, to sweep away the nation...which had now come to be a rotting abomination'.

87. *The Gospel of Luke* (NCB; London: Marshall, Morgan & Scott, 1974), p. 212. Ellis does make cross reference to 21.20 where Luke alludes to the Roman destruction of the city. It is sometimes argued that Lk. 21.20-36 is an independent oracle which was penned during the traumatic years of the First Jewish Revolt. See V. Taylor, 'A Cry from the Siege: A Suggestion Regarding a Non-Marcan Oracle Embedded in Lk XXI 20-36', *JTS* 26 (1925), pp. 136-43, for a classic discussion along these lines. Alternatively, it is not infrequently argued that the passage from Luke predates the fall of Jerusalem, as B. Reicke, 'Synoptic Prophecies on the Destruction of Jerusalem', in D.A. Aune (ed.), *Studies in New Testament and Early Christian Literature: Essays in Honor of Allen F. Wikgren* (NovTSup, 33; Leiden: Brill, 1972), pp. 121-34, serves to illustrate.

88. *The Gospel of Matthew* (NCB; London: Marshall, Morgan & Scott, 1972), p. 322. Why it is 'unlikely' is never explained.

Some have thought that ὁι ἀετοί refers to the eagles of the Roman legions swooping down on Jerusalem during the first Jewish revolt (AD 66–73); but the context in Luke has nothing about the destruction of Jerusalem, and Matthew focuses attention on the Son of man's coming rather than on the destruction of the city.[89]

What is singularly unsatisfying about a remark such as Gundry's is its failure to recognize the nature of Jesus' declaration in Mt. 24.28/Lk. 17.37 as evidence of the wider concerns of apocalyptic expectation. Just because Luke does not happen to mention the destruction of Jerusalem here, or Matthew concentrates on the christological implications of the coming of the Son of Man instead of the cataclysm of Jerusalem with which it is associated in Jesus' mind, does not mean that there is no connection between the saying of Jesus and the destruction of the city of Jerusalem at the hands of the Roman legions. Indeed, one could make a good case for exactly the opposite; namely that the saying of Jesus recorded in Mt. 24.28/Lk. 17.37 has at its root the idea that the legionary eagles will be the instrument whereby the 'corpse' of Judaism (as personified by its capital Jerusalem) will be devoured. Such an interpretation fits well with other passages, particularly in the Gospel of Luke, where allusions to the destruction of Jerusalem by the Roman legions are integrated with material based on Jesus' Olivet discourse contained in Mark 13. The classic instance of this is, of course, Lk. 21.20.[90]

Only occasionally do commentators of Matthew and Luke seriously break from this approach of denying or downplaying the connection between the legionary *aquilae* and Jesus' saying about the eagles. For example, A.R.C. Leaney focuses on the term 'eagles' and comments that

---

89.   *Matthew: A Commentary on his Handbook for a Mixed Church under Persecution* (Grand Rapids, MI: Eerdmans, 1994, 2nd edn), p. 487. D.A. Carson, 'Matthew', in F.E. Gabelein (ed.), *The Expositor's Bible Commentary*, VIII (Grand Rapids: Zondervan, 1984), p. 503, is of a similar opinion when he says that the verse 'relates to Parousia, not the Fall of Jerusalem'.

90.   Follow the discussion in G. Braumann, 'Die lukanische Interpretation der Zerstörung Jerusalems', *NovT* 6 (1963), pp. 120-27; F.O. Francis, 'Eschatology and History in Luke–Acts', *JAAR* 37 (1969), pp. 49-63; J.A. Fitzmyer, *The Gospel according to Luke X–XXIV* (AB, 28B; New York: Doubleday, 1985), pp. 1342-47. Strangely, A. Plummer, *The Gospel according to St Luke* (ICC; Edinburgh: T. & T. Clark, 1922, 5th edn), p. 410, comments that 'reference to the eagles of the Roman standards is not the point here, although it is possible [in] Mt. xxiv. 28'.

However originally intended, [it is] apparently taken by Luke to be the Roman standards... This is further evidence that the day to which Luke looks forward in this passage (xvii. 22-37) is that of the destruction of Jerusalem, the consummation of the 'seasons' of the Gentiles, after which the Son of Man will appear (xxi. 24-27).[91]

Similarly, J.A. Fitzmyer remarks on Lk. 17.37, 'There may be an allusion in this reference to 'eagles' to the image of an eagle carried by the Roman armies.'[92] Given the range of opinion about the possibility of the Roman military image as a background to the saying of Mt. 24.28/Lk. 17.37, I turn now to discuss the passage in more detail. Three main issues arise in the interpretation of the saying itself. The first concerns the use of the term ἀετός and the fact that it can be rendered as either 'eagle' or 'vulture'. The second concerns the differences between Matthew's version of the saying and that contained in Luke. The third concerns the meaning of the saying within the larger context of the apocalyptic material in which it is located. Each of these areas is worth considering briefly in order to set the stage for an interpretation which focuses on the Roman legionary *aquilae* as a key to understanding the saying.

First, with regard to the meaning of ἀετός, it is sometimes suggested that the saying suffers from mistranslation in that the Aramaic *nisra* can mean either 'vulture' or 'eagle'.[93] This alleged mistranslation is used by some to explain how a saying which was originally about vultures becomes one about eagles. This is judged to be necessary since (so the argument goes) eagles do not eat carrion and that is clearly an element central to the saying as a whole. In short, an Aramaic saying of Jesus about carrion-eating vultures is mistranslated in Greek into one about eagles. However, the argument does not really stand up to scrutiny and can be faulted both on lexical grounds (the LXX always renders the Hebrew נשׁר as ἀετός) and on ornithological grounds (eagles *do* sometimes eat carrion).[94] In any event, we should not assume that a hard and fast distinction was maintained between eagles and vultures in the ancient world; it would be virtually impossible to distinguish one from the other

91.   *The Gospel according to St Luke* (London: A. & C. Black, 1958), p. 232. Also note J. Drury, *Luke* (JBPC; London: Collins, 1973), p. 167.

92.   *Luke*, p. 1173. He alludes to Josephus, *War* 3.6.2 as a parallel.

93.   J. Jeremias, *The Parables of Jesus* (London: SCM Press, 1972, 2nd edn), p. 162.

94.   See J.S. Kloppenborg, *The Formation of Q* (SAC; Philadelphia: Fortress Press, 1987), pp. 161-62, for details.

when they were soaring high in the sky. The interesting passage on birds from Job 39.26-30 (LXX) also illustrates something of the overlap between the two birds. The section forms part of the Lord's defence of his creative design which is directed at Job as he speaks out of the whirlwind (38.1). More specifically, 39.27 sets out a parallelism between the eagle (ἀετός) and the vulture (γύψ) in successive poetic phrases:

39.26	ἐκ δὲ τῆς σῆς ἐπιστήμης ἔστηκεν ἱέραξ ἀναπετάσας τὰς πτέρυγας ἀκίνητος καθορῶν τὰ πρὸς νότον;
39.27	ἐπὶ δὲ σῷ προστάγματι ὑψοῦται ἀετός; γὺψ δὲ ἀπὶ νοσσιᾶς αὐτοῦ καθεσθεὶς αὐλίζεται
39.28	ἐπ' ἐξοχῇ πέτρας καὶ ἀποκρύφῳ;
39.29	ἐκεῖσε ὢν ζητεῖ τὰ σῖτα, πόρρωθεν οἱ ὀφθαλμοὶ αὐτοῦ σκοπεύουσιν;
39.30	νεοσσοὶ δὲ αὐτοῦ φύρονται ἐν αἵματι, οὗ δ' ἂν ὦσι τεθνεῶτες, παραχπῆμα εὑρίσκονται.

Unfortunately the parallelism set up between the eagle and the vulture in v. 27 does not occur in the MT and is lost in most English translations. Most of them, based on the MT, follow the lead of the RSV and make vv. 27-30 refer to a single bird, the eagle (or hawk).

39.26	Is it by your wisdom that the hawk soars, and spreads his wings toward the south?
39.27	Is it at your command that the eagle mounts up and makes his nest on high?
39.28	On the rock he dwells and makes his home in the fastness of the rocky crag.
39.29	Thence he spies out the prey; his eyes behold it afar off.
39.30	His young ones suck up blood; and where the slain are, there is he.

The passage from Job 39 is certainly interesting, and many point to 39.30 as a possible source for the proverbial saying Jesus seems to be citing in Mt. 24.28/Lk. 17.37. This is frequently suggested, even though neither Mt. 24.28 nor Lk. 17.37 share a single word with the LXX of Job 39.30. However, this need not overly concern us since the Q saying may originally have been uttered by Jesus in Aramaic; as a result, we should not necessarily expect any correspondences in Greek terminology. There is little need to rule out absolutely any influence of Job 39.30 upon the saying of Jesus under discussion, even though it is impossible to say how and in what way it may have shaped Jesus' original declaration.

Second, we note the differences between Matthew's version and Luke's version of the saying. Most agree that the original saying was

part of the so-called Q Apocalypse and that it has been integrated with
other apocalyptic material from Mark in both Matthew and Luke.
Matthew is probably responsible for the insertion of the subjunctival ἐὰν
ᾖ. It is commonly thought that Lk. 17.37a ('And they said to him,
"Where, Lord?" He said to them') is redactional and sets up the eagle
saying which follows. Matthew has a different word for 'body' in the
saying, substituting πτῶμα ('corpse') for the less vulgar σῶμα contained in Luke (Luke also avoids the use of πτῶμα in his parallel to Mk
15.45).[95] Matthew's term is probably more original given that the saying
is concerned with flesh-consuming birds.

Matthew and Luke appear to have slightly different emphases by
including the eagle saying as they have. For Matthew the stress is on the
sudden revelation of the Son of Man, as the connection with the saying
about lightning flashing from the east to the west in the prior verse
(24.27) indicates; for Luke the stress is on the *imminent judgment* of the
Son of Man, as the two-part saying about two people being separated on
the critical day (17.34-35) indicates.[96] This emphasis on the theme of
judgment in Luke also helps to explain how vv. 25-33 have come to
occupy the place that they do in the Gospel. What is important for my
purposes is that recognition of the judgment motif within these intervening verses in Luke allows us to bring together the saying about lightning

95.   An interesting parallel to this is found in two sayings within the *Gospel of
Thomas*. Logion 56 reads, 'Whoever has known the world has found a corpse
(πτῶμα), and whoever has found a corpse (πτῶμα), of him the world is not
worthy'; logion 80 reads, 'Whoever has known the world has found the body
(σῶμα), and whoever has found the body (σῶμα), of him the world is not worthy.'
Logion 60 also contains an enigmatic use of πτῶμα which may echo the Q saying:
'They saw a Samaritan carrying a lamb on his way to Judaea. He said to his
disciples, "Why does this man carry the lamb with him?" They said to him, "In
order that he may kill it and eat it." He said to them, "As long as it is alive, he will
not eat it, but only if he has killed it and it has become a corpse (πτῶμα)." They said,
"Otherwise he will not be able to do it." He said to them, "You yourselves, seek a
place for yourselves in repose, lest you become a corpse (πτῶμα) and be eaten."'
Clearly πτῶμα here carries a christological sense which is not explicit in the Q
saying, although many commentators do interpret the verses in that way. It is
perhaps worth noting that the very next saying in the *Gospel of Thomas* (logion 61)
begins with an image which may be drawn from Lk. 17.34-35/Mt. 20.40-41. It
reads, 'Jesus said, "Two will rest on a bed: the one will die, the one will live."'

96.   G.R. Beasley-Murray, *Jesus and the Kingdom of God* (Exeter: Paternoster
Press, 1986), pp. 321-22, and H.O. Guenther, 'When "Eagles" Draw Together',
Foundations and Facets Forum 5 (1989), pp. 140-50, both discuss this.

(17.24) and the eagle saying (17.37), just as they have been preserved in Matthew's account (24.27-28).[97] In other words, there is something to be said for taking the two sayings (lightning and eagle) as originally belonging together.[98] They share a common theme, the sudden and unmistakable arrival of the Son of Man who comes in judgment, and they use stock metaphors drawn from the world of apocalyptic literature to express this conviction.[99] Let us assume then that there is some justification for maintaining a direct link between the lightning saying and the eagle saying in precisely the manner that Matthew has them. What of the difference in the way that the lightning saying is expressed in Matthew as compared to Luke? Matthew says, 'the lightning comes from the east and shines as far as the west' (ἡ ἀστραπὴ ἐξέρχεται ἀπὸ ἀνατολῶν καὶ φαίνεται ἕως δυσμῶν), while Luke says, 'the lightning flashes and lights up the sky from one side to the other' (ἡ ἀστραπὴ ἀστράπτουσα ἐκ τῶς ὑπὸ τὸν οὐρανὸν εἰς τὴν ὑπ' οὐρανὸν λάμπει). How does this change come about? It is sometimes suggested that Matthew's imagery is more suitable to the sun than to lightning insofar as the sun's light moves from the east to the west. It may well be that this confusion of imagery is precisely the reason why Luke alters the description to a more generalized one more conducive to lightning which is not restricted to such an east-west pattern. On the other hand, it could be that the idea of lightning coming 'from the east' in Mt. 24.27 is not so much an image about thunderstorms as a veiled reference to the arrival of an apocalyptic Son of Man figure from the east. The fact that there is a well-established tradition of the anti-Christ, the Nero *redivivus*, as coming to Judaea from the east (Parthia?) may

97.   It is sometimes suggested that Luke has moved 17.37b to the end of the pericope in order to avoid an unpleasant comparison between the Son of Man and the eagles/vultures. On this see S. Schulz, *Q: Die Spruchquelle der Evangelisten* (Zürich: Theologische Verlag, 1972), p. 280, who describes such a comparison as 'indecent' (anstößig).

98.   H.E. Tödt, *The Son of Man in the Synoptic Tradition* (London: SCM Press, 1965), p. 50, goes so far as to suggest that the eagle saying is a commentary on the lightning saying in Q. R. Schnackenburg, 'Der eschatologische Abschnitt Lk. 17:20-37', in A. Descamps and A. de Halleux (eds.), *Mélanges Bibliques: En Hommage au R.P. Béda Rigaux* (Gembloux: Duculot, 1970), pp. 213-34, disagrees, arguing instead that 17.37b was linked with Lk. 17.34-35 in Q.

99.   D. Catchpole, *The Quest for Q* (Edinburgh: T. & T. Clark, 1993), pp. 253-55, discusses the use of the image of lightning as a symbol of judgment in a number of Jewish texts.

also be taken as tangential evidence of such an interpretation. That is to say, widespread expectations that the anti-Christ would come from the east could easily be connected to apocalyptic traditions about the arrival of the Son of Man on the day of judgment. However, this is all highly speculative and we may be trying to squeeze more from the cryptic saying about lightning than it is reasonable to expect.

One final point is worth noting when we consider the association between the saying about eagles (Mt. 24.28/Lk. 17.37) and the saying about lightning (Mt. 24.27/Lk. 17.24). It has to do with the fact that in many coin representations of the Roman eagle the creature is portrayed as clutching a bolt of thunder/lightning in its claws. Again this was a standard image in Roman art and is well documented in a variety of media from the first and second centuries, including literature, sculpture, paintings, cameos and so forth. The bolt of thunder/lightning (and the distinction between the two need not bother us too much; the ancients knew as well as we do how close the two are in the natural world!) is intimately associated with Jupiter, chief of the Roman pantheon. As J.R. Fears remarks, 'The god's thunderbolt epitomized the entire conception of divine power exerted against the forces of barbarous hubris and on behalf of civilized existence.'[100]

The coin evidence depicting a divine thunderbolt is also quite striking and includes examples from as early as the second century BCE, as well as Imperial issues from the reigns of such Emperors as Augustus

Figure 23

Figure 24

(27 BCE–14 CE), Tiberius (14–37 CE), Galba (68–69 CE), Domitian (81–96 CE) and Antoninus Pius (138–161 CE). Four examples will serve to illustrate the point for my purposes. The first comes from the Republican period, notably the period 167–155 BCE when an extensive series of gold coins were issued in three different values (60 asses, 40 asses, 20 asses). The obverse and reverse of all three values were the same: the obverse depicted a helmeted bust of the bearded god Mars and the reverse depicted an eagle with wings outstretched, standing on a lightning bolt,

100. 'The Theology of Victory at Rome: Approaches and Problems', *ANRW*, II.17.2, p. 817.

with the word ROMA standing in exergue (Figure 23). Second, there is an aureus of the moneyer Cn. Cornelius Lentulus Marcellinus, dated to 87 BCE, which has a reverse portrayal of an eagle clutching a lightning bolt in its claws. An abbreviated form of the moneyer's name, CN LENTVL, is at the bottom of the scene while the head of the god Jupiter is on the obverse (Figure 24). Third, there is a typical military reverse on a denarius issued by the moneyer Q. Salvius in 40 BCE. It depicts a lightning bolt, vertically presented, with rays of energy going forth toward the top and bottom of the coin. The surrounding inscription is Q. SALVIVS IMP COS DESIG (Figure 25). Similarly, on an as from the reign of Tiberius we see an enlarged depiction of the vertical lightning bolt so prevalent in earlier issues of denarii. Here the letters S C stand in exergue (Figure 26).[101] The exact same reverse type also appears on a dupondius from the reign of Antoninus Pius. It shows the bolt with wings and four rays of energy going forth and the words PROVIDENTIAE DEORVM surrounding the scene, together with the letters S C in exergue (Figure 27). Fourth, there is an aureus from Domitian's reign which shows on its obverse the representation of an eagle with a lightning bolt in its claws surrounded by the inscription P(ontifex) M(aximus) TR POT III IMP(erator) V COS X P(ater) P(atriae) (Figure 28).[102]

Figure 25   Figure 26   Figure 27   Figure 28

Summary

Throughout this chapter I have been concerned with the idea of legionary *aquilae* as a background to one particular saying of Jesus recorded in the New Testament. In order to do this I have examined in some detail key events in Roman military history where the legionary *aquilae* figured prominently in imperial propaganda associated with them. In particular, I have looked at numismatic evidence surrounding these three military episodes. I began by noting the so-called 'legionary

101.   *RIC* Tiberius 83.
102.   *RIC* Domitian 49.

denarii' issued by Mark Antony just prior to the battle of Actium in 32–31 BCE. This series of coins, one of the most extensive issues from antiquity, clearly demonstrates how important the image of the legionary *aquilae* series was for the military. I have also examined the sources which describe the historical circumstances surrounding the question of the Parthian Eagles, and have sought to demonstrate, to some degree, the extent of the turmoil such an episode had inflicted upon the Roman psyche. We have also seen how Augustus redeemed Roman military pride and restored national honour via his negotiated return of the captured legionary standards. I have noted how prominently this theme figures within the Augustan poets as the glories of Augustus were proclaimed by them, and have sought to relate all of these matters to the set of silver cistophori issued from Pergamum in 19–18 BCE which commemorate this diplomatic triumph of Augustus. The avenging of the so-called 'Varian disaster' which took place in Germany in 9 CE, and in which three legionary aquilae were captured, was also discussed briefly. Here the coinage later issued by Caligula celebrating the military victory was the focus of my concern, notably the coins which proclaim the triumph of the Roman commander responsible for the return of the *aquilae*, Caligula's father Germanicus.

Finally, I have suggested that the image of Roman legionary *aquilae* may help to provide a conceptual background to the cryptic statement by Jesus recorded in Mt. 24.28 and Lk. 17.37. In addition, I have tentatively put forward the suggestion, based on the numismatic imagery of the legionary aquilae, that Mt. 24.27-28 and Lk. 17.24, 37 belong together as a single unit. Such a suggestion allows us to understand more clearly why and how Luke has composed his version of the so-called Q apocalypse, breaking the unity of the two-part saying so as to stress the judgment of the Son of Man.

Chapter 2

THE APOTHEOSIS OF THE ROMAN EMPEROR

New Testament scholars have spent a great deal of energy in recent years trying to trace the development of christology, the theological interpretation of the person and work of Jesus.[1] How is it that the man Jesus of Nazareth was eventually declared by the Church to partake of the very nature of God? More to the point, how much, if at all, can we rely upon the New Testament documents as initiating or supporting such a belief? Certainly these questions are much too complicated to try and answer in one brief chapter, but I would like to call attention to one category of evidence that is often overlooked in attempts to fathom the complexities associated with the rise and development of christological thought in early Christianity. The category to which I refer is the apotheosis, or deification, of the Roman Emperor, and the suggestion is that this religious practice may prove to be a small, but not insignificant, piece of the larger christological puzzle. The practice of apotheosis of the Roman Emperor was certainly widespread and influential enough to have touched upon the lives of some of the early Christians. Thus, it is perhaps not too far-fetched to suggest that a fresh look at the practice might shed some light on the way in which many common people living in the first and second centuries CE might have conceived of the relation-ship between god and humankind. Such a look might also help to illuminate some of the ideas that helped shape the development of New Testament christological thought.

The deification of the Roman Emperor eventually became a standard religious practice in Roman religion and was confirmed by senatorial vote.[2] Ratification generally followed the death of the Emperor and was

1. J.D.G. Dunn, *Christology in the Making* (London: SCM Press, 1980), provides a helpful guide to most of the main issues involved.
2. The literature on this subject is immense. Among the more important studies on the subject are L.M. Sweet, *Roman Emperor Worship* (Boston: Gorham Press,

virtually guaranteed unless the Emperor did something during his reign to offend the Senate and thereby jeopardize his chances of being enrolled with the gods. Of the first twelve Emperors, the ancient biographer Suetonius mentions five as having apotheosis conferred upon them after death: Julius Caesar, Augustus (Octavian), Claudius, Vespasian[3] and Titus. Thus, it is as important to see who is *not* accorded divinity by the Senate as it is to note who is granted that honour; non-admittance into the pantheon is a fairly reliable guide that some shameful or unacceptable activity on the part of the Emperor had occurred. Little wonder then that Caligula, Nero and Domitian are among the main figures con-

1919); L.R. Taylor, 'The Worship of Augustus in Italy during his Lifetime', *TPAPA* 51 (1920), pp. 116-33; *The Divinity of the Roman Emperor* (Middletown, Connecticut: American Philological Association, 1931); C. Bailey, *Phases in the Religion of Ancient Rome* (London: Oxford University Press, 1932), pp. 144-76; A.D. Nock, 'Religious Developments from the Close of the Republic to the Death of Nero', *CAH*, X (1934), pp. 465-511; M.P. Charlesworth, 'Some Observations on Ruler-Cult', *HTR* 28 (1935), pp. 5-44; J. Ferguson, 'The Sacred Figure of the Emperor', in *idem, The Religions of the Roman Empire* (New York: Cornell University Press, 1970), pp. 88-98; S. Weinstock, *Divus Julius* (London: Oxford University Press, 1971); D. Fishwick, 'The Development of Provincial Ruler Worship in the Western Roman Empire', *ANRW*, II.16.2, pp. 1201-1253; D.L. Jones, 'Christianity and the Roman Imperial Cult', *ANRW*, II.23.2, pp. 1023-1054; A. Wardman, *Religion and Statecraft among the Romans* (London: Granada, 1982); G.W. Bowerstock, 'Augustus and the East: The Problem of the Succession', in F. Millar and E. Segal (eds.), *Caesar Augustus: Seven Aspects* (Oxford: Clarendon Press, 1984), pp. 169-88; B.W. Jones, *The Emperor Titus* (Beckenham: Croom Helm, 1984), pp. 152-57; E.J. Bickermann, 'Die Römische Kaiserapotheose', in *idem, Religions and Politics in the Hellenistic and Roman Periods* (repr.; Como: Edizioni New Press, 1985 [1929]), pp. 1-34; D. Fishwick, *The Imperial Cult in the Latin West: Studies in the Ruler Cult of the Western Provinces of the Roman Empire* (2 vols.; Leiden: Brill, 1987, 1991); B.W. Winter, 'The Imperial Cult', in D.W.J. Gill and C. Gempf (eds.), *The Book of Acts in Its First Century Setting.* II. *Graeco-Roman Setting* (Grand Rapids, MI: Eerdmans, 1994), pp. 93-103; A.J.S. Spawforth, 'The Achaean Federal Cult Part I: Pseudo-Julian, Letters 198', *TB* 46 (1995), pp. 151-68; B.W. Winter, 'The Achaean Federal Cult II: The Corinthian Church', *TB* 46 (1995), pp. 169-78. D. Earl, 'The Imperial Cult', in *idem, The Age of Augustus* (London: Ferndale Editions, 1980), pp. 166-76, offers a readable introduction to the topic.

3.   The date of the consecration of Vespasian is contested. See G.W. Clarke, 'The Date of the Consecration of Vespasian', *Historia* 15 (1966), pp. 318-27; T.V. Buttrey, 'Vespasian's Consecration and the Numismatic Evidence', *Historia* 25 (1976), pp. 449-57.

spicuous by their absence; each had a controversial reign in which excessive claims to divinity were made, and each was treated with derision by the Senate following his death. As E. Lohse says,

> Caligula and Nero, however, abandoned all reserve. Caligula was pictured on coins with the halo of the sun-god Helios, and Nero was represented as Apollo. Yet the way in which these two emperors conducted them-selves after the pattern of the Hellenistic divine kingship met stiff resistance in Roman circles.[4]

Certainly by the time of the Emperor Domitian (81–96 CE) the demands of the Imperial cult were a matter of extreme concern among Christians wishing to remain faithful to their own religious commitments and beliefs.[5] Suetonius's remark about Domitian's insistence that he be addressed as both 'our Lord and god' (*dominus et deus noster*)[6] is a well-known focal point for the clash between Christian belief and the Roman Imperial cult. This text, together with Pliny's letter to the Emperor Trajan seeking advice about how to handle the conduct of worshipping Christians,[7] are among the most discussed texts from antiquity, particularly by those

---

4. *The New Testament Environment* (London: SCM, 1976), p. 220.

5. M.P. Charlesworth, 'Some Observations', pp. 5-44, suggests that the cult took a decisive turn during the reign of Domitian. S.J. Friesen, *Twice Neokoros: Ephesus, Asia and the Cult of the Flavian Imperial Family* (Leiden: Brill, 1993), also follows this line, concentrating on the cult as it was expressed in the city of Ephesus. More recently Winter, 'Imperial Cult', pp. 93-103, argues that the reign of Claudius (41–54 CE) was the focus of conflict over the Imperial cult, particularly as Jewish leaders attempted to force a confrontation between Christians and Roman officials in the matter. According to Winter this was an attempt to get the Christian movement declared illegal and thus distinguish it from Judaism which enjoyed the status of *religio licita*. The incident in Corinth between Paul and Gallio, the proconsul of Achaea (Acts 18.12-21), is central to Winter's proposal.

6. *Domitian* 13.2.

7. *Epistles* 10.96. Pliny was governor of the province of Bithynia at the time. See K. Scott, 'The Elder and Younger Pliny on Emperor Worship', *TPAPA* 63 (1932), pp. 156-65; A.N. Sherwin-White, *Fifty Letters of Pliny* (Oxford: Oxford University Press, 2nd edn, 1969), pp. 68-71 and 171-79. Pliny's letter raises questions about the persecution of Christians by Romans for their refusal to worship the Emperor. On this matter follow the debate between A.N. Sherwin-White, 'Early Persecutions and Roman Law Again', *JTS* 3 (1952), pp. 199-213; 'Why Were the Early Christians Persecuted?—An Amendment', *PP* 27 (1964), pp. 23-27; and G.E.M. de Ste. Croix, 'Why Were the Early Christians Persecuted?', *PP* 26 (1963), pp. 6-38; 'Why Were the Early Christians Persecuted?—A Rejoiner', *PP* 27 (1964), pp. 28-33.

wishing to trace the practice of Christian belief and worship within its historical setting. Yet two other pieces of information must also be kept in mind if we are to try and gain an overall picture of the development of the Imperial cultus. Each of these two items to consider provides an important extra-biblical source of information and helps to set up a discussion of the numismatic evidence relevant to the present discussion. The first concerns an intriguing archaeological discovery of this century, and the second concerns an oft-cited text from the third century.

First, there is the discovery of an important cache of papyrus documents by an archaeological team from Yale University working in Dura-Europos on the Euphrates in 1931–32. Included within this find is a small papyrus scroll, containing four columns in Latin, listing religious festivals. This list, known as the *Feriale Duranum*,[8] dates to the reign of Severus Alexander (224–235 CE) and is, effectively, a military calendar, providing dates upon which religious ceremonies in honour of the various gods and goddesses of the Empire[9] would have been observed by the Roman auxiliary unit stationed in this border region, the Twentieth Palmyrene Cohort. Such observance would have been standard practice throughout the Empire and was an important feature of the discipline of the military legions; it was one means whereby the soldiers demonstrated their continued obedience to the State and to the Emperor.[10] From this document it is possible to determine that in 224 CE some twenty people were worshipped as divine figures (*divi*), including six women and,

8.   A critical edition of the papyrus can be found in R.O. Fink, A.S. Hoey, and W.S. Snyder, 'The *Feriale Duranum*', *YCS* 7 (1940), pp. 1-222. See also H.W. Benario, 'The Date of the *Feriale Duranum*', *Historia* 11 (1962), pp. 192-96.

9.   R.M. Ogilvie, *The Romans and their Gods in the Age of Augustus* (New York: W.W. Norton & Co., 1969), pp. 70-99, provides an overview of the religious festivals which would have been celebrated during the year.

10.   A.D. Nock, 'The Roman Army and the Roman Religious Year', *HTR* 45 (1952), p. 238, comments, 'the deified Emperors have the disciplined order of a legally constituted Hall of Fame'. I.A. Richmond, 'The Roman Army and Roman Religion', *BJRL* 45 (1962–63), pp. 185-97; C. Martin, 'The Gods of the Imperial Roman Army', *History Today* 19 (1969), pp. 255-63; M. Grant, *The Army of the Caesars* (London: Weidenfeld & Nicolson, 1974), p. 79; Helgeland, 'Roman Army Religion', pp. 1470-1505; and J.B. Campbell *The Emperor and the Roman Army (31 BC–AD 235)* (Oxford: Clarendon Press, 1984), pp. 99-101, offer some helpful comments on the matter. A.S. Hoey, 'Official Policy Towards Oriental Cults in the Roman Army', *TPAPA* 70 (1939), pp. 456-81, discusses the apparent exclusion of Oriental gods from the official pantheon and notes that 27 out of the extant 43 entries in the *Feriale Duranum* relate to the Imperial cult.

somewhat surprisingly, the military hero Germanicus.[11] Most agree that the basic idea of a military calendar such as this derives from the time of Augustus, who carried through a large-scale restructuring of the military; the *Feriale Duranum* simply slots into an Augustan idea of an up-dated list of divine personages to be worshipped.

The second item concerns an interesting passage from a third-century document. By chance we have one historian's account of the apotheosis ceremony. Herodian of Syria, a biographer writing during the third century CE, composed his *History*, an account of Imperial rule covering the time of Marcus Aurelius in 180 CE to the death of Gordian III in 238 CE. Included in Herodian's work is an account of the ritual ceremony of the apotheosis of Septimius Severus which took place in 211 CE. The relevant passage (IV.2.1-11) reads,

> It is normal Roman practice to deify Emperors who die leaving behind children as their successors. The name they give to this ceremony is apotheosis. All over the city expressions of grief are displayed, combined with a festival and a religious ceremony. The body of the dead Emperor is buried in a normal way with a very expensive funeral. But then they make a wax model exactly like the dead man and lay it on an enormous ivory couch raised up on high legs at the entrance to the palace, and spread golden drapes under the effigy. This model lays there pale, like a sick man, and on either side of the couch people sit for most of the day. On the left is the entire senate dressed in black cloaks and on the right all the women who hold a position of high honour because of the distinction of their husbands or fathers. None of these women appear wearing gold ornaments or necklaces; they wear only a plain white dress to show they are in mourning. For seven days the above-mentioned ceremonies continue. Each day the doctors come and go up to the couch, and each day they pretend to examine the patient and make an announcement that his condition is deteriorating. Then, when it appears he is dead, the noblest members of the equestrian order and picked young men from the senatorial order lift the couch up and take it along the Sacred Way to the old forum, and there they set it up at the place where Roman magistrates swear themselves out of office. On either side stands are put up in tiers,

11. J.H. Oliver, 'The Divi of the Hadrianic Period', *HTR* 42 (1949), pp. 35-40, and J.F. Gilliam, 'The Roman Military *Feriale*', *HTR* 47 (1954), pp. 183-96, discuss this. Although officially the apotheosis of Germanicus was never confirmed by the Senate, it seems his memory was particularly cherished within the army, no doubt based upon his legendary exploits as a military commander on the Rhine during the early years of Tiberius's reign.

on which there are two choirs, one made up of children from noble and
patrician families, and opposite them one composed of women of
honourable reputation. Each group sings hymns and chants that are set to
solemn rhythms of mourning in honour of the dead man. Next, the bier is
carried out of the city to the Campus Martius, where there has been set up
in the most open part of the plain a square building, which consists
entirely of vast wooden beams put together to make a kind of house.
Inside, the building is completely filled with brushwood, and outside it is
decorated with gold-embroidered drapery, ivory carvings and a variety of
paintings. On top of this structure there is another one of the same shape
and with the same decoration, but smaller and with open windows and
doors. On top of this there is a third and a fourth tier, each smaller than
the last, until finally comes, the smallest of all. One might compare the
shape of the structure to the lighthouses which stand at the harbours and
guide ships at night to safe anchorage; the general name for these
lighthouses is Pharos. The bier is taken up and placed on the second
storey. Every perfume and incense on earth and all the fruits and herbs
and juices that are collected for their aroma are brought up and poured out
in great heaps. Every people and city and prominent persons of distinction
vies with each other to send these last gifts in honour of the Emperor.
When an enormous pile of these aromatic spices has been accumulated
and the entire place has been filled, there is a cavalry procession around
the pyre in which the whole equestrian order rides in a circle round and
round in a fixed formation, following the movement and rhythm of the
Pyrrhic dance. Chariots, too, circle round in the same formation with their
drivers dressed in purple-bordered togas. In the chariots are figures
wearing masks of all the famous Roman generals and Emperors. After
this part of the ceremony the heir to the principate takes a torch and puts it
to the built-up pyre, while everyone else lights the fire all around. The
whole structure easily catches fire and burns without difficulty because of
the large amount of dry wood and aromatic spices which are piled high
inside. Then from the highest and topmost storey an eagle is released, as
if from a battlement, and soars up into the sky with the flames, taking the
soul of the Emperor from earth to heaven, the Romans believe. After that
he is worshipped with the rest of the gods.[12]

Herodian's account is probably too late to have been directly influential
upon any of the writers of the New Testament; even 2 Peter is likely to
have been completed by the death of Septimius Severus in York on
4 February 211 CE. Nevertheless, Herodian's work may still be of some
value insofar as it presents a description of a religious ritual which had

12. A similar account of the apotheosis of the Emperor Pertinax (193 CE) is
recorded in Cassius Dio, *Hist.* 75.4.1–5.5.

been practised for many years, indeed, as far back as the earliest days of the Christian church.

It is worth noting that the story mentions, at the climax of the ceremony, two interesting motifs which help to convey something of the religious significance of the ritual. The first is that of the funeral pyre upon which the deceased is placed, and the second is the releasing of an eagle to symbolize the ascent into the heavens. Both motifs appear regularly on Imperial coins of the Antonine and Severan periods, and beyond that, well into the third century. For example, there is a sestertius issued by Marcus Aurelius (161–180 CE) in honour of his predecessor Antoninus Pius (138–161 CE). The coin depicts on its reverse an elaborate, three-layered funeral pyre which has at its top a quadriga containing an effigy of the deceased Emperor. The inscription CONSECRATIO surrounds the scene with the customary letters SC standing in exergue (Figure 1).[13] The image of an eagle carrying the deceased to the heavens is also quite common. For example, the Emperor Valerian I (253–260 CE) minted an antoninianus between 257-258 CE which uses this motif (Figure 2). The reverse shows his son Valerian II, who dies as a boy, being carried to heaven on the back of an eagle; the accompanying inscription reads CONSECRATIO. The obverse is a portrait of the boy with the inscription DIVO VALERIANO CAESAR (The Divine Caesar Valerian). Apotheosis was also accorded to privileged members of the Imperial household. A good case in point is Sabina, the wife of Hadrian (117–138 CE), who was deified following her death in 137 CE. A sestertius minted to commemorate her has as its reverse a depiction of the Empress being carried to the heavens on the back of an eagle with the inscription CONSECRATIO as a surround and the letters SC in exergue (Figure 3). The eagle motif, as we shall see in due course, figures frequently in artistic portrayals of apotheosis dating from the Julio-Claudian Emperors of the New Testament period, including representations on coins and gem-stones.

13. *RIC* Marcus Aurelius 1266. The obverse design is used in connection with a number of other deified Emperors, including Hadrian (117–138), Marcus Aurelius (161–180 CE), Lucius Verus (161–169 CE), Commodus (177–192 CE), Pertinax (193 CE), Septimius Severus (193–211 CE) and Caracalla (198–217 CE).

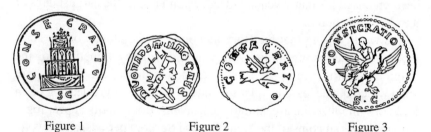

Figure 1   Figure 2   Figure 3

The rest of this chapter is primarily concerned with the period 45 BCE to 68 CE, from the end of Julius Caesar's reign to the death of Nero. The Julio-Claudian period is most relevant to the formulation of New Testament theology as some of the most significant christological developments undoubtedly took place during this period. Coins constitute one of the most important primary sources of evidence for this period and I will use numismatic evidence as the major primary guide, although one or two other interesting pieces of first-century art will be mentioned first in order to help to set the stage for this study. We can be fairly confident that early Christians scattered throughout the various provinces and territories would have had daily contact with Roman coins and thus would have been regularly exposed to the Imperial propaganda that such coinage displayed, including that promulgating the Imperial cult. It is hoped that this brief exploration will sensitize students of the New Testament to the contribution that numismatic evidence has made to the subject of christology. First let me turn to some ways in which the apotheosis of the Emperor was portrayed in sculpture and engraving from the Julio-Claudian period.

1. *Artistic Evidence from the Julio-Claudian Period*

The apotheosis of the Emperor also found its way into Roman sculpture and art as well as literary accounts such as that of Herodian of Syria cited above. Most of us have seen a picture of the Arch of Titus (79–81 CE) which shows the spoils of the first Jewish revolt being carried off by the conquering Romans. Less well known is another carved scene in the interior of the arch which depicts the apotheosis of Titus. Here the figure of Titus is presented with a Roman eagle whose wings are outstretched before him, as if preparing to carry him to heaven. Many similar examples of sculpture are also extant. The image of apotheosis also appears in numerous carved cameos, three of the most famous of which I mention here.

First, the apotheosis of Augustus is the subject of a very beautifully carved sardonyx cameo, known as the *Gemma Augustea*, part of the collection of antiquities housed in the Kunsthistorisches Museum in Vienna.[14] The cameo, frequently attributed to the engraver Dioscurides, is one of the most beautiful from Roman times and contains some twenty figures (Figure 4). It depicts on its upper scene a semi-nude Augustus, in the guise of the god Jupiter, sharing a throne with Roma and being crowned by the personification Oikoumene (representing the civilized world).[15] The crowning stands as a symbol of the Emperor's divinity,

Figure 4

as does the association with the goddess Roma. The fact that Augustus holds in his right hand a *lituus* also serves to symbolize the connection with Jupiter, for this augur's staff was the instrument whereby the will of the god was communicated to his earthly representative. The *Gemma*

14. The cameo is 19 x 23 cm in size and is made of white and brown Arabian sardonyx.

15. See O. Brendel, 'The Great Augustus Cameo at Vienna', *AJA* 43 (1939), pp. 308-309; Hannestad, *Roman Art*, pp. 78-82; Zanker, *Power,* pp. 230-32. J.R. Fears, 'The Cult of Jupiter and Roman Imperial Ideology', *ANRW*, II.17.1, pp. 57-58, also discusses the *Gemma Augustea* and gives a full bibliography.

Augustea probably dates from about 9 CE and commemorates Tiberius's victory in Dalmatia; the lower scene, where a group of Roman legionaries are erecting a military trophy amidst a number of bound captives, suggests this historical setting. Tiberius himself appears on the left of the upper scene, where he is portrayed as a victorious general, stepping down from a chariot in order to receive his triumph at the hands of the Jupiter-like Augustus. He wears a laurel wreath as a symbol of his victory. Standing between Tiberius and the seated figure of Roma is Germanicus, Tiberius's adopted son who was later to prove himself an extremely able military commander. A Roman eagle crouches beneath the throne of Augustus while the astrological sign of Capricorn is placed at the top between the figures of Roma and Augustus. This is a reminder of Augustus's title and the fact that he assumed power on the 16th of January during the time of the sign of Capricorn.

Second, the cameo known as *The Grand Camée* in the Cabinet des Médailles of the Bibliothèque Nationale in Paris depicts a similar scene (Figure 5). Here it is the character of Tiberius who occupies the central place of the cameo, which contains three distinct levels. Tiberius, in the guise of Jupiter, is seated alongside the figure of Livia, his mother. He holds a staff upright in his left hand while his right hand is outstretched to receive gifts from the assembled household figures who surround him. Immediately before him is the figure of Germanicus, dressed in military gear. Behind him is Agrippina, his wife, and, on the extreme left of the central section of the cameo, their young son Gaius, better known as the future Emperor Caligula. Above them all in the heavens is the deified Augustus, wearing a laurel crown and also holding an Imperial staff in his right hand, looking down on the scene with Tiberius below. Augustus is surrounded by other figures of the Imperial family, including Tiberius's son Drusus on the left, who is in military dress and carries a shield. In a reclining position in front of Augustus is a representation of Alexander the Great, symbolic figure of cosmic rulers, holding a globe in his hand and garbed in Graeco-Persian dress. Below the central scene of Tiberius and Livia we are presented (as was the case with the *Gemma Augustea*) with a number of figures representing peoples subdued in war. It is this feature of the cameo which provides us with a clue to the date of the scene presented. It probably refers to the return of Germanicus from the Rhine to Rome in triumph on 26 May 17 CE following his successful suppression of the German rebellion.[16] Once again we are

16. J.P.V.D. Balsdon, 'Gaius and the Grand Cameo of Paris', *JRS* 26 (1936),

presented with an intriguing scene involving the deified Emperor Augustus.

Figure 5

Third, there is a cameo contained in the Cabinet des Antiques in Paris (Figure 6).[17] It depicts the military leader Germanicus being crowned by a winged Victory, and riding on the back of an eagle who is carrying him to heaven. In his right hand he holds a lituus and in his left arm he cradles a cornucopia. What is significant here is that the cameo again indicates that apotheosis was not only accorded to the Emperors alone, but was also granted to select members of the Imperial household.

All of these examples of artistic endeavour illustrate that the idea of apotheosis was apparently very much more widespread in the first-century world than we sometimes realize. However, such cameos as I have been discussing were probably private gifts intended for members of the Imperial household and would have been seen by only a handful

pp. 152-60, discusses alternative interpretations. The article also has an excellent photograph of the cameo (Plate 10).

17. The cameo is approximately 10 x 11 cm in size.

Figure 6

of people. We have no guarantee that the particular images they portrayed would have been known by the public at large, although there is every indication that their subject matter forms part of a consistent pattern.

I turn now to consider some of the numismatic evidence which also addresses the topic of apotheosis. The fact that coins served as the medium of commerce and were thus intended for a general audience means that they are much firmer evidence for apotheosis as a generally understood and well-known idea among the citizens of the Empire.

2. Numismatic Evidence from the Julio-Claudian Period

For the purposes of this chapter, I will limit myself mainly to a consideration of coins issued by moneyers of the late Republic or those produced by the Imperial mints, although the Greek influence on the coinage is readily apparent. Rome permitted many Greek cities and states to mint their own coins, and they often reflect a much more fluid understanding of how great rulers were accorded divine status than was traditional in Rome. The Greeks had a long history of deifying their kings, a practice that is traceable in coinage at least as far back as the reign of Alexander the Great (336–323 BCE).[18] Some kings actively promoted such a policy during their reign, perhaps the most famous example being

18. M. Grant, *From Alexander to Cleopatra* (London: Weidenfeld and Nicolson, 1982), pp. 91-104, discusses the process of the deification of Hellenistic monarchs. Also see the seminal study by J.P.V.D. Balsdon, 'The "Divinity" of Alexander', *Historia* 1 (1950), pp. 363-88.

the Seleucid king Antiochus IV (175–163 BCE). He minted silver tetradrachma (Figure 7) which carried a reverse inscription declaring ΒΑΣΙΛΕΩΣ ΑΝΤΙΟΧΟΥ ΘΕΟΥ ΕΠΙΦΑΝΟΥΣ ΝΙΚΗΦΟΡΟΥ (King Antiochus, God Made Manifest, Conqueror). The inscription surrounds a figure of Zeus, seated on a throne, with his left hand supporting a staff and his right arm outstretched to receive the figure of Nike. The obverse of the coin has a laureated head of Antiochus facing to the right. Antiochus's claim of divinity brought him into conflict with his Jewish subjects, and helped set the stage for the ensuing Maccabean Revolt.[19]

As the Romans absorbed the remnants of Alexander the Great's empire, the succeeding generals and provincial governors often found themselves the objects of divine honours and acclaim. This was especially true of Pompey the Great and Julius Caesar. Following Caesar's victory at the Greek city of Pharsalus in 46 BCE, his statues often bore inscriptions that proclaimed him a god. An inscription from Ephesus in the province of Asia, for instance, calls him ΘΕΟΣ ΕΠΙΦΑΝΗΣ (God Made Manifest). Such divine honours abounded in the East and were generally received by military victors as a matter of course.

Returning to the early imperatorial period, we should point out that religious practice operated on several different levels in the Empire. Many of the associations that were made between the great leaders and deities of the East would have been unacceptable in the West. It was acceptable for Roman generals to be showered with divine honours when they were in the eastern half of the Mediterranean world, but such honours were frowned upon in Rome and the West. Therefore, whenever we see significant senatorial developments toward apotheosis of the Emperor, we can be certain that such developments had long been a part of religious activity in the East. In a way, by examining the official senatorial steps toward apotheosis we give ourselves a starting point from which to understand what must have been a more popular perception among many eastern peoples of the Empire.

Following the precedents of the eastern provinces in relating kingship and divinity, we find that a series of senatorial honours were decreed on Julius Caesar from 45 to 44 BCE. These honours established a pattern that was to culminate in his full enrolment into the pantheon. Although not

---

19. See A.D. Nock, 'Notes on the Ruler-Cult, I-IV', *JHS* 48 (1924), pp. 21-43; Ø. Mørkholm, *Studies in the Coinage of Antiochus IV of Syria* (Copenhagen: 1963), pp. 68-74; J.G. Bunge, '"Theos Epiphanes"', *Historia* 23 (1974), pp. 57-85, for discussion of the offending title.

Figure 7   Figure 8

technically constituting deification, all of these honours contributed to an atmosphere of public adulation of Caesar's rule in a manner and scale previously unknown in Rome. Until 44 BCE no living person had ever appeared on Roman coinage; yet in that year many moneyers minted coins with Caesar's portrait on them. The obverse of one denarius (Figure 8)[20] portrays Caesar as a priest and bestows a fatherly character on the Emperor with the inscription CAESAR PARENS PATRIAE (Caesar, Father of the Nation). This title was one of many senatorial honours given to Caesar prior to his death in March 44 BCE. Another accolade bestowed on Caesar was the placing of his statue, with the inscription DEO INVICTO (To the Unconquered God), in the temple of Quirinus. This quasi-divine honour was considered in bad taste by many Romans and prompted Cicero to make some sarcastic comments in several of his *Letters to Atticus*. Note, for example the following two examples:

> I wrote to you about your 'neighbour' Caesar, because I learned about it from your letters. I would rather see him sharing the temple (σύνναιον) of Quirinus than of Safety.
>
> (Book 12, letter 45, dated 17 May 45 BCE)[21]

Here Cicero alludes to the fact that the temple of Salus (Safety) was also on the Quirinal hill, as was the house of his correspondent Atticus.

> Why, don't you see that even that pupil of Aristotle, in spite of his high ability and his high character, became proud, cruel, and ungovernable, after he got the title king? How do you suppose this puppet messmate of Quirinus will like my moderate letters? Let him rather look for what I do not write than disapprove of what I have written.
>
> (Book 13, letter 28, dated 26 May 45 BCE)

20. *CRR* 1069.

21. A.D. Nock, 'ΣΥΝΝΑΟΣ ΘΕΟΣ', *HSCP* 41 (1930), pp. 1-62, offers a full discussion of this passage as well as others from the Hellenistic world which contain similar ideas of temples either erected to human figures or into which images of human rulers were placed.

In this excerpt Cicero continues an on-going discussion with Atticus about whether or not he should write to Caesar and congratulate him for his successes. He compares Caesar with the 'pupil of Aristotle'; that is, Alexander the Great. There is much to suggest that Caesar was consciously styling himself after Alexander, particularly when it came to proclaiming publicly his military accomplishments.[22]

Caesar's statue was associated with other gods and other temples as well. The obverse of one Roman denarius (Figure 9),[23] for example, depicts the temple of Clementia and Caesar together with the surrounding inscription CLEMENTIAE CAESARIS. Although this temple has never been located (and some even doubt that it ever existed), its image on the coin speaks of the ready association of Caesar with the gods of the Roman capital. The identification of Caesar with Jupiter is certainly another example of the way in which the Roman leader and god were merging in the popular imagination. Let us not forget that Suetonius wrote that on the night before Caesar was murdered he had a dream in which he ascended the heavens and shook hands with the god Jupiter.[24] We also remember that according to Suetonius the mob wanted to cremate Caesar's body and inter his ashes in the temple of Jupiter located on the Capitoline hill.[25]

One final senatorial honour is represented on the coinage of the time. Just prior to Caesar's assassination, between January 26 and February 9 of the year 44 BCE, the Senate awarded Caesar the title *Dictator Perpetuus* (Dictator for Life) and granted him a gold crown and a gold throne for use in public displays and theatres. These actions could be construed as according Caesar quasi-divine rights and no doubt offended the religious sensitivities of many in Rome at the time. The crown and throne are subjects of a denarius reverse from the coinage of Octavian, Caesar's adopted heir and successor (Figure 10).[26] The crown is portrayed as resting on the throne which has an inscription on its base reading CAESAR DIC(tator) PER(petuus). Many other denarii from this time show a portrait of Caesar on their obverse together with an inscription proclaiming his dictatorship. For example, we note a coin from the

22. S. Weinstock, 'Victor and Invictus', *HTR* 50 (1957), pp. 211-47, discusses this.
23. *CR* 1076.
24. *The Deified Julius* 81.3
25. *The Deified Julius* 84.3.
26. *CRR* 1322.

moneyer C. Maridianus which shows Caesar, his head veiled and
and laureated, with the surrounding inscription CAESAR DICT IN
PERPETVO (Figure 11).[27]

Figure 9   Figure 10   Figure 11

It was not until after the assassination of Julius Caesar in March of 44
BCE, however, that the Roman Senate took the official step of
deification. On 1 January 42 BCE, Caesar was officially declared a god, a
move no doubt prompted by his adopted heir Octavian who saw in
the act a means of consolidating his own power. Octavian was involved
at the time in a desperate political struggle with Mark Antony, who
vigorously opposed the deification of Julius Caesar, and Octavian used
the deification of Caesar as a way of legitimizing and elevating his own
position over that of his rival. Octavian was quick to capitalize on his
adoptive status and issued a series of coins proclaiming his position as
son of the Divine Caesar.[28] One such coin was an aureus issued following
Octavian's victory over Antony at Actium in September of 31 BCE. The
obverse shows the head of Octavian facing left while the reverse shows
the triumphant figure of Octavian riding in a victory chariot drawn by a
quadriga of horses. The CAESAR DIVI F(ilius) (Caesar, Son of the
Divine One) stands in exergue (Figure 12).[29]

One of the most interesting coins issued by Octavian commemorates
the appearance of a comet during the games he held in honour of Julius
Caesar's military victories at the battle of Thapsus in July of 44 BCE.
The comet appeared on the first day of the games, which lasted for
seven days. Its appearance was conveniently interpreted as being the

27. *CRR* 1068.

28. S.R.F. Price, 'Gods and Emperors: The Greek Language of the Roman
Imperial Cult', *JHS* 104 (1984), pp. 79-95, discusses the subtle but all-important
distinction between *divus* and *deus* in Roman religious thought. He notes (p. 83),
'From the cult of the deceased Julius Caesar onwards *divus* referred exclusively in
official terminology to former emperors and members of their family. They were
thus distinguished from the traditional *dei*.' It is also significant that, according to
Price, a linguistic distinction must be made between the Greek understanding of
theos and the Latin understanding of *divus*.

29. *RIC* Augustus 258.

soul of Caesar ascending to heaven.[30] The comet, or star, became a common feature in the subsequent coinage of Octavian (Augustus), again as a means of emphasizing his relationship to the Divine Caesar. All of the coins containing star or comet images are charged with religious and political symbolism—the kind of symbolism that can be used to great political advantage.[31] Thus note a denarius minted under Augustus's authority which contains the so-called *sidus Iulium*, the comet of Julius. The coin[32] (Figure 13) dates to 19–18 BCE and has as its obverse the head of Augustus with the inscription CAESAR AVGVSTVS surrounding the portrait; the reverse shows the comet of Julius Caesar with the inscription DIVVS IVLIVS (Divine Julius). The *sidus Iulium* also appears on the reverse of another interesting coin, probably issued in 36 BCE by the mint in Carthage in Africa. The coin, which was struck in both gold and silver, depicts the tetrastyle temple of the Divine Julius, including the

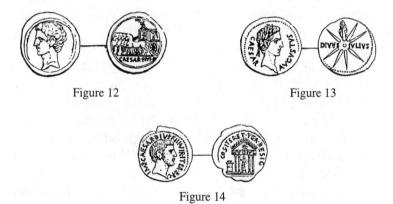

Figure 12   Figure 13

Figure 14

cultic statue of Julius himself in the centre. The entablature above contains the inscription DIVO IVL(ius) and the Julian comet is plainly visible on

30. Oster, 'Numismatic Windows', pp. 208-212, provides a detailed study of this, describing it as 'the nativity comet' (p. 208). See also K. Scott, 'The *Sidus Julium* and the Apotheosis of Caesar', *CP* 36 (1941), pp. 257-72. According to Suetonius, *Claudius* 46.1 a comet was also seen after the death of Claudius in 54 CE.

31. A.D. Nock, 'The Emperor's Divine *Comes*', *JRS* 37 (1947), pp. 102-116, traces how this idea of a divine ally, the guiding protection of the gods symbolized by a star or comet, was used in the coinage of various Roman Emperors up to and including Constantine the Great. Nock describes it as 'one manifeststion of the growth of a theology of imperial rule' (p. 116).

32. *RIC* Augustus 37a and 102.

the pediment of the temple.[33] The coin also has an altar in the field to the left of the temple and bears the inscription COS ITER ET TER DESIG around the scene (Figure 14). The temple itself was dedicated by Augustus on 18 August 29 BCE and was centrally located in the Forum of Rome. The obverse of the coin has a portrait of Augustus facing right surrounded by the inscription IMP CAESAR DIVI F III VIR ITER R P C. Augustus appears bearded on the coin, alluding to the tradition that as a sign of mourning for the loss of Julius Caesar he did not shave until after the battle of Naulochus in September 36 BCE. This feature of the coin helps to date it.

In 27 BCE, when the Roman Senate granted Octavian the title of Augustus, the Roman Empire, properly speaking, began. It was at this time, within the eastern provinces of the Empire, that the first logical step toward the practice of worshipping the son of a god as a god was taken.[34] The province of Bithynia, located along the northwest coast of Asia Minor, and the province of Asia, located along Asia Minor's western coast, were the first areas authorized by Rome to build temples to the god Augustus, perhaps indicating an identification between the Emperor and the legendary figure Romulus so foundational to the mythology of Rome.[35] They were allowed to build the temples in the cities of Nicaea and Ephesus respectively on the proviso that worship would also be accorded to the goddess Roma.[36] In so stipulating, Augustus was at the same time, of course, strengthening the provincial allegiance to Rome—a remarkably perceptive and politically astute move. Temples were also soon raised by the cities of Nicomedia and Pergamum. The temple in Pergamum is depicted on the reverse of a silver cistophorus,

33. Zanker, *Power*, pp. 33-37, discusses the importance that such comet imagery had in Octavian's attempts to portray himself as the rightful successor to Julius Caesar. Several of the relevant coins are pictured in the book.

34. There are hints of such deification in the Augustan poets of the time. Thus Horace, *Odes* 1.2 lines 41-48, speaks of Augustus as the manifestation of Mercury, avenging the assassination of Julius Caesar before returning to his home in the heavens. This Ode was probably composed in 29 BCE following Augustus's return to Rome after his victories in the East.

35. As K. Scott, 'The Identification of Augustus with Romulus-Quirinus', *TPAPA* 56 (1925), pp. 82-105, argues.

36. D. Magie, *Roman Rule in Asia Minor to the End of the Third Century after Christ* (Princeton, NJ: Princeton, 1950), p. 471, notes that in no less than eleven of the cities of Asia Minor Augustus was worshipped in conjunction with Roma.

dating to 19 BCE (Figure 15).[37] The inscription on the temple pediment, ROM(a) ET AVGVSTVS, stands for Rome and Augustus, and alludes to the suggestion by Suetonius that Augustus did not want the worship of himself to be independent of that given to the personification of the ruling city of the Empire.[38] The other part of the inscription, COM ASIAE (shorthand for COMMVNE ASIAE), indicates that the coin was issued by the common league of the province of Asia. The obverse portrait is that of Augustus, facing right, with the surrounding inscription IMP IX TR PO V declaring his titles (*Imperator* nine times, holding *Tribunicia Potestas* five times).

The first western province to institute a similar cult was Gaul, a region comprising much of modern France, Belgium and northern Italy. At Lugdunum, capital of the three districts of Gaul, an altar was erected to the gods Roma and Augustus in 10 BCE. This altar is depicted on a number of coins issued by several of the Julio-Claudian Emperors, commencing with Augustus himself. An example is a sestertius issued by Augustus (Figure 16)[39] which has his portrait on the obverse, laureated and facing right. The inscription on the obverse reads, CAESAR AVGVSTVS DIVI F PATER PATRIAE. The coin depicts on its reverse the front of the altar decorated with the *corona civica* (awarded to Augustus by the Senate on 13 January 27 BCE[40]) between two laurel wreaths. The altar is flanked by two winged victories, who face each other and hold laurel crowns in their hands. Similar temples and altars were subsequently erected in Germany, Spain and elsewhere. Another important development concerned Augustus's reorganization of the traditional worship of the Roman household gods, the Lares. In about 10 BCE the practice of erecting statues dedicated to Augustus's spirit, his *genius*, among those of the household Lares began to become widespread. This worship of Augustus's spirit was tantamount to worshipping Augustus himself, and marked a subtle, but very significant, shift in religious custom. Probably for many people of the day the difference between worshipping Augustus's genius and worshipping Augustus himself was exceedingly

37. *RIC* Augustus 506.

38. Suetonius, *Augustus* 53. S.R.F. Price, 'Between Man and God: Sacrifice in the Roman Imperial Cult', *JRS* 70 (1980), pp. 28-43, discusses this.

39. *RIC* Augustus 231.

40. The oak-wreath was awarded *ob cives servatos* ('for saving citizens') and appears regularly on coinage of Augustus. Maxfield, *Military Decorations*, pp. 70-76, discusses the award.

difficult, if not impossible, to describe. Some scholars of Roman religion attempt to make a theological distinction between the worship of the Emperor's *genius* (his personal spirit) and the worship of his *numen* (his divine power) in order to help make sense of what was meant by religious worship of the Emperor.[41] But a hard-and-fast distinction between

Figure 15   Figure 16

the two seems forced when all of the evidence is considered; the terms *genius* and *numen* are used interchangeably in many texts and inscriptions of the time. In short, there seems every indication that the dividing line between man and god was somehow breached by Augustus, at least in the minds of many of the people living in the early years of his reign. This is true even if, technically speaking, Augustus is more properly described as *possessing* numen rather than *being* a numen.[42]

Augustus was not deified in Rome until after his death in 14 CE, and his successor Tiberius (14–37 CE) was largely responsible for propagating the cult of the Divine Augustus.[43] Many important centres of religion within the eastern half of the Empire included worship of the deified Augustus as part of their cultic practices, including Aphrodisias in Caria in Asia Minor where a recently discovered temple dedicated to Aphrodite and the Julio-Claudian emperors has been identified.[44] There

41. D. Fishwick, '*Genius* and *Numen*', *HTR* 62 (1969), pp. 356-67, argues that the two ideas were never wholly identical. In any event, such a theological distinction is strikingly reminiscent of the christological debates concerning Jesus' relationship to God, and reflects the ways in which religious language is ever attempting to define the divine–human encounter.

42. Much in the same way as saying that a Christian declaring 'Jesus is the wisdom of God' was to affirm that Jesus is an agent through whom God's divine actions are channeled, rather than an assertion that Jesus was God himself.

43. Many of the Augustan poets, including Ovid, Virgil, Horace and Propertius, also had an important role to play in advancing the Imperial cult. See K. Scott, 'Emperor Worship in Ovid', *TPAPA* 61 (1930), pp. 43-49.

44. This temple, conventionally known as the Sebasteion, was uncovered in 1979

are a number of official coin issues which also reveal the trend toward a cult of Augustus and are worth noting. One interesting aureus (Figure 17)[45] from the reign of Tiberius bears on its reverse side a portrait of the Divine Augustus with the inscription DIVI F DIVOS AVGVST(us) (the Divine Augustus, Son of the Divine Caesar). The characteristic ascension star is placed above the head of Augustus, recalling Augustus's own use of the comet or star on his coins to emphasize his relationship to the Divine Julius. Tiberius also issued throughout his reign a number of asses and dupondii which commemorated the Divine Augustus and bore his head, sometimes wearing a radiate crown, on their obverse. The inscription surrounding the head of Augustus is DIVVS AVGVSTVS PATER (Figure 18). It is generally accepted that Tiberius wished to strengthen his own position by promoting the cult of Augustus, his adoptive father, who had designated him as heir in 4 CE. However, he does not appear to have been terribly interested in promoting his own position within the cult; in fact there are indications that he actively opposed it.[46] Even so, in 26 CE the city of Smyrna in Asia Minor was allowed to build a temple in honour of Tiberius, Livia and the Senate.[47]

Figure 17

Figure 18

by K.T. Erim. For more details, see R.R.R. Smith, 'The Imperial Reliefs from the Sebasteion at Aphrodisias', *JRS* 77 (1987), pp. 88-138 + Plates 3-26; J.M. Reynolds, 'New Evidence for the Imperial Cult in Julio-Claudian Aphrodisias', *ZPE* 43 (1981), pp. 317-27; K.T. Erim, *Aphrodisias* (Istanbul: Net Turistik Yayinlar, 1989), pp. 52-64. The discoveries at Aphrodisias are featured in two colourful articles in *National Geographic*: J. Blair and K.T. Erim, 'Ancient Aphrodisias and its Marble Treasures', *National Geographic* 132 (August 1967), pp. 280-94; and 'Aphrodisias: Awakened City of Ancient Art', *National Geographic* 141 (June 1972), pp. 766-91.

45. *RIC* Tiberius 23.

46. Tacitus, *Annals* 4.37-38 and Suetonius, *Tiberius* 26.1, both mention this. See also L.R. Taylor, 'Tiberius' Refusals of Divine Honours', *TPAPA* 60 (1929), pp. 87-101; K. Scott, 'Tiberius' Refusal of the Title "Augustus"', *CP* 27 (1932), pp. 43-50.

47. This is mentioned in Tacitus, *Annals* 4.55-56.

Tiberius's successor Caligula (37–41 CE) attempted to bestow the honour of deification upon his great-uncle, although the Senate opposed this. Neither did the Senate confirm the apotheosis of Caligula, thus we have no coins proclaiming the divinity of either Emperor. Nevertheless, Caligula still holds an important place in our study of the apotheosis of the Emperor. For one thing, he continued Tiberius's policy of issuing coins to support the cult of the Divine Augustus. He also accorded quasi-divine status to his three sisters, Agrippina, Drusilla and Julia (with whom he had incestuous relationships), by portraying them as the personifications of Securitas, Concordia and Fortuna respectively. This is seen on the reverse of a sestertius issued in 37–38 CE (Figure 19).[48] The names of the three sisters frame the scene and the customary letters S C are at the base of the coin. Caligula was particularly attached to Drusilla and did all he could to promote her elevation to the gods[49]—as indeed it appears that he attempted to do for himself by insisting on his equality with Jupiter.[50] It is well known that he caused a near revolt in Judaea in 39 CE by insisting that his statue be placed within the Holy of Holies in the Jerusalem Temple.[51] This was but one example of how Caligula's twisted mind worked in trying to promote his own divinity during his reign. Another was his proposal to have the great statue of Zeus removed from its temple in Olympia and transferred to his temple on the Palatine in Rome where it could be fitted with a new head bearing Caligula's own likeness.[52] Fortunately, from the standpoint of political

48. *RIC* Gaius 33.

49. See P. Herz, 'Diva Drusilla', *Historia* 30 (1981), pp. 324-36, for a discussion. After her death in 38 CE Caligula promoted her deification as the goddess Panthea, and Cassius Dio reports that a Senator, Livius Geminus, swore under oath that he had seen her ascending to heaven and conversing with the gods of Olympia (59.11.3; cp. Seneca, A*pocolocyntosis of Claudius* 1.3).

50. J.P.V.D. Balsdon *The Emperor Gaius (Caligula)* (Oxford: Clarendon Press, 1934), pp. 157-72; C.J. Simpson, 'The Cult of the Emperor Gaius', *Latomus* 40 (1981), pp. 489-511.

51. The alarm the incident caused among Jews is reflected in Philo's *Embassy to Gaius*. Balsdon, *Gaius,* pp. 111-45; E.M. Smallwood, 'The Chronology of Gaius's Attempt to Desecrate the Temple', *Latomus* 16 (1957), pp. 3-17; A.A. Barrett *Caligula: The Corruption of Power* (London: Guild Publishing, 1989), pp. 182-91; and A. Ferrill, *Caligula: Emperor of Rome* (London: Thames & Hudson, 1991), pp. 140-48, all deal with the matter.

52. This story is related in Suetonius, *Gaius* 22.2; Josephus, *Ant.* 19.8-10 and Cassius Dio, *Hist.* 59.28.3-4. Also worth considering is K. Scott, 'The Significance of Statues in Precious Metals in Emperor Worship', *TPAPA* 62 (1931), pp. 101-23.

harmony, he was assassinated before either proposal was acted upon. Given these megalomaniac ideas it is hardly surprising that the Roman Senate repudiated his reign by refusing his apotheosis. However, the monstrosity of what Caligula had proposed lingered for a long time in the memory and we find allusions to it in many apocalyptic writings written by both Jews and Christians. It forms part of the historical background for the idea of the 'abomination of desolation' (τὸ βδέλυγμα τῆς ἐρημώσεως) mentioned in Mk 13.14.[53] Indeed, some have suggested that part of Jesus' apocalyptic discourse—namely Mk 13.14-22—was originally an independent source dating back to this critical episode with Caligula.[54]

One other coin from Caligula's reign is also worth noting (Figure 20).[55] A sestertius depicts the temple of the deified Augustus in the background with a representation of Caligula in the foreground, second figure from the right, standing by an altar as he prepares to make a sacrifice of a bull in honour of his Imperial predecessor. The inscription

53. The phrase is quite an unusual one and is almost certainly to be associated with the desecration of the Jewish temple by Antiochus Epiphanes in 168–167 BCE as well as Pompey's violation of it in 64 BCE. For more on the subject, see C.H. Dodd, 'The Fall of Jerusalem and the "Abomination of Desolation"', *JRS* 37 (1947), pp. 47-54; B. Rigaux, 'βδέλυγμα τῆς ἐρημώσεως Mc 13,14; Mt. 24,15', *Biblica* 40 (1959), pp. 675-83; D. Daube, *The New Testament and Rabbinic Judaism* (New York: Arno Press, 1973), pp. 418-37; D. Ford, *The Abomination of Desolation in Biblical Eschatology* (Washington, DC: University Press of America, 1979). Not to be missed is the highly entertaining piece by I. Asimov entitled 'Pompey and Circumstance', in *idem, The Left Hand of the Electron* (New York: Dell, 1974), pp. 199-213.

54. This so-called 'Little Apocalypse' theory concerning Mk 13 has had a great deal of attention given to it. Important studies include G.R. Beasley-Murray, *Jesus and the Future: An Examination of the Criticism of the Eschatological Discourse, Mark 13, with Special Reference to the Little Apocalypse Theory* (London: Macmillan, 1954); *A Commentary on Mark Thirteen* (London: Macmillan, 1957), pp. 54-72; L. Hartman, *Prophecy Interpreted: The Formulation of Some Jewish Apocalyptic Texts and of the Eschatological Discourse Mar 13 Par* (Uppsala: Gleerup, 1966); R. Pesch, *Naherwartungen: Tradition und Redaktion in Mk 13* (Düsseldorf: Patmos, 1968); L. Gaston, *No Stone on Another: Studies in the Significance of the Fall of Jerusalem in the Synoptic Gospels* (Leiden: Brill, 1970); D. Wenham, *The Rediscovery of Jesus' Eschatological Discourse* (Gospel Perspectives, 4; Sheffield: JSOT Press, 1984); N.T. Wright, *The New Testament and the People of God* (London: SPCK, 1992), pp. 390-96.

55. *RIC* Gaius 36.

DIVO AVG (for 'Divine Augustus') is found on the edges of the scene with the letters S C in exergue. The obverse of the coin depicts a personification of Pietas, veiled and seated on a throne, facing left and holding a patera in her right hand while a small figure crouches under her left arm. The surrounding inscription reads C CAESAR AVG GERMANICVS PM TR POT and the combination of the titles allows the coin to be dated precisely to 37–38 CE. The inscription PIETAS stands in exergue.

Figure 19   Figure 20

Next to take the throne was Claudius (41–54 CE). By a strange coincidence Claudius was born in Lugdunum on 1 August 10 BCE, the very day on which the famous altar to the Divine Augustus and Roma was dedicated in the city (or at least so ancient sources would have us believe). As Emperor, Claudius appears to have revived the Lugdunum altar coinage which was so extensively used in Augustus's time, possibly in celebration of his own fiftieth birthday. An interesting bronze coin from the city of Philippi is also worth considering. The coin has an obverse bust of Claudius facing left with a surrounding inscription which reads TI CLAVDIVS CAESAR AVG PM TR P IMP. The reverse shows the figures of Julius Caesar and Augustus standing on a platform which has the words DIVVS AVG on it. Surrounding the statues are the words COL(onia) AVG(usti) IVL(ia) PHILIP(ensis) (Figure 21).[56] The choice of reverse type on the coin records the role that Augustus had in

Figure 21

56. Sear, *Greek Imperial*, p. 40, lists this coin as 428.

resettling the colony in 30 BCE following his victories over Mark Antony, as well as marking the family connection that Claudius had to both the deified Julius Caesar and the deified Augustus.

In the main Claudius shunned the excesses of his predecessor Caligula and did not promote his own position within the Imperial cult. Indeed, in one very interesting papyrus letter which has survived, written in 41 CE by Claudius to the city of Alexandria in response to their request to show honours to him, he declares,

> I deprecate the appointment of a high priest to me and the building of temples, for I do not wish to be offensive to my contemporaries, and my opinion is that temples and such forms of honour have by all ages been granted as a prerogative to the gods alone.

Somewhat ironically, an Alexandrian official named Lucius Aemilius Rectus undercuts Claudius's point when he adds a preface to the letter and says,

> I have deemed it necessary to display the letter publicly in order that reading it one by one you may admire the majesty of *our god Caesar* (τοῦ θεοῦ ἡμῶν Καισαρος) and feel gratitude for his goodwill towards the city.[57]

However, one development in the divine cult which took place during the reign of Claudius was the deification of Livia, the wife of Augustus and grandmother of Claudius.[58] Livia had already appeared on a variety of coin types, usually as a personification of Roman virtues and divine attributes. For instance, Tiberius in 21–22 CE issued a series of dupondii

---

57. Emphasis is mine. An English translation of the full text of the letter and its preface is found in C.K. Barrett, *The New Testament Background: Selected Documents* (London: SPCK, 1956), pp. 44-47. The Greek text is available in M.P. Charlesworth, *Documents Illustrating the Reigns of Claudius and Nero* (Cambridge: Cambridge University Press, 1939), pp. 3-5.

58. G. Grether, 'Livia and the Roman Imperial Cult', *AJP* 67 (1946), pp. 222-52. The Emperor Galba (68–69 CE) also issued a similar series of coins in honour of Livia. Apparently, Livia was Galba's patroness and bequeathed him a large sum of money. In a similar vein, Oliver, 'Divi', pp. 35-40, discusses aspects of the sub-sequent development of the Imperial cult, notably the elevation to divine status in Hadrian's day of Marciana (died 112 CE), Matidia (died 119 CE) and Plotina (died 122 CE). All three women were related to Hadrian's adoptive father Trajan, whom he succeeded as Emperor. The deification of the women may have helped to solidify Hadrian's political position, especially given the fact that there were rumours about the legitimacy of his adoption by Trajan.

depicting Livia as the personification of key Roman virtues, namely Iustitia, Pietas and Salus.[59] The obverse of these coins shows the head of Livia, dressed in costume suited to the personification, with the name of the virtue underneath (Figure 22 shows the three personifications).[60] Claudius went one step further by actually petitioning the Senate to grant Livia deification, something neither Tiberius her son nor Caligula her great-grandson ever attempted. The Senate complied, and Claudius celebrated this honour by minting a pair of dupondii, one of which bears

Figure 22

Figure 23

on its obverse a portrait of Divus Augustus and on the reverse Diva Augusta; Livia is represented as seated on a throne and holding a sceptre. Claudius also honoured his mother Antonia by minting coins bearing her portrait on the obverse and on the reverse displaying her as a personification of the virtue Constancy.[61] These coins are similar to

59. A. Wallace-Hadrill, 'The Emperor and his Virtues', *Historia* 30 (1981), pp. 298-323, discusses the way in which personifications of ethical virtues are used on Imperial coinage. The article includes a discussion of the Livia coinage and contains 2 plates, one of which has examples of the dupondii of Tiberius, as well as the sestertius of Caligula mentioned above. Also worth consulting is J.R. Fears, 'The Cult of Virtus and Roman Imperial Ideology', *ANRW*, II.17.2, pp. 827-948. M.B. Flory, 'Honorific Statues for Women in Rome', *TPAPA* 123 (1993), pp. 287-308, discusses some of the public honours awarded to figures such as Octavia and Livia.

60. *RIC* Tiberius 43.

61. N. Kokkinos, *Antonia Augusta: Portrait of a Great Roman Lady* (London: Routledge & Kegan Paul, 1992), pp. 87-107, discusses the presentation of Antonia on coinage. Similar honours appear to have been accorded to Augustus's sister Octavia in Athens, perhaps between 40–32 BCE while she was still married to Mark

Caligula's sestertia, mentioned previously, in which the Emperor bestowed quasi-divine honours on his three sisters.

Claudius died on 13 October 54 CE and was succeeded by his adopted son Nero (54–68 CE). Shortly after taking power, Nero issued a series of coins to commemorate his adoptive father whose rule was deemed worthy enough by the Senate to allow them to confer upon him the honour of apotheosis. Suetonius tells us that Nero later annulled the honour but it was eventually restored by the Emperor Vespasian (*Claudius* 45). Apparently Nero's opinion of Claudius was more favourable in the beginning of his reign than it was at the end because he minted the commemorative series in 54–55 CE. A good example of this series is the didrachma from the mint in Caesarea in Cappadocia (Figure 23).[62] The obverse is a portrait of Claudius with the inscription DIVOS CLAVD AVGVST GERMANIC PATER AVG. The reverse of the coin is a portrait of Nero and it carries the inscription NERO CLAVD DIVI CLAVD F CAESAR AVG GERMANI.

Not even the comparatively benevolent rule of Claudius was without its critics. One of the most vocal was the philosopher Seneca, who wrote a satirical work on the subject called the *Apocolocyntosis of Claudius*, frequently translated as the 'pumpkinfication of Claudius', in which he poked fun at the idea of the apotheosis of Claudius. Seneca sets the satire in heaven where a discussion is going on about Claudius's being made a god, managing to score some political points of his own in the process.[63] Even the dedication of a temple to the divine Claudius in Camulodunum (modern Colchester) a month after his death in 54 CE[64] is made the subject of ridicule. At one point Seneca has the deified Augustus stand up and speak:

Antony. See A.E. Raubitschek, 'Octavia's Deification in Athens', *TPAPA* 77 (1946), pp. 146-50.

62. *RIC* Nero 620.

63. Claudius had banished Seneca to the island of Corsica in 41 CE, ostensibly for being an accomplice in the debaucheries of Julia, the daughter of Germanicus. He was to spend eight years in exile on the island before returning to Rome in order to become the tutor of the youthful Nero. M. Altman, 'Ruler Cult in Seneca', *CP* 33 (1938), pp. 198-204, discusses Seneca's hatred of Claudius in light of the philosopher's Stoic views about deification.

64. M.P. Charlesworth, 'Deus Noster Caesar', *CR* 39 (1925), pp. 113-15, discusses this. Tacitus, *Annals* 14.31.6, mentions the temple in connection with a native uprising in 60 CE.

> Inasmuch as the blessed Claudius murdered his father-in-law Appius
> Silanus, his two sons-in-law, Pompeius Magnus and L. Silanus, Crassus
> Frugi his daughter's father-in-law, as like him as two eggs in a basket,
> Scribonia his daughter's mother-in-law, his wife Messalina, and others
> too numerous to mention; I propose that strong measures be taken against
> him, that he be allowed no delay of process, that immediate sentence of
> banishment be passed on him, that he be deported from heaven within
> thirty days, and from Olympus within thirty hours.

Claudius's successor Nero fell out of Senatorial favour because of his
mismanagement of rule, and ended up committing suicide on 8 July 68
CE in the midst of the first Jewish revolt against Rome (66–70 CE).
Nero was never deified by the Roman Senate, and no coins display his
apotheosis.[65] With his death the rule of the Julio-Claudian house came to
an end.

We turn now to consider briefly the implications that the practice of
apotheosis may have had upon early Christian thought. We must reckon
that the elevation of the Emperor (or one of his family) to the heavenly
pantheon was not only a political but also a religious act, and as such
would have occasioned reactions from within the Church.

3. *Political Aims and Monotheistic Reactions*

The development of the Divine Man cult was by no means peculiar to
the Roman Empire, although during the Imperial period this worship
system reached unparalleled heights. The roots of Emperor worship lay
deep in many ancient Near Eastern cultures in which great rulers were
seen to take on divine qualities. Nevertheless, Rome had its own contribution to make; ruler worship was organized and refined into a unifying
political force. The worship of the Roman Emperor as a personification
of divinity was used to great political advantage, particularly as a means
of welding various peoples and cultures into a single Empire. The political dynamic of the divine cult cannot be overlooked. It is central to any
proper understanding of how the cult functioned within the Roman
Empire, particularly during the time of Augustus when the civilized
world, yearning for relief after decades of civil war, sought in the young
Emperor a deliverer from turmoil and bloodshed. There is no better

---

65. K. Scott, 'Plutarch and the Ruler Cult', *TPAPA* 60 (1929), pp. 117-35, discusses Plutarch's special dislike for Nero and the way in which he ridicules the
Emperor's pretensions to divinity in his work.

example of the statesman's approach to religion than in the person of Augustus. He more than any other Emperor utilized religion as a means of unifying the far-flung provinces and peoples, forging out of them a vast new Empire.

This situation brings up an important consideration: the reactions of persons from traditionally monotheistic faiths to the development of this Imperial cult. It is important to remember that a significant number of Jews and Christians lived within the boundaries of the Roman Empire during the Julio-Claudian period. Judaea first came under Roman rule during the time of Pompey the Great in 63 BCE, and the reign of Herod the Great and his sons amounted to little more than a temporary respite from direct Roman rule. With Augustus's appointment of Coponius as prefect in 6 CE, Judaea once again became a province under direct Roman control and continued to be so throughout the Julio-Claudian period. This period is perhaps one of the most formative in terms of the development of Christianity, a new faith that began as a messianic sect within the confines of Judaism. How did the monotheistic faith of Judaism and its offspring Christianity react to the developing Imperial cult? What responses can we trace within Judaism and Christianity to this religio-political cult focusing on the person of the Emperor? Would it be true to say that the idea of a man becoming god, apotheosis, was acceptable to Christianity but not to Judaism? Could this have been what eventually made Christianity more acceptable to the Roman world? To return to the primary question regarding the Imperial cult, how did the monotheistic faith that was the foundation of both Judaism and Christianity react to the developing Imperial cult? The major difference in reaction seems to be christologically derived. This does not mean that a straightforward equation can be asserted between the 'Son-language' of the Roman cult, the declaration that an Emperor was the 'son of the deified Caesar', for example, and the 'Son of God' language which is applied to Jesus of Nazareth in the New Testament. That is far too simplistic and does not pay enough attention to the essential differences between religious praxis in Rome and religious praxis in the Hellenistic world to the east.[66] However, it does suggest that many Christians found that the incarnational basis of their faith was readily synthesized with the prevailing religious system of the Romans, which included the apotheosis of the Emperor. The Roman concept of apotheosis moved a man from

66. As Price, 'Gods', pp. 79-95, rightly argues. M. Hengel, *The Son of God* (London: SCM Press, 1976), pp. 28-30, also discusses this.

earth toward heaven, whereas the Christian concept of incarnation moved God from heaven toward earth, but the two are similar in that they both deal with the relationship between the human and the divine. It is important to note that the barrier between humans and God was transcended in Christianity in a way that it was not in Judaism. Perhaps this aspect more than any other allowed Christianity to gain a foothold in the life of the average Roman citizen in a way that Judaism was unable to do.

What essentially began as a welding together of the religious life of the Empire, based on political expedience, eventually culminated in the continuing practice of the apotheosis of the Emperor. This meant that Christianity, with its belief in transcending the barrier between human and divine through the incarnation of Jesus Christ, was able to find fruitful ground and flourish within the Roman world.

Summary

From the brief survey presented here, it seems clear that the apotheosis of the Roman Emperor and its attendant implications were very much a part of the religious heritage of many peoples of the early Roman Empire. Numismatic evidence is an important if often neglected source for the conception of apotheosis, and presents a wide variety of images of it. Such a heritage must take its proper place in any attempt to trace the development of New Testament christological thought, recognizing that such development must be set against the backdrop of the religious ideas of the Roman Empire.

Part II

THE WORLD OF PAUL THE APOSTLE

Chapter 3

A NUMISMATIC CLUE TO ACTS 19.23-41:
THE EPHESIAN CISTOPHORI OF CLAUDIUS AND AGRIPPINA[*]

The Emperor Claudius (41–54 CE) is mentioned by name twice in the Acts of the Apostles (11.28 and 18.2). Both instances are supported in their historicity by passing references made within the writings of the Roman biographer Suetonius. The first of these references in Acts is in connection with a severe famine which occurred during Claudius's reign (compare Suetonius, *Claudius* 18). The second deals with his edict of expulsion of Jews from Rome in 49 CE (compare Suetonius, *Claudius* 25). In addition, Claudius is alluded to by the mention of 'Caesar' in Acts 17.7. Each of these three references to Claudius and his influence upon the events recorded within the Acts of the Apostles has been well discussed by New Testament scholars.[1] Are there other indications of Claudius's influence upon the events recorded within this earliest of

* I would like to acknowledge that the impetus for researching this matter came through a letter from K. Hewitt which came across the desk of Professor G. Stanton of King's College, London. Professor Stanton, knowing of my interest in Roman coinage, passed it on to me for comment.

1. An introductory survey is to be found in F.F. Bruce, 'Christianity under Claudius', *BJRL* 44 (1961–62), pp. 309-26. A study of Claudius is important in two other areas related to New Testament research: the situation involving the Alexandrian Jews following Gaius's 'abomination of desolation' incident in which Claudius writes to the Alexandrian authorities, and the so-called 'Nazarene inscription' concerning the desecration of graves which is sometimes thought to have been issued in Claudius's reign. Bruce's discussion includes both of these areas of interest. An older article by K.S. Gapp, 'The Universal Famine under Claudius', *HTR* 28 (1935), pp. 258-65, argues for the historicity of Luke's description of the famine as worldwide on the basis of extra-biblical sources. D. Slingerland, 'Suetonius *Claudius* 25.4, Acts 18, and Paulus Orosius' *Historiarum Adversum Paganos Libri VII*: Dating the Claudian Expulsion(s) of Roman Jews', *JQR* 83 (1992–93), pp. 127-44, discusses the problems of dating the incident alluded to in Acts 18.2.

Christian histories? It would not be unreasonable to expect traces of such influence within Acts since during much of the period covered by its account Claudius reigned as the supreme ruler of the Empire in which Christianity was born, spread and flourished. His policies and actions would undoubtedly affect the residents of those far-away regions of Judaea, Syria and Asia Minor. Only rarely, however, do we see any evidence of how Imperial policy *directly* helped to shape the events recorded within the Acts of the Apostles. Yet, there is one *indirect* indication of Claudius's Imperial policy which needs to be examined more closely in connection with an episode recorded in Acts 19.

That incident is found in Acts 19.23-41 and involves the riot of Demetrius in response to Paul's presence and activity in Ephesus. It just so happens that an issue of commemorative coins was struck at Ephesus during Claudius's reign, and this may prove helpful in understanding the political dynamics which lie behind the incident described in Acts 19. We note once again at this point that New Testament scholars have gene-rally been slow to embrace the contribution that numismatic evidence has to make to their discipline.[2] It is astonishing that hardly any of the major commentaries on Acts allude to numismatic evidence in connec-tion with Acts 19.23-41. I suspect that this oversight is due to sheer ignorance of such evidence, or at least to a reluctance to enter into the seemingly complicated field of ancient coinage. This chapter is an attempt to relate one instance in which numismatic evidence may con-tribute indirectly but significantly to our understanding of a specific New Testament passage. The particular coin issues to be discussed are all silver commemorative coins produced by Claudius through the mint of Ephesus. Of special note in connection with the incident at Ephesus recorded in Acts 19.23-41 is the relationship of the Emperor Claudius to Agrippina the Younger.

Claudius married Agrippina the Younger in 49 CE following the execu-tion of his previous wife Messalina in the preceding year. There is some evidence to suggest that the marriage was politically motivated and specifically designed to 'heal the wounds caused by the Julio-Claudine strife'.[3] Agrippina was an excellent choice in this regard for her family connections were impeccable. She was the daughter of Claudius's brother

2. Crawford, 'Numismatics', pp. 185-233, has attempted to demonstrate how numismatic evidence can be properly employed in historical research and study.

3. V.M. Scramuzza, *The Emperor Claudius* (Cambridge, MA: Harvard University Press, 1940), p. 91.

Germanicus by Agrippina the Elder,[4] the sister of the Emperor Caligula (37–41 CE), and could claim to be descended from both Agrippa and Augustus himself. In addition, she brought with her an equally well-placed son and she was anything but reserved in promoting his adoption by Claudius in preparation for his succession to the Imperial throne. As it turns out, she was successful in her endeavours—we now know this son as the Emperor Nero (54–68 CE).

A beautifully executed cameo of the first century CE has survived which illustrates something of the political import of the marriage between Claudius and Agrippina the Younger. This cameo, known as the *Gemma Claudia*, is made out of sardonyx and is part of the collection of the Cabinet of Antiquities in the Kunsthistorisches Museum in Vienna. It depicts four figures, two pairs facing each other with an Imperial eagle between them (Figure 1). On the left we are presented with the figures of Claudius in the foreground and Agrippina the Younger in the background. Facing them are the parents of Agrippina the Younger, namely Germanicus in the foreground and Agrippina the Elder in the background. It has been suggested that the cameo was made by an unknown artist in 48–49 CE as a gift for the wedding between Claudius and Agrippina the Younger.[5]

The marriage of Claudius and Agrippina was also commemorated in Ephesus by the issue of two cistophori. These two small issues[6] may shed valuable light on the religious and political climate in Ephesus surrounding the marriage in a manner illustrative to New Testament

4. Thus she was Claudius's niece. If the account of the marriage given by Tacitus in *Annals* 12.5-6 is anything to go by, the incestuous marriage created quite a stir within the Roman Senate. On this whole issue of Claudius's marriage to his niece, see M.S. Smith, 'Greek Precedents for Claudius's Actions in AD 48 and Later', *CQ* 57 (1963), pp. 139-44.

5. S. Wood, '*Memoriae Agrippinae*: Agrippina the Elder in Julio-Claudine Art and Propaganda', *AJA* 92 (1988), p. 422. See also S. Fuchs, 'Deutung, Sinn und Zeitstellung des Wiener Cameo mit den Fruchthornbüsten', *RM* 51 (1936), pp. 233-36; E. Fantham, H.P. Foley, N.B. Kampen, S.B. Pomeroy and H.A. Shapiro, 'Women, Family, and Sexuality in the Age of Augustus and the Julio-Claudines', in *idem, Women in the Classical World* (Oxford: Oxford University Press, 1994), pp. 294-329.

6. Judging from the number of examples which have survived, the number of each of the two coins struck could not have been very large, perhaps only a few thousand of each. The British Museum collection contains a total of six examples of the two issues.

interests. The two relevant cistophori issues from Ephesus have Latin inscriptions which may serve as some indication of their semi-official status and their production in a local setting under the auspices of the Roman state.

Figure 1

Both of these cistophori bear the portrait of Agrippina as well as that of the Emperor himself. The first cistophorus (Figure 2)[7] has as its obverse a laureated bust of Claudius facing to the right with the inscription TI CLAVD CAESAR AVG PM TR PX IMP XIIX. This titular inscription, via its reference to Claudius's tenth year of tribunicial power and his eighteenth imperatorship, allows the coin to be positively dated to 50 or 51 CE. The reverse of the coin bears a finely executed portrait bust of Agrippina facing right with the inscription AGRIPPINA AVGVSTA CAESARIS AVG. The second cistophorus (Figure 3)[8] has an obverse jugate portrait of Claudius and Agrippina with the inscription TI CLAVD CAES AVG AGRIPP AVGVSTA. The reverse is a representation of the cult-figure of Diana[9] of the Ephesians standing in ceremonial dress with a ball-polos on her head and long bracelets descending from her wrists

7.   Listed as *RIC* Claudius 117. The British Museum collection includes three examples of this issue (one of which is holed).

8.   *RIC* Claudius 119. The British Museum collection also contains three examples of this issue.

9.   Generally known as Artemis within the Greek-speaking world.

Figure 2   Figure 3

to the ground.[10] The reverse inscription reads DIANA EPHESIA. This second cistophorus does not contain any precise inscriptional clue which helps to determine its exact date. However, its similarity in style and execution of lettering does seem to indicate that it was issued at the same time as the first cistophorus and it therefore can also be dated to 50 or 51 CE. The use of the term AVGVSTA with reference to Agrippina in the inscriptions of both coins is significant and is worthy of further investigation. Both Tacitus and Cassius Dio record that the title 'Augusta' was accorded to Agrippina by Claudius around the year 50 CE.[11] These two literary sources are corroborated by epigraphic evidence as well. The most important example is a 12-line inscription from Ilium in Troas (*Corpus Inscriptionum Graecarum* 3610).[12] The introduction of this inscription, when reconstructed, reads:

(Line 1)   Τιβε]ριω Κλαυδιω καισαρι Σ[εβ
(Line 2)   αστω] Γερμανικω και Ιουλι[α] Σ[ε
(Line 3)   βα]στῆ Αγριππεινη

10. For a discussion of the artistic representation of Artemis/Diana within history, see C. Seltman, 'The Wardrobe of Artemis', *NC* 12 (1952), pp. 33-51 + Plates 5-6; L.R. LiDonnici, 'The Images of Artemis Ephesia and Greco-Roman Worship: A Reconsideration', *HTR* 85 (1992), pp. 389-415. In particular, the many egg-shaped objects on the torso of surviving images of Artemis/Diana have led some to interpret her as a fertility goddess, assuming that these objects represent breasts. B.L. Trell, *The Temple of Artemis at Ephesos* (New York: American Numismatic Society, 1945) offers a full discussion of the various coin issues from antiquity which depict the temple and the cultic figure of Artemis.

11. Tacitus, *Annals* 12.26 and Cassius Dio, *Hist.* 61.33.2a.

12. The translation of the full inscription is given in D.C. Braund, *Augustus to Nero: A Sourcebook on Roman History (31 BC–AD 68)* (London: Croom Helm, 1985), p. 89. Braund also cites a similar relevant Latin inscription which was discovered in Rome.

It should be noted that the critical term within the epigraphic inscription is Σεβαστή instead of *Augusta*. This need not overly concern us since the two are virtually synonymous within both epigraphic and numismatic contexts (with Σεβαστός functioning as the standard Greek translation of *Augustus*).[13] We should not underestimate the significance of the application of this title to Agrippina. It constitutes the first time that the title *Augusta* (or its Greek equivalent Σεβαστή) was borne by a living wife of the reigning Emperor. Previously, only Livia, the wife of Augustus himself, enjoyed the title during the last years of her life; and even then it was only after the death of her husband.[14] The unprecedented step of Agrippina's elevation to *Augusta* is emphasized when we consider that Claudius's previous wife Messalina was specifically denied that title by her husband (Cassius Dio, *Hist.* 60.12.5). Perhaps the reason such a high privilege was granted to Agrippina was that it helped to legitimize the adoption of her son Nero as the designated successor to the Imperial throne. In any case, both Tacitus and Cassius Dio mention Agrippina's elevation to *Augusta* within the larger context of Nero's rise to power.

What is the significance of the issue of these two coins for the situation at Ephesus? What was the purpose of their issue? A partial answer can perhaps be found when we consider the other cistophoric issues of Asia Minor during the reign of Claudius. Basically there are three other relevant coin types which must be considered. The first of these cistophori (Figure 4)[15] bears an obverse portrait of Claudius facing left with the inscription TI CLAVD CAES AVG. The reverse of this coin shows a tetrastyle temple (obviously the Artemision) with the cult figure of Diana of the Ephesians standing within the temple cella and a shortened inscription DIAN EPHE. Unfortunately, these vague inscriptions do not allow us to date the coin precisely within the reign of Claudius. C.H.V. Sutherland suggests[16] that it was issued in 41 or 42 CE in connection with Claudius's rise to power. Although this is a probable suggestion it cannot be proven. In any event, the subject matter of the reverse of the coin clearly points to the city of Ephesus as its issuing source.

---

13. It may be that Σεβάστη carries with it a slightly stronger hint of religious reverence than *Augusta* via its association with the idea of εὐσεβεία.

14. Cassius, Dio *Hist.* 61.33.12, specifically mentions Agrippina's desire to have all the respect and official titles that Livia had, and more.

15. *RIC* Claudius 118.

16. *RIC*, p. 130.

The second relevant cistophorus (Figure 5)[17] issued during Claudius's reign is slightly more difficult to assess. It bears exactly the same obverse portrait and inscription as the undateable 'Temple' issue from Ephesus just described. The reverse, however, does not betray any specific connection with the temple of Diana at Ephesus. Instead, it shows a distyle temple of Roma and Augustus with the standing figure of the Emperor (Claudius?) on the left being crowned by a female figure (a personification of Asia?) on the right. The Emperor holds a spear in his right hand while the female figure holds a cornucopia in her left. The temple pediment is inscribed ROM(a) ET AVG while the inscription COM(mune) ASI(ae) is found in the field of the coin. The provenance of this coin is a debated point. In terms of style, weight, size and portrait execution it is

Figure 4   Figure 5

remarkably similar to the three known Ephesian cistophori already discussed. Indeed, most of the older coin catalogues and studies list this coin as an issue from the city mint at Ephesus. For instance, the standard catalogue of the British Museum collection lists all four of the cistophori under discussion as issues of the Asia Minor mint at Ephesus.[18] More recently, however, Sutherland has argued that this fourth cistophorus type is much more likely to have been issued from Pergamum.[19] This seems probable when we consider that the inscription COM(mune) ASI(ae) points to that city as it was the Roman capital of the province of Asia and the only city within the province which is known to have had a

17. *RIC* Claudius 120.

18. H. Mattingly (ed.), *Coins of the Roman Empire in the British Museum*. I. *(Augustus to Vitellius)* (London: Trustees of the British Museum, 1923), pp. 196-98.

19. *The Emperor and the Coinage: Julio-Claudine Studies* (London: Spink & Son Ltd, 1976), p. 54. This argument is also assumed in Sutherland's revision in *RIC*, p. 120. This is a reversal of Sutherland's earlier opinion found in *Coinage in Roman Imperial Policy* (London: Methuen, 1951), p. 135, where Mattingly's assignment of the type to Ephesus is accepted.

temple dedicated to both Roma and Augustus.[20] In other words, the fact that in 29 BCE Pergamum was known to have dedicated a temple to Roma and Augustus and instituted a yearly festival in Augustus's honour is decisive in Sutherland's assigning the cistophorus to that city as the capital of the Commune Asia. The inscriptions ROM(a) ET AVG(ustus) and COM(mune) ASI(ae) on the reverse of the coin seem to support this conclusion.

Furthermore, if Sutherland is correct in dating this cistophorus type to 41 or 42 CE in celebration of Claudius's accession, then a deliberate reason for its issue seems indicated. We know that as a general rule the accession of any Emperor was immediately followed by official issues from the Imperial mints which proclaimed the appropriate virtues and qualities of the man concerned. It seemed a matter of political expedience to advertise Claudius's assumption of power within these two most important cities in Asia Minor, Ephesus and Pergamum, and to do so in such a way as to emphasize both their close ties to Rome and the beauty and splendour of their respective city temples. In other words, these two brief commemorative issues represent a clever but effective way of binding both cities more closely in their allegiance to the new Emperor himself and yet allowing the cities the privilege of further extending their own prominence and prestige. Thus it appears that the issue was politically motivated and designed to help consolidate Claudius's authority and power within the province. It certainly was not needed in terms of economics since the vast cistophoric issues of Augustus minted in Asia Minor from 28–18 BCE sufficed to meet any local monetary needs.

Instead, we must remember that coinage represented a most effective means of Imperial propaganda at the time. It was a convenient means of emphasizing official policies and ideas and was, by its very economic nature, guaranteed to touch every level of society. In short, the minting of these coins represents a mutually beneficial arrangement between the Emperor and these two major cities of Asia Minor. The claims of the new Emperor were thereby effectively broadcast, as were the glories of the two privileged cities called upon to serve as minting centres— Ephesus and Pergamum. It appears that precisely the same dynamic was in operation with respect to the third cistophorus from Asia Minor which demands our attention. This coin (Figure 6)[21] has as its obverse a

20. Cassius Dio, *Hist.* 61.20.6-9, mentions this in connection with the establishment of the Imperial cultus in the time of Augustus.
21. *RIC* Claudius 121.

portrait of a young bareheaded Nero with the dedicatory inscription
NERONI CLAVD CAES DRVSO GERM. The reverse depicts a shield
within a laurel wreath. An inscription on the shield reads, in three lines,
COS DES PRINCI IVVENT. The occasion of this coin, which incidentally Sutherland assigns to Pergamum, is probably the adoption of Nero
by Claudius in 51 CE as the heir-apparent to the throne. All three of
these coin issues have as their common theme the proclamation of
Imperial rights in terms of reigning authority and thus serve an obviously
political interest.

Figure 6

With this salient fact of political expedience in mind let us turn once
more to the first two cistophoric issues with which we began our discussion. We have suggested that both were minted in commemoration
of Agrippina's marriage to Claudius and her unprecedented elevation to
Augusta in 50 or 51 CE. Claudius had not allowed (or initiated?) the
minting of any Ephesian or Pergamene silver with Latin inscriptions for
nearly ten years (i.e. since the minting of cistophori in commemoration
of his accession in 41 CE). Why now is this dual issue emphasizing
Agrippina's position commissioned? And why does it clearly emphasize
the significance of Diana of the Ephesians? Sutherland throws out the
attractive suggestion that 'Ephesus tended towards a syncretism of
Agrippina with Diana'.[22] Such a possibility is certainly in keeping with
what we know to have been true of Agrippina's desire for official
recognition of power and Imperial titles. No doubt the close association
with the great goddess Diana would have been an attractive prospect for
her. At the same time it does the city of Ephesus little harm by high-
lighting the association of that city with the centre of Imperial policy and
decision making.

Sutherland's suggestion is given further weight when we consider that
there also exists a series of indigenous bronze coins minted in Ephesus
which bear Greek inscriptions and also contain portrait busts of Claudius

22. *RIC*, p. 120.

and Agrippina. These bronze coins were in all likelihood struck at the same time as the cistophori commemorating the royal marriage and were probably designed to supplement the official silver issues within the local context. One particularly relevant example[23] bears an obverse dual portrait of the facing heads of Claudius and Agrippina and the remarkable inscription THEOGAMIA ('The Marriage of the Gods'). The reverse of the coin once again shows the cultic statue of Artemis/Diana and carries with it the inscription EPHESIA. This coin issue adds further weight to the suggestion that a religious syncretism was indeed in operation and that a mutually beneficial arrangement between the Emperor Claudius and the city of Ephesus was reached via the minting of such commemorative issues.

To turn now to the New Testament, is it possible that this atmosphere of affinity between Rome and Ephesus helps to explain the experiences of Paul as recorded in Acts 19? We know that the episode involving the riot of Demetrius in Acts 19.23-41 focused on Paul's insult to the established marketing practices associated with the Artemision. The specific bone of contention is the manufacture and sale of silver temples of Artemis/Diana (ναοὺς ἀργυροῦς ᾿Αρτέμιδος) and the effect that Paul has on their sale throughout the province of Asia.[24] Such silver souvenirs, of course, have no direct relationship to the minting of silver cistophori under Imperial authority. But no doubt the minting of such coins may help to explain the climate of hostile reaction Paul receives from the Ephesians at the instigation of the silversmith Demetrius. Such a rare Imperial move as the minting of commemorative cistophori may have helped to foster an aggressive pride among the Ephesians with regard to the temple of Artemis/Diana. Perhaps we see something of this patriotic fervour being made manifest in the riot of Acts 19. One can almost imagine the Ephesians saying, 'How dare this foreign Jew come here

23. The British Museum has a specimen which is noted in the *Catalogue of Greek Coins of Ionia in the British Museum* (London: Trustees of the British Museum, 1892), pp. 73, 207. Unfortunately, it is in such a poor state as to render any useful artistic reproduction impossible. This coin is also cited as 234 in Braund, *Augustus*, p. 94.

24. L.R. Taylor, 'Note XXII. The Asiarchs', in F.J. Foakes-Jackson and K. Lake (eds), *The Beginnings of Christianity*, V (5 vols.; London: Macmillan, 1933), p. 255, comments: 'the cult of Artemis was in eclipse as a result of Paul's preaching, and the Ephesians were trying to guard the prestige of their divinity'. Also see Sherwin-White, *Roman Foreign Policy*, pp. 83-92; R.F. Stoops, 'Riot and Assembly: The Social Context of Acts 19.23-41', *JBL* 108 (1989), pp. 73-91.

and criticize our sacred and holy temple of Artemis? Does he not know that even the Empress herself has recently declared the greatness of Artemis and identifies herself with the goddess? Look, we even have official Roman coins to prove it!'

In short, the Agrippina cistophoric issues may offer a brief numismatic glimpse into the highly-charged atmosphere in Ephesus, an atmosphere which was consumed with pride over the Imperial honour granted to their city and the fact that they, as the guardians of the most important temple of Artemis/Diana in the world,[25] were brought that much closer to the source of Imperial power and majesty by the Empress's association with the goddess. This suggestion is not at all incompatible with recent studies in the chronology of Paul's life. For instance, the thorough attempt by R. Jewett to establish Pauline chronology suggests that Paul's Ephesian ministry stretched from late 52 to early 55 CE.[26] The imprecise chronological introduction of the account of the riot of Demetrius in Acts 19.23 (ἐγένετο δὲ κατὰ τὸν καιρὸν ἐκεῖνον) allows us to place the episode at any point within the Ephesian ministry of Paul.[27] This means that without great difficulty it is possible to imagine Paul's confrontation with Demetrius and his crowd occurring within a year or so of the appearance of the Claudian cistophoric issues. We could, of course, attribute this to 'mere coincidence'. Perhaps this might suffice as an explanation, but one or two other brief indications within the story in Acts 19.23-41 deserve further consideration.

The first involves the role that the Asiarchs play in calming the riotous mood within the Ephesian theatre by advising Paul not to enter into the theatre itself (19.31). We should note that the Asiarchs were extremely influential officials, chosen from the most respected and aristocratic circles within the province of Asia, whose specific job was service in the

25. See R.E. Oster, 'The Ephesian Artemis as an Opponent of Early Christianity', *JAC* 19 (1976), pp. 23-45; and 'Ephesus as a Religious Center under the Principate I: Paganism before Constantine', *ANRW*, II.18.3, pp. 1661-1728, for a full discussion of the worship of Artemis over many centuries, stressing the importance of the cult for the life and development of the city of Ephesus. P. Trebilco, 'Asia', in D.W.J. Gill and C. Gempf (eds.), *The Book of Acts in Its First Century Setting*. II. *Graeco-Roman Setting* (Grand Rapids, MI: Eerdmans, 1994), pp. 302-357, is also well worth consulting and provides up-to-date bibliographical information.

26. *Dating Paul's Life* (London: SCM Press, 1979).

27. Although it seems to me that the incident was so severe that it was probably toward the end of Paul's ministry at Ephesus and was responsible, at least in part, for his leaving the city.

Roman Imperial cult.[28] They would have had a vested interest in making sure that nothing occurred within the religious life of the city of Ephesus which might be seen to be damaging to the peaceful and prosperous propagation of the Imperial cultus.

The reference to the Asiarchs in Acts 19.31 describes some of their number as friends of Paul (τινὲς δὲ καὶ τῶν 'Ασιαρχῶν). One is tempted to assume that this oblique comment implies a prior acquaintance between Paul and the Asiarchs concerned. However, this remark may be nothing more than an after-the-fact reflection of their benevolent instrumentality in saving Paul's life (and at the same time preventing any further disruption to the smooth operation of the Imperial cultic activities in the city).[29] It seems to me that the presence of the Asiarchs within the account of Acts 19.23-41, which is very compressed and gives us only the bare bones of the story, indicates that a far deeper religious/political battle was raging than is at first evident. My suspicion is that Paul was much closer to extreme bodily harm, perhaps even death, than we sometimes think in this episode, and I remain sceptical of those who assert that 2 Cor. 1.8 and 1 Cor. 15.32 are totally unrelated to this incident in Ephesus.[30] The presence of the Asiarchs within the story suggests a dynamic involving the Imperial cultus which is easily overlooked. This brings me to my second observation.

The second supporting point involves the consistent tension between Jews and Christians, often focusing on Paul, which seems on show throughout the book of Acts. It is remarkable that on several occasions the Imperial angle is brought out and Paul's ministry is rejected and condemned because it treads upon accepted Roman practices including, in all likelihood, the local expressions of worship of the Emperor. Note for instance the episode in Philippi recorded in Acts 16 (especially vv. 20-21) and the episode in Thessalonika recorded in Acts 18.5-9. These incidents suggest that the complicated tangle of Jewish/Christian relations was such that some of the Jews disaffected by Paul's preaching and

28. On this, see Taylor, 'Note XXII', pp. 256-62.

29. R.A. Kearsley, 'The Asiarchs', in D.W.J. Gill and C. Gempf (eds.), *The Book of Acts in Its First Century Setting. II. Graeco-Roman Setting* (Grand Rapids, MI: Eerdmans, 1994), pp. 363-76, stresses the civic, as opposed to the provincial, nature of the Asiarchs' responsibilities.

30. Follow the discussion in R.E. Osborne, 'Paul and the Wild Beasts', *JBL* 85 (1966), pp. 225-30; A.J. Malherbe, 'The Beasts at Ephesus', *JBL* 87 (1968), pp. 71-80; D.R. MacDonald, 'A Conjectural Emendation of 1 Cor. 15.31-32: Or the Case of the Misplaced Lion Fight', *HTR* 73 (1980), pp. 265-76.

ministry were not above subtly indicting him among the common people as a threat to the local religious conventions involving the worship of the Emperor. This tension helps to provide a very broad background against which to examine the specific incident of Paul's clash with such local conventions in Ephesus.

Summary

We have, in the unusual cistophoric coins of Ephesus minted in commemoration of Agrippina's marriage to Claudius in 50–51 CE, a tantalizing numismatic clue to the episode in Acts 19.23-41. These coins, which coincide remarkably well with recent attempts to establish Pauline chronology in relation to the Ephesian ministry, suggest that the Empress's syncretistic association with the goddess Artemis/Diana (as implied by the coins) could help to explain the surge of popular fervour and support for the temple cultus which occurred in reaction to Paul's ministry in Ephesus.

Chapter 4

NERO'S ROME: IMAGES OF THE CITY ON IMPERIAL COINAGE

That the apostle Paul intended to visit Rome on his way to Spain is clearly recorded in his letter to the Roman church (Rom. 15.24). Whether he ever did manage to get as far as Spain, and when, is a matter of considerable scholarly debate.[1] Certainly we know that Paul eventually made it to Rome and stayed there for a substantial length of time, perhaps as long as two years or more (Acts 28.11-31). But the account in Acts breaks off so abruptly that we are left wondering what happened to Paul afterwards. In all probability he was executed in Rome under Nero in late 64 or early 65 CE in the turmoil following the great conflagration.[2] By the end of the first century and the beginning of the second century CE Christian writers were already beginning to speak of Paul's martyrdom in Rome under the Emperor Nero (54–68 CE) as a factual matter.[3] Assuming that this early tradition about Paul's martyrdom rests on historical fact, we can safely deduce that Paul did indeed manage to visit Rome as he had hoped, but that he was prevented in his plan to preach the gospel message to the ends of the earth (Spain) by his execution, an execution performed under Nero's command. This means that Paul was to spend the last years of his life in Rome in confinement awaiting trial. Perhaps it is not too far-fetched to suggest that Paul would have had

1.   On this question, see Jewett, *Dating*, pp. 44-46.
2.   Jewett, *Dating*, p. 46, suggests a date range for Paul's execution from spring of 62 CE to August 64 CE.
3.   *1 Clem.* 5, written about 96 CE, speaks of both Peter and Paul as martyred saints in language which seems to suggest that they had recently been killed; that is to say, within living memory of those being addressed. The most likely setting for this martyrdom would have been the Neronic persecutions which arose following the great fire in Rome in July of 64 CE. Similarly, Ignatius, *Rom.* 4.2-3 (written about 110 CE), speaks of his own impending martyrdom and compares himself with both Peter and Paul in this context. The Muratorian Canon lines 38-39 (written about 200 CE?) also speak of Paul's intended journey to Rome.

occasion during that two-year period to see something of Rome even
while under house arrest.

What was Nero's Rome like then? What might Paul have seen while
walking through the streets there? What evidence is there from that time
which helps us to understand the Rome of Nero's reign that Paul would
have encountered? Fortunately there is a great deal of archaeological and
literary evidence which has helped to fill out the picture fairly accurately.
However, I would here like to call attention to some of the numismatic
evidence from Nero's Imperial mints which also gives us a few brief, but
suggestive, glimpses of the Imperial City at that time, the Rome that the
Apostle Paul might have seen, the Rome in which he lived and eventually died. The Imperial capital in the early 60's CE must have been a
hive of activity, as we might expect any capital of the ancient world to
be. One can easily imagine that there was a tremendous amount of excitement in the air, with many crucial political issues, both domestic and
foreign, circulating as hotly debated topics of discussion. What might
some of these topics have been? Do we have any way of knowing?

As I have already noted, in the ancient world coinage served as a
major propaganda tool, a means of communication to the masses. Nero
followed the precedents that had been set by other Emperors in this area
and used his coinage as a means of proclaiming his military victories,
asserting his political ideas and advertising his construction and rebuilding
programmes. Within this chapter I want to call attention to seven reverse
types in which Nero does just that. The examples chosen all come from
64–67 CE and thus coincide with the precise period during which I have
suggested that Paul might have been imprisoned in Rome. In examining
the coins more closely we gain an insight not only into some of the
issues which must have been talked about in Rome at the time, but also
some rare insights into some of the architectural features of that city and
its environs. Through the coins we may be seeing things that Paul
himself saw, or at least seeing things about which he had participated in
discussion. The numismatic evidence can therefore become a means of
our penetrating the mists of time, of seeing Paul's world in its own
terms, however limited the picture and however imperfect our vision
may be. The coinage stands as a concrete piece of evidence, an invaluable
resource which we should not overlook in our attempt at understanding
the world of two millennia ago. As R. Oster has said, 'NT historians
must admit that since we have far less primary data at our disposal then
we would like, we cannot afford to ignore the whole range of numismatic

documents.'[4] What of the Roman coinage of Paul's day? It is clear that following the great fire in July of 64 CE Nero was responsible for a complete reorganization of the coinage system of the Empire, including a reduction in the weight of the standard gold and silver coinage, the aureus and the denarius. Another very important feature of this reform was the reintroduction of bronze coins of various denominations, including sestertia, asses and dupondii, all of which were struck in large numbers. Special attention was given to the aesthetic quality and beauty of presentation of the coins within the reform. Commenting on the Imperial coinage produced under Nero, E.A. Sydenham has said, 'It is during the Nero period that the coins of the Roman Empire unquestionably reach their highest point of artistic excellence.'[5] As an illustration of this artistic excellence, note the obverse presentation of a sestertius (Figure 1) with its finely-executed portrait of Nero wearing a laurel-wreath and facing to the right. The inscription of the coin reads, NERO CLAVD(ius) CAESAR AVG(ustus) GER(manicus) P(ontifex) M(aximus) TR(ibunicia) P(otestas) IMP(erator P(ater) P(atriae). Because of its large size, the sestertius was a perfect vehicle for the die-cutter to express his skill and expertise. In particular, the reverses of the sestertia became a major platform of the Imperial propaganda machine, and served as an ideal publicity medium for the Emperor.

Allow me now to examine six reverse types of sestertia, together with the slightly smaller bronze asses and dupondii, before moving on to consider one particular reverse type which appeared on aureii and denarii. All of this evidence provides us with a small insight into the sights of the Rome of Paul's imprisonment. At the same time we see something of the political concerns of the day by the choice that is made about subject matter for the reverses. Having looked at the seven reverse types I will make suggestions about a couple of particular passages in the captivity epistles of Paul which may be illuminated by the numismatic evidence.

1. *The Harbour at Ostia Reverse*

The first example is a sestertius[6] which bears on its obverse the inscription NERO CLAVD(ius)CAESAR AVG(ustus) GER(manicus) P(ontifex)

4.   'Numismatic Windows', p. 218.

5.   *The Coinage of Nero* (London: Spink & Son, 1920), p. 34. The most recent study of Nero's coinage is contained in Sutherland, *RIC*, pp. 133-87.

6.   *RIC* Nero 178-183. Also see *RIC* Nero 440-441, 513-514, 586-589.

M(aximus) TR(ibunicia) P(otestas) IMP(erator) P(ater) P(atriae) (see Figure 1). Sutherland dates this coin to 64–65 CE. The reverse (Figure 2) is most revealing in that it depicts the Roman harbour city of Ostia. The whole of the reverse is taken up with a very artistic presentation of the harbour, the central area containing a number of ships while the outer border is a circular presentation of the harbour sea wall and accompanying warehouses and buildings. The inscription of the reverse helps

Figure 1   Figure 2

to complete the border of the scene and is in two parts: the top inscription is AVGVSTI while the bottom contains the words POR(tus) OST(iae) between the letters S C. Thus the inscription declares 'The Imperial Port of Ostia'. The harbour lighthouse, topped by a statue, possibly one of Neptune, is also depicted toward the top of the coin, the figure projecting into the letters of the top inscription. In the foreground is a personification of the river Tiber, reclining and facing to the left, holding a rudder and a dolphin. He is larger than the statue of Neptune in a deliberate attempt to convey perspective and distance. The central area of the coin is filled with a number of ships of various sizes and types. The number of ships depicted varies from one coin to another, some examples of the sestertius containing as many as 13 separate ships and boats.

Noting the perspective that the die-cutter of the coin is attempting to convey in his work, L. Breglia suggests that he is drawing from direct observation and comments,

> I would like, above all, to draw the reader's attention to the bird's-eye perspective he has employed. This particular angle of incidence is a fairly popular device with Roman artists, both for relief work and in graphic design, when they want to portray the inside of something, especially something (e.g. an amphitheatre or a camp perimeter) which has a circular ground plan.[7]

7. *Roman Imperial Coins: Their Art and Technique* (London: Thames & Hudson, 1968), pp. 76-77. An enlarged photograph of the sestertius is also provided. A full-page colour photograph of the sestertius can also be viewed in M.J. Price

Nero took over the Ostia harbour building project from his predecessor Claudius (41–54 CE), intending to expand it by building a canal from Rome to the harbour itself, a distance of some 10 miles.[8]

We have no record of Paul ever having been in Ostia, but it is not unreasonable to suggest that he might have visited it at some stage during his imprisonment. Certainly some of the visitors he received in Rome would have passed through this famous port on their way to the city of Rome itself. The extensive reconstruction programme pursued by Nero there would have undoubtedly been a major talking-point of the day.

2. *The Praetorian Guard Reverse*

Moving on from the Ostia reverse type we have on another coin reverse a glimpse of part of the architectural building of the city of Rome itself. At the same time the reverse type provides us with an extremely suggestive setting and highlights the reliance of the Emperor upon the loyalty and allegiance of his soldiers. The second example is a sestertius[9] which also bears on its obverse the Nero portrait and the inscription NERO CLAVD(ius) CAESAR AVG(ustus) GER(manicus) P(ontifex) M(aximus) TR(ibunicia) P(otestas) IMP(erator) P(ater) P(atriae) (see Figure 1). The reverse (Figure 3) is an interesting presentation of Nero addressing a cohort of the praetorian guard, his personal bodyguard, from a raised platform. Nero stands bare-headed and wearing a toga on the right side of the scene, his arm raised in dramatic fashion as if he were in the midst of a speech. Alongside him is a praetorian prefect, also bare-headed and wearing a toga. Below them are three soldiers in military gear and bearing standards. In the background to the whole scene is a building supported by pillars with what appears to be an oval-shaped roof. The building may be a representation of the praetorium.[10] The

(ed.), *Coins: An Illustrated Survey—650 BC to the Present Day* (London: Hamlyn, 1980), p. 86.

8.   Suetonius, *Claudius* 20.1-3; *Nero* 16.1; 31.3; Cassius Dio, *Hist.* 60.11.1-4. An inscription from Ostia itself (*Corpus Inscriptionum Latinarum* xiv. 85), dated to 46-47 CE, is also relevant. M.K. Thornton, 'Nero's Quinquennium: The Ostian Connection', *Historia* 38 (1989), pp. 117-19, discusses Nero's completion of the project begun by Claudius in 42 CE and describes the construction of the harbour as one of the greatest of his achievements in his first five years of power.

9.   *RIC* Nero 95. Also see *RIC* Nero 96-97, 130-136, 371, 386-388, 429, 489-492, 564-565.

10.   Sutherland, *RIC*, p. 156, describes it as a 'pillared building below battlemented

inscription ADLOCVT(io) COH(ortium) is in exergue with the letters
S C in the field on either side of the scene. This coin dates to 64 CE
although the reverse type first appeared the previous year.

Figure 3   Figure 4

The headquarters of the praetorian guard in Rome, the praetorium,
was located on the northeastern outskirts of the city near the Viminal
Gate. We know that there were nine cohorts of the praetorian guard
stationed in Rome and Italy and that they were the backbone of the
Emperor's strength in rule. The fact that Nero chose as a reverse type a
representation of the praetorian guard stands as an index as to how
important it was to maintain their loyalty and good favour.

3. *The Temple of Janus Reverse*

The third example builds on the historic event of the closing of the doors
of the temple of Janus in the Roman Forum, an event which Suetonius
says took place in 66 CE on the occasion of Tiridates' visit to Rome.[11]
The fact that Tiridates, as king of Armenia, had in 63 CE paid symbolic
homage to the Roman authorities in the East was a cause of great
rejoicing and celebration in Rome. It meant that the state of hostilities
between Armenia and Rome had ceased and that peace was finally at
hand. The event was commemorated in a variety of ways including the
minting of sestertia, asses and dupondii which depict the temple of Janus
on their reverse.[12] It was a particularly suitable choice for a reverse type

crescent-shaped structure (? the praetorian camp)'.

11. *Nero* 13.1-2.

12. *RIC* Nero 50, 58, 263-271, 283-291, 300-311, 323-328, 337-342, 347-350,
353-355, 362, 366-367, 421, 438-439, 468-472, 510-512, 537-539, 583-585. See
D.W. MacDowall, 'The Organisation of the Julio-Claudian Mint at Rome', in R.A.G
Carson and C.M. Kraay (eds.), *Scripta Nummaria Romana: Essays Presented to
Humphrey Sutherland* (London: Spink & Son Ltd, 1978), pp. 32-46, for a discus-
sion of variations in the depiction of the temple.

because Roman tradition had long before decreed that the doors to the temple of Janus could not be closed as long as there was a war going on in which Rome was involved.[13] The Imperial mint clearly wished to call attention to the great diplomatic triumph involving Tiridates' submission to Roman rule and the peace that ensued by minting this coin with its highly symbolic reverse. The coin bears an obverse portrait of Nero with an inscription reading NERO CAESAR AVG(ustus) IMP(erator) TR(ibunicia) P(otestas) XI P(ater) P(atriae), which allows the coin to be dated between December of 64 CE and December of 65 CE.[14]

The reverse of the coins show the front of the temple of Janus itself with a latticed window and a set of closed doors from which a garland is hung. There is a variety of ways in which the temple of Janus is depicted; sometimes the door is on the left, sometimes on the right, for instance (Figure 4 shows two examples both of which have the door on the right). The inscription on all versions reads, PACE P(opuli) R(omani) TERRA MARIQ(ue) PARTA IANVM CLVSIT, with the letters S C sometimes appearing in the field of the coin on either side of the temple building. Judging by the description that is given in all of the ancient sources about the Tiridates incident, it must have been quite an issue for popular discussion throughout Rome during the time of Paul's imprisonment there.

4. *The Triumphal Arch Reverse*

The fourth example is a sestertius[15] which bears on its obverse the Nero portrait and inscription NERO CLAVD(ius) CAESAR AVG(ustus) GER(manicus) P(ontifex) M(aximus) TR(ibunicia) P(otestas) IMP(erator) P(ater) P(atriae) (Figure 1). The coin dates to 64–65 CE. The reverse depicts an ornamental triumphal arch surmounted by a figure of the Emperor riding in a quadriga (Figure 5). Alongside the quadriga are figures of Victory and Pax: Victory on the right holding a wreath and palm, and Pax on the left holding a caduceus and a cornucopia. The arch itself is garlanded and has on its left side, in a niche, the figure of Mars

---

13. Suetonius, *Augustus* 22; Cassius Dio, *Hist.* 51.20.4 and 53.27.1.

14. M.T. Griffin, *Nero: The End of a Dynasty* (London: B.T. Batsford, 1984), p. 122, discusses some of the chronological problems this poses with regard to the actual date when the doors of the temple were closed.

15. *RIC* Nero 143. Also see *RIC* Nero 144-50, 392-93, 432-33, 498-500, 573-75.

holding a spear. The letters S C stand in the field on either side of the arch. From Tacitus[16] we learn that the eastern victories were being celebrated in Rome by the establishment of many monuments and that the Triumphal Arch was being worked on in 62 CE. It was probably completed by 64 CE with the minting of the sestertius as part of the celebrations surrounding its completion. It seems certain that the Triumphal Arch has an integral link to the Tiridates incident.

5. *The Macellum Magnum Reverse*

The fifth example is a reverse type which appears on dupondii issued by the mints in Rome and Lugdunum dating from 63–65 CE. It depicts the great market (*macellum*) of Rome which was completed by Nero in 59 CE. The market was located on the Caelian hill and the reverse type presents us with a representation of a large domed building which contains two storeys. A flight of stairs is visible leading up to an arched doorway in the centre of the first storey. A nude male statue, probably of a god, stands in the doorway. The words MAC(ellum) AVG(usti) are above the scene while the letters S C are on either side of the building. The obverse of the dupondii shows a portrait of Nero facing right, wearing a radiate crown, surrounded by the inscription NERO CLAVD(ius) CAESAR AVG(ustus) GERM(anicus) TR(ibunicia) P(otestas) P(ater) P(atriae) (Figure 6).[17]

Figure 5   Figure 6

6. *The Ara Pacis Augustae Reverse*

The sixth example is a reverse type which appears on sestertia and asses issued by the imperial mint in Rome. It depicts the famous Altar of Peace ordered erected by Augustus (Figure 7).[18] This altar, the *Ara Pacis*

16. *Annals* 25.18.1.
17. *RIC* Nero 109. See also *RIC* Nero 110-11, 184-89, 373-74, 399-402.
18. *RIC* Nero 418. See also *RIC* Nero 456-461, 526-531. An as depicting the

Augustae, was situated on the Campus Martius and was dedicated on 30 January 9 BCE. It was erected to celebrate the return of Augustus from Spain and Gaul in 13 BCE, and is mentioned in the *Res Gestae* 12. The altar is one of the most important artistic monuments which has survived from the Julio-Claudian period, and sets forth the ideals of the Augustan age in striking fashion.[19] It has been the subject of intense interest for many years and was restored in 1937–38 (although some scholars do not feel that all of the marble fragments which have survived actually belong to the altar itself).[20] The bronze sestertia and asses which illustrate the altar were issued by the mint in Lugdunum between 64–67 CE. The coins show the altar, including ornamentation on the top and decorations on the front panels which stand on either side of the central double doors. The words ARA PACIS stand at the base of the scene and the letters S C are in the field of the coin.

The proclamation of Augustus as the one who brought peace to the Roman world, the Pax Romana, was extremely important in terms of political propaganda. The Julio-Claudian successors of Augustus traded upon this fact, freely taking advantage of the opportunity to present themselves as rulers anxious to carry on the best Augustan traditions. Nero was certainly no exception in this regard; he is said to have modelled his principate on that of Augustus, as Suetonius, *Nero* 10.1, makes clear: 'To make his good intentions still more evident, he declared that he would rule according to the principles of Augustus, and he let slip no opportunity for acts of generosity and mercy, or even for displaying his affability.' Clearly the association of the person of the Emperor Nero with the Pax Romana seems intended by the deliberate issue of these coins. The coinage harks back to the era of peace inaugurated by the Divine Augustus, a peace which was readily celebrated by the erection of the Ara Pacis which bore his name. The role of the Julio-

altar was issued in 86 CE by the Emperor Domitian, probably to celebrate the military victories over Germany and Britain. See *RIC* Domitian 336 for details of the coin.

19. For details see E. Strong, 'The Art of the Augustan Age', *CAH*, X, pp. 546-50; G. Moretti, *The Ara Pacis Augustae* (Rome: Instituto Poligrafico Dello State, 1961); Hannestad, *Roman Art,* pp. 62-74; J. Elsner, 'Cult and Sculpture: Sacrifice in the Ara Pacis Augustae', *JRS* 81 (1991), pp. 50-61 + Plates 1-7; D. Castriota, *The Ara Pacis Augustae and the Imagery of Abundance in Later Greek and Early Roman Imperial Art* (Princeton, NJ: Princeton University Press, 1995).

20. This is discussed in S. Weinstock, 'Pax and the Ara Pacis Augustae', *JRS* 50 (1960), pp. 44-58; J.M.C. Toynbee, 'The Ara Pacis Reconsidered', *PBA* 39 (1953), pp. 67-96; 'The "Ara Pacis Augustae"', *JRS* 51 (1961), pp. 153-56.

Claudian house as a peacemaking force in the Roman world is thereby asserted.

7. *The Temple of Vesta Reverse*

The seventh example is a reverse type which appears on aurei and denarii issued by the mint in Rome in 65–66 CE. The reverse of these coins depicts a domed, six-sided temple of Vesta which has a set of steps leading into the entrance. In the central nave of the temple, which is depicted as having six columns built in Ionic style, is a draped statue of the goddess, seated and facing to the left. In her right hand she extends a patera and in her left she holds a long sceptre; this representation is characteristic of the way in which the goddess was portrayed in art. The word VESTA stands above the scene.[21] Most numismatic specialists feel that the statue is there simply to assist in identifying the temple as that belonging to Vesta since the actual temple did not contain such a statue. Nero was responsible for rebuilding the temple of Vesta following the disastrous fire of Rome in 64 CE. The temple was the sixth dedicated to the goddess in Rome and it survived until 191 CE.

The Emperor Vespasian (69–79 CE) also depicted the rebuilt temple of Vesta on several coins between the years 73–75 CE; these include aurei and asses which bear obverse portraits of Vespasian, Titus and Domitian. The temple is here depicted as having four Ionic columns with the same

Figure 7   Figure 8

central statue of the goddess; the word VESTA is presented in two halves, one on either side of the temple itself, as are the letters S C (Figure 8).[22]

---

21. *RIC* Nero 61 (aureus) and 62 (denarius).

22. *RIC* Vespasian 59, 69, 157, 162, 171, 180, 230, 249, 304 (aurei); 548, 659, 690, 705 (asses).

Three New Testament Parallels?

By way of suggestion, I would like to draw attention to several interesting passages in the Pauline letters which may be illuminated by this discussion about these coins from Nero's reign. First note the fact that mention is made in Phil. 1.13 of the praetorian guard (ἐν ὅλῳ τῷ πραιτωρίῳ).[23] It has often been suggested that the epistle to the Philippians was written while Paul was imprisoned in Caesarea where the Palace of Herod served as the 'praetorium' (Acts 23.35). But it is equally as plausible that what is meant is the Roman praetorium, a possibility which shifts us away from the theory that Philippians was written during the Caesarean captivity of Paul and suggests instead that a Roman confinement is what Paul speaks of when he describes himself as being imprisoned (Phil. 1.7, 12-26). If this is indeed so, and it appears to me very possible, then we have in the reverse of the sestertia a representation of the praetorium and part of the cohort itself dating from roughly the same time as when Paul was imprisoned there. It is certainly an interesting numismatic illustration paralleling the Pauline letter.

Secondly, in Col. 2.15 the author is describing God's ultimate victory through Christ over evil and uses a metaphor drawn from the Roman practice of a triumphal procession in which prisoners of war are led by their vanquishers.[24] Many commentators on Colossians have noted the metaphor,[25] but no one to my knowledge has suggested that the his-

---

23. It is difficult to decide if what is meant here is the praetorian guard or their camp, although the former seems more likely. J.-F. Collange, *The Epistle of Saint Paul to the Philippians* (London: Epworth, 1979), p. 54, notes that 'the meaning given to the word here depends on the view which is adopted as to the place of origin of the letter'. See the extended discussion in J.B. Lightfoot, *Saint Paul's Epistle to the Philippians* (London: Macmillan, 1885), pp. 99-104. Also note the reference to Caesar's household (οἱ ἐκ τῆς Καίσαρος οἰκίας) in 4.22.

24. The same imagery is used in 2 Cor. 2.14-15, but not with quite the same degree of ridicule and public disgrace which seems to me to underlie the parallel in the Colossian letter. Is it the anticipated ignominious treatment of Tiridates by Nero which underlies the description of the triumph in Col. 2.15? On the parallel in 2 Cor. see A.T. Hanson, *The Paradox of the Cross in the Thought of St Paul* (JSNTSup, 17; Sheffield: JSOT Press, 1987), pp. 108-15.

25. Follow this discussion in P.T. O'Brien, *Colossians, Philemon* (WBC, 44; Waco, TX: Word Books, 1982), pp. 128-29; S.J. Hafemann, *Suffering and the Spirit: An Exegetical Study of 2 Cor. 2.14-3:3 within the Context of the Corinthian Correspondence* (WUNT, 19; Tübingen: Mohr [Paul Siebeck], 1986), pp. 18-39.

torical setting underlying the use of the image might well be the expected arrival of Tiridates in Rome following the events of 63 CE as described above.[26] This was an event which, after all, was proclaimed loudly and clearly as a victory and a triumphal occasion by the Imperial authorities; the sestertia related to this event bear ample testimony to that fact. Could it be that here, in the form of the sestertia discussed, we have uncovered another numismatic hint (and it must remain nothing more than that) as to the occasion of the triumph imagery of Col. 2.15?[27] And could we be so bold as to move a step beyond that and suggest that this lends weight to traditional arguments which took Colossians to be a genuine epistle of Paul written during his captivity in Rome c. 64 CE?

Thirdly, note how central the image of peacemaking is within the thought of another Pauline letter, namely Eph. 2.14-16. In this deutero-Pauline letter the death of Jesus Christ is presented as the supreme act of peacemaking whereby opposing parties are brought together and forged into a new humanity. The thought here is generally explained as one which arises out of the division between Jews and Gentiles, with the imagery of the dividing wall of the Second Temple serving as a backdrop.[28] Yet it is not difficult to imagine how this Jewish–Gentile reconciliation might itself be seen as dependent upon the larger *Pax Romana* for its inspiration and central motif of peacemaking. It is difficult to read this paragraph from Eph. 2 without having one's mind recall the words of Jesus recorded in Mt. 5.9, one of the most memorable of the Beatitudes: 'Blessed are the peacemakers, for they shall be called children of God.' It is perhaps worth noting that the word here translated as 'peacemakers' (εἰρηνοποιοί) is a *hapax legomenon* in the New Testament. Yet it is precisely this word that Cassius Dio applies to Julius Caesar, the founder of the Julio-Claudian house who attempted to bring an end to the warring madness which characterized the end of the Roman Republic. Cassius Dio, *Hist.* 44.49.2, has Mark Antony describe

26. Cassius Dio, *Hist.* 63.14, discusses the triumph associated with the victory over Tiridates in 66 CE.

27. C.F.D. Moule, *The Epistles to the Colossians and to Philemon* (Cambridge: Cambridge University Press, 1957), p. 100, specifically notes that the Greek verb θριαμβεύειν corresponds to the Latin verb *triumphare*.

28. The Greek term translated as 'dividing wall' (τὸ μεσότοιχον) occurs only here in the New Testament. A.T. Lincoln, *Ephesians* (WBC, 42; Dallas, TX: Word Books, 1990), p. 143, discusses the term and the suggestion that it refers to the balustrade separating the Court of the Gentiles from the inner courts and the Holy of Holies within the Jerusalem Temple complex.

Julius Caesar as a 'peacemaker' (εἰρηνοποιός) during his funeral oration over the assassinated leader:

> This father, this high priest, this inviolable being, this hero and god, is dead, alas, not by the violence of some disease, nor wasted by old age, nor wounded abroad somewhere in some war, nor caught up inexplicably by some supernatural force, but right here within the walls as the result of a plot—the man who had safely led an army into Britain; ambushed in this city—the man who had enlarged its pomerium; murdered in the senate-house—the man who had reared another such edifice at his own expense; unarmed—the brave warrior; defenceless—the promoter of peace (ὁ εἰρηνοποιός).

Taken together these seven coin reverses offer us a suggestive glimpse into the Rome of Paul's day, the Rome in which Nero reigned supreme. According to Acts 25.1-12 it was to the Emperor Nero that Paul appealed when he stood before the Roman governor Porcius Festus, accused with charges arising out of his preaching ministry among the Jews in Jerusalem. Paul demanded to have his case heard by the reigning Emperor, and to the city of Rome, to Nero's Rome, he was delivered.

Chapter 5

ROMAN TRIUMPH IMAGERY IN THE PAULINE LETTERS:
THE BACKGROUND OF 2 CORINTHIANS 2.14-16
AND COLOSSIANS 2.15

The precise meaning of the verb θριαμβεύειν, which appears in the Pauline letters only in 2 Cor. 2.14 and Col. 2.15, has long been a matter of scholarly interest. Most commentators accept that the idea of a Roman military triumph is probably at its core. Nevertheless, something of the ambiguity implied by the verb is reflected in the various translations of 2 Cor. 2.14 and the way in which they communicate the force of this military image. Many translations take the central image to be a positive one wherein the believer either triumphs in Christ, or is said to triumph through Christ, or joins in the divine triumphal procession as one of the victors. A few modern translations reverse this triumphalistic note, however, and focus on the idea of the believer as one who is led as a captive in God's triumphal procession. Thus the NEB renders the phrase, 'But thanks be to God, who continually leads us about, captives in Christ's triumphal procession.'[1] Similarly, the JB renders the verse '[Christ] has stripped the sovereignties and the ruling forces, and paraded them in public, behind him in his triumphal procession'.

In short, the question is, Does the triumph image focus on the participants in the celebration as *victorious conquerors* or as *vanquished enemies*? F.W. Farrar may well have been right when he said, 'St. Paul was so possessed by the metaphor that he did not pause to disentangle it.'[2] Nevertheless, many interpreters of 2 Corinthians have applied themselves to the arduous task of disentanglement, and I will endeavour to follow the main directions of their deliberations.

---

1.   L. Williamson, 'Led in Triumph: Paul's Use of Thriambeuo', *Int* 22 (1968), p. 317, queries whether the shift away from triumphalism in modern translations is 'due simply to a theological trend which finds it more Christlike to lose than to win'.
2.   *The Life and Work of St. Paul* (London: Cassell & Co., 1919), p. 410.

Much of the recent scholarly debate about θριαμβεύειν has revolved around the proper use of lexical evidence in interpretation. The fact that the verb is quite rare in Hellenistic Greek makes it a prime target for such speculation. Many recent interpretations of the enigmatic verb have been put forward, most of which are forced to employ some specialized approach, or adopt a more comprehensive analysis of Paul's argument in 2 Corinthians and Col. 2.15, or beyond, in order to offer an explanation for what is in effect a puzzling linguistic metaphor. Yet what is striking about a number of these interpretations is the way in which they each try to relate the imagery of the two passages (whatever they might be!) to the question of Paul's apostolic ministry. For example, L. Williamson turns to the variety of instances in Paul's letters in which paradoxical statements are made in order to support the contention that the image intended by the use of 'to triumph' (θριαμβεύειν) is that of the believer as a conquered slave who is part of Christ's victory triumph and yet, at the same time, a joyful participant in the Lord's celebration parade.[3] In effect, Paul's life as an apostle is an expression of precisely this paradox of defeat/victory and weakness/power. Williamson's ideas have been quite influential and are often cited as a definitive interpretation of 2 Cor. 2.14, although he has not been without his critics. For example, R.B. Egan questions the very foundation of the interpretation, namely that the verb θριαμβεύειν was understood as an image intimately linked to the Roman military triumph. Instead Egan argues that the verb is best translated as 'to reveal', or 'to make manifest', or to 'publicize', and that this was how it was understood by most early Christian commentators and translators. He suggests that a better translation of the verse is, 'But thanks be to God who is always making us known in Christ and revealing through us the odor of his knowledge in every place.'[4] It is to be noted that while this interpretation dissolves any alleged connection with the military triumph imagery, it nevertheless does still maintain a strong link to the theme at hand, effectively constituting an introduction to Paul's apologia for his apostleship (contained in 2.14-6.4).

However, not all have been so willing to surrender the military imagery underlying θριαμβεύειν in 2.14, although the need to relate the metaphor to the larger concern of Paul's apostleship is something about which

3.   'Led in Triumph', pp. 317-32.
4.   R.B. Egan, 'Lexical Evidence on Two Pauline Passages', *NovT* 19 (1977), p. 50.

there is general agreement. Thus, S.J. Hafemann in his *Suffering and Ministry in the Spirit*[5] associates both the triumph imagery (focusing on the word θριαμβεύειν) and the fragrance imagery (focusing on the words 'fragrance', ὀσμή, and 'aroma', εὐωδία) with the larger issue of Paul's apostolic authority which is being addressed in 2 Cor. 2.14–6.4. Inherent in the triumph image, Hafemann insists, is the idea of the captives who are in the procession being led to their deaths by their conquerors. This leads him to take the military image as one in which Paul sees himself as a slave who has been conquered and who is being led in the triumphal procession by the conqueror (Jesus Christ himself) with the apostle's life being offered to God as sacrificial incense. In effect, Paul's view of his apostolic ministry is as a vanquished slave who is being led to his death by the conquering Christ; his life is to be consumed as an offering to his victorious Lord.[6] This is a position of extreme weakness/death which paves the way for the triumph of God through the power of the cross. Death gives way to life, and this, according to Hafemann's reading of Paul, is the basis for a truly apostolic ministry which follows the path of the crucified Christ. The greatest strength of Hafemann's interpretation is the way in which it integrates the triumph imagery of 2.14a and the sacrificial imagery of 2.14b–16a within the wider argument of 2.14–4.6, and beyond that, sees this theme of Paul's weakness as an apostle to be central to the Corinthian correspondence as a whole.

A crucial element of an interpretation such as Hafemann's is the assumption that Roman triumph imagery was widespread within the Roman world, and that it would have been readily known and understood by the congregations to which he was writing in the cities of Corinth and Colossae (presuming Pauline authorship of Colossians). There is much that suggests this is exactly the case. My task within this chapter is to examine some of the numismatic evidence which gives us a better understanding of how Roman military victories were popularly conceived.

I shall examine the coin reverses under four separate but related headings: 1) triumphal arches; 2) triumphal chariots and quadrigae; 3) subjected enemies and captured arms; 4) other public processions. Each

5. Grand Rapids, MI: Eerdmans, 1990; esp. pp. 16-83.
6. J.M. Scott, 'The Triumph of God in 2 Cor. 2.14: Additional Evidence on Merkabah Mysticism in Paul', *NTS* 42 (forthcoming), offers a slightly different interpretation in which God and Christ share the triumphal chariot within the procession. Some interesting coin evidence is marshalled in support.

of these four areas will help to fill out the general picture of how Roman military conquest, and the public celebration of such conquests and related games, was officially commemorated. I shall have space to discuss only a sampling of the more important examples of each group. Following my brief survey of these matters I shall conclude with one or two observations about the triumph imagery in the Pauline letters which are based on the numismatic evidence.

1. *Triumphal Arches*

The celebration of a triumph was an honour rarely granted to victorious military leaders by the Roman Senate, particularly during the New Testament period with which we are concerned.[7] Julius Caesar was awarded a quadruple triumph in 45 BCE in connection with his victories over Gaul, Egypt, Pontus and Africa; Augustus was awarded a triple triumph in 27 BCE in connection with his victories in Illyrium, Egypt and Actium; Tiberius was awarded a triumph in 8–7 BCE and another in 12 CE in connection with his endeavours in Germany and Pannonia, as was Germanicus in 17 CE. Similarly, the Emperor Claudius was awarded a triumph in 44 CE in connection with his campaigns in Britain, as was the Emperor Nero in connection with his military victory over Tiridates in 62 CE. Perhaps most interesting in terms of New Testament studies is the fact that Vespasian and his son Titus celebrated a triumph in June of 71 CE in connection with the victories over the Jews in Judaea following the fall of Jerusalem on 7-8 September 70 CE.[8] Several of these Emperors issued coins which depict triumphal arches associated with these military victories. In addition, a number of other army commanders figure on coins which proudly announce their achievements and show triumphal arches erected in their honour. A good example is the triumphal arch which appears on both aurei and denarii issued by Claudius to honour the fiftieth anniversary of the death of his father Nero Claudius

---

7.   There are many important studies on the place that the military triumph had within Roman society. Among them are H.S. Versnel, *Triumphus: An Inquiry into the Origin, Development and Meaning of the Roman Triumph* (Leiden: Brill, 1970); Fears, 'Theology of Victory', pp. 736-826; Campbell, *Emperor*, pp. 133-42; and R. Payne, *Rome Triumphant: How the Empire Celebrated Its Victories* (New York: Barnes and Noble, 1993).

8.   Josephus, *War* 7.116-157, purports to be an eye-witness account of this celebration. Jones, *Titus*, pp. 77-79, discusses the 'double triumph'.

Drusus, the hero of the military successes in Germany in 14–9 BCE.
These coins depict the Arch of Drusus, probably erected over the Via
Appia in Rome shortly after the general's untimely death in 9 BCE. The
obverse of these coins (Figure 1)[9] shows a laureated portrait of Drusus,
facing left, with the surrounding inscription NERO CLAVDIVS DRVSVS
GERMANICVS IMP(erator). The reverse shows a triumphal arch
surmounted by an equestrian statue of the figure of Drusus brandishing
a spear in his right hand. The arch also has military trophies on either
side of the mounted Drusus and the words DE(victis) GERM(anis)
appear on the arch. Related aurei and denarii depicting the same triumphal arch reverse, with slightly different representations of the equestrian
figure and the military trophies, are also extant. These coins (Figure 2)[10]
have the slightly enlarged inscription DE(victis) GERMANIS on the architrave of the arch and have an obverse portrait of the Emperor Claudius.
The obverse inscription is TI CLAVD CAESAR AVG PM TR P.[11]

Figure 1   Figure 2   Figure 3

Claudius's victories in Britain were also commemorated by a triumphal
arch erected in Rome in 51–52 CE. Little of the arch itself has survived
beyond some inscription fragments, some decorative materials and a few
sculptural scenes of soldiers on parade.[12] Gold coins representing this
arch were first issued by the Imperial mint in Rome in 46–47 CE. These
aurei have an obverse portrait of Claudius surrounded by the inscription
TI CLAVD CAESAR AVG PM TR P VI IMP X.[13] The reverse has a

9.   *RIC* Claudius 69-70.

10.   *RIC* Claudius 3-4.

11.   Another issue of the aureus (*RIC* Claudius 35) was produced in 46–47 CE
with the inscription TI CLAVD CAESAR AVG PM TR P VI IMP XI.

12.   L. Keppie, *Understanding Roman Inscriptions* (London: B.T. Batsford,
1991), pp. 46-47, offers a reconstruction of the text of the arch. G. Webster, *The
Roman Invasion of Britain* (London: Book Club Associates, 1980), pp. 168-71, also
discusses Claudius's triumphal arch and the circumstances surrounding its erection.

13.   *RIC* Claudius 30. Later aurei and denarii with different obverse inscriptions
are also known. There are coins which alter the inscription to TR P VI IMP XI (*RIC*
Claudius 33-34 from 46–47 CE) and TR P VIIII IMP XVI (*RIC* Claudius 44-45
from 49–50 CE).

single-span arch topped by a figure riding a horse with trophies on either side; the words DE(victis) BRITANN(is) are on the architrave (Figure 3). The chapter of Julio-Claudian interest in triumphal celebrations was concluded when Nero erected a triumphal arch in c. 64 CE to commemorate his victory over Tiridates (I discussed this coin type in Chapter 4).

The Emperor Galba (68–69 CE) issued one very interesting sesterius in December 68–January 69 CE which depicts on its reverse a triumphal arch on the top of which the Emperor is being crowned by Victory as he manages a quadriga. The coin bears the inscription XXXX REMISSA together with the letters S C in exergue (Figure 4).[14] The coin commemorates Galba's remission of the customs tax on goods transported into Gaul, probably in appreciation of the province's support for him in the revolt of Vindex against the Emperor Nero in April 68 CE.

Figure 4

Titus's victories over the Jews were marked by the erection of two triumphal arches, only one of which has survived. This is the Arch of Titus in the Forum in Rome, perhaps best known by students of the New Testament because of the depiction of Roman soldiers carrying off the spoils from the Temple in Jerusalem which is contained on one of the reliefs on the underside of the monument. Here we see a startling image of the seven-branched candlestick, as well as the Ark of the Covenant, in the hands of the conquering soldiers (Figure 5). This arch was erected by Titus's brother, the Emperor Domitian (81–96 CE), on the highest point of the Via Sacra overlooking the Forum, and serves more as an epitaph to Titus than as a monument recording his triumph over the Jews. The second arch of Titus, which marked the triumph proper, stood near the Circus Maximus but has not survived. However, we do find a depiction of it on the reverse of a sestertius from the reign of Trajan (98–117 CE), issued in 103 CE to celebrate Trajan's rebuilding

14. *RIC* Galba 134.

Figure 5

of the Circus area in the centre of Rome. This coin shows various public
buildings around the Circus Maximus, which stands in the foreground.
Trajan's column holds the centre place on the coin while Titus's triumphal arch can be seen on the left of the coin, and is identifiable by the
quadriga which stands on top of the arch. The inscription S P Q R
OPTIMO PRINCIPI surrounds the scene and the letters S C stand in
exergue (Figure 6).[15]

Figure 6

Figure 7

Domitian also issued a sestertius in 95–96 CE which bears an interesting
scene on the reverse. It shows a triumphal arch surmounted by two
quadrigae of elephants with the customary letters S C on either side of

15. *RIC* Trajan 571. Domitian also had several triumphal arches erected in Rome
to celebrate his various military successes. An interesting discussion of the numismatic evidence for this is contained in F.S. Kleiner, 'An Arch of Domitian in Rome
on the Coins of Alexandria', *NC* 149 (1989), pp. 68-81 + Plates 20-21.

the scene (Figure 7).[16] There is some debate about the precise location of this arch within Rome, but it is generally thought to have stood at the intersection of the Via Flaminia and the Vicus Palacinae. Domitian is known to have erected an arch there in 85 CE in connection with his military successes in Germany.

2. *Triumphal Chariots and Quadrigae*

One of the most remarkable representations of an Imperial triumphal procession is that contained on the so-called Boscoreale Cups, presently on exhibition in the Louvre Museum in Paris after nearly a century of absence from public view. This pair of finely executed silver drinking cups was discovered in 1895 in a hoard of silver within a villa near the modern town of Boscoreale on the southeastern slopes of Mount Vesuvius. It seems clear that the original owners hid the cups before fleeing the eruption of the volcano in August of 79 CE. The two cups are among the most detailed silver-work of the Julio-Claudian period; one depicts scenes from the life of Augustus while the other depicts scenes from the life of Tiberius.[17] It is the Tiberius Cup which is of interest to us, for the major scene presented is of Tiberius's triumph of 8–7 BCE. The Emperor is presented as riding in his triumphal chariot pulled by four horses. He is accompanied in the chariot by a *servus publicus* who holds a laurel crown over Tiberius's head; traditionally this slave was to whisper in the ear of the person celebrating the triumph the words *hominem te esse memento* ('remember you are a man') so as to keep him humble. Preceding the triumphal chariot is a sacred ox which is to be sacrificed to Jupiter Capitolinus in the culminating ceremony of the triumph. It was customary that this sacrifice was offered on the Capitoline Hill. A host of other attendant figures surround the chariot containing the Emperor.

The victories of Claudius in Britain were commemorated by a special coin issue from the mint in Caesarea in Cappadocia. The mint at Caesarea

16. *RIC* Domitian 416.

17. A.L. Kuttner, *Dynasty and Empire in the Age of Augustus: The Case of the Boscoreale Cups* (Berkeley, CA: University of California Press, 1995), offers the most thorough discussion available of this important treasure. In particular, she challenges the traditional assessment of the scenes depicted on the cups, suggesting that they were made before the accession of Tiberius in 14 CE. The prominence of Drusus within the central scene on the Augustus cup, together with the presence of a slave alongside the Emperor in the quadriga on the Tiberius cup, support such an interpretation. Also worth noting is the discussion contained in Zanker, *Power,* pp. 227-30.

was especially noted for its production of coins containing military themes, particularly during the reigns of Tiberius and Caligula.[18] This silver coin, generally described as a didrachma, is dated to about 45–46 CE and depicts on its obverse a bust of Claudius, laureated and facing left, surrounded by the inscription TI(berius) CLAVDIVS CAESAR AVG(ustus) GERM(anicus) P(ontifex) M(aximus) TR(ibunicia) P(otestas). The reverse shows Claudius in a chariot drawn by four horses, holding a spear in one hand; the inscription DE(victis) BRITANNIS stands in exergue (Figure 8a, b shows two examples).[19]

Figure 8a   Figure 8b

One of the most interesting coins issued in connection with the Roman military defeat of the Jews is a sestertius from Titus's reign in 80 CE, probably issued on the tenth anniversary of the victory. The obverse of the coin shows a bust of the Emperor, laureated and facing left with the inscription IMP(erator) T(itus) CAES(ar) VESP(asianus) P(ontifex) M(aximus) TR(ibunicia) P(otestas) P(ater) P(atriae) COS VIII. The reverse depicts Titus standing in a triumphal chariot being pulled by four horses. He has an olive branch in one hand and a sceptre appears tucked under his arm; the letters S C stand in exergue (Figure 9).[20]

Figure 9

18. Sutherland, *RIC*, p. 120, comments, 'All these didrachms of Caesarea Cappadociae are rare, and it may be that their purpose was at least to stimulate legionary loyalty.'

19. *RIC* Claudius 122. For some strange reason these coins are very often distorted in shape. This may have to do with the way that they were produced (with a rolling flan?).

20. *RIC* Titus 101.

3. *Subjected Enemies and Captured Arms*

Much of the coinage of the Roman Republic displays military motifs, particularly on the reverses of the various issues. One of the more common reverse types involves the depiction of a military trophy, symbol of a successful conquest by the Roman army. Thus, the standard coins of the period 195–187 BCE bear as their reverse a representation of the winged Victory crowning a trophy with a laurel wreath while the word ROMA stands in exergue. The obverse of these coins shows a portrait of one of the gods of the Roman pantheon, usually Jupiter who wears a laurel crown. It is not surprising, given this reverse type, that such a coin is known as victoriatus. These were issued in different denominations, the double victoriatus being equivalent to a denarius, the single being equivalent to a quinarius, and a demi victoriatus being equivalent to a sestertius (Figure 10a, b shows the double and the single victoriatus).

The military triumph of Julius Caesar over insurgent tribes in Gaul is well represented in coinage and occurs frequently to symbolize the conquest of Rome's enemies. For example, a denarius from 48 BCE, issued by the moneyer L. Hostilius Saserna, celebrates Caesar's victory over the charismatic leader Vercingetorix. This coin shows on its obverse a portrait of the rebel leader, including wind-swept hair and a wild-looking beard; behind the portrait is a Gaulish shield. The reverse of this coin

Figure 10a   Figure 10b

shows a naked warrior, holding a shield and riding in a horse-drawn chariot, with the words L. HOSTILIVS and SASERN above and below the scene (Figure 11).[21] It seems clear that this particular coin honours the heroic struggle of the Gauls against the Roman legions and in a roundabout way celebrates the ability of the Roman army to conquer even the most formidable of foes.

Another denarius from 46–45 BCE also commemorates the victories in Gaul, presenting on its obverse a stylized portrait of the goddess

21. *CRR* 952.

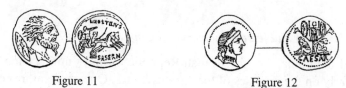

Figure 11   Figure 12

Venus Genetrix to whom Caesar attributed his success in the province. The reverse of this coin is of particular interest for my concerns in that it presents a representation of a captured military trophy, including armaments and shields, while the word CAESAR stands in exergue. Under the trophy are two seated figures, in positions of subjugation. These figures probably represent a personification of Gallia on the left and Vercingetorix on the right (Figure 12).[22]

Among the most famous of the coins which depict Rome's conquered peoples are those associated with the victory of Vespasian and Titus over the Jewish insurgents.[23] This is an extensive series of coins, dating from 69–70 CE onwards, which present striking images of Roman domination over the conquered Jewish nation.[24] The range and importance of this coinage has prompted H.St.J. Hart to describe them as 'the official commentary' by Rome on the Jewish War.[25] Many of these coins depict

---

22. *CRR* 1014.

23. F. Millar, *The Roman Near East (31 BC–AD 337)* (Cambridge, MA: Harvard University Press, 1993), pp. 70-80, deals with the Jewish War of 66–70 CE. On the triumph of Vespasian and Titus, Millar remarks (p. 79), 'It was the only triumph ever to celebrate the subjugation of the population of an existing province.'

24. The treatment of the Jews by all three of the Flavian Emperors has been widely discussed. The question of the extent to which the military subjugation carried over into political persecution of the Jews by the Flavian Emperors is a matter of considerable debate. On these matters see S.J. Case, 'Josephus' Anticipation of a Domitianic Persecution', *JBL* 44 (1925), pp. 10-20; E.M. Smallwood, 'Domitian's Attitude Towards the Jews and Judaism', *CP* 51 (1956), pp. 1-13; L.W. Barnard, 'Clement of Rome and the Persecution of Domitian', *NTS* 10 (1963–64), pp. 251-60; K.H. Waters, 'The Character of Domitian', *Phoenix* 18 (1964), pp. 49-81; and M.H. Williams, 'Domitian, the Jews and the "Judaizers"—A Simple Matter of Cupiditas and Maiestas?', *Historia* 39 (1990), pp. 196-211.

25. 'Judaea and Rome: The Official Commentary', *JTS* 3 (1952), pp. 172-98. Also on the subject see C.M. Kraay, 'The Bronze Coinage of Vespasian: Classification and Attribution', in R.A.G Carson and C.M. Kraay (eds.), *Scripta Nummaria Romana: Essays Presented to Humphrey Sutherland* (London: Spink & Son Ltd, 1978), pp. 47-57. T.V. Buttrey, 'Vespasian as Moneyer', *NC* 12 (1972), pp. 89-109 + Plates 12-13, discusses how Vespasian utilized the coin types of his predecessors, notably Augustus, to advance his own aims.

both male and female figures, representing the people of the conquered province of Judaea, on their reverse. A case in point are the aurei and denarii which show an image of a dejected female personification of the province either sitting beside a trophy of arms or under a palm tree, often with her arms bound behind her; the inscription IVDAEA stands in exergue beneath the scene. The obverse of these coins typically shows the laureated bust of Vespasian surrounded by the inscription IMP CAESAR VESPASIANVS AVG (Figure 13a, b shows the obverse and two versions of the reverse).[26] There is also a version of the scene which has the female figure standing to the left of the palm tree with her hands bound in front of her; the reverse inscription reads IVDAEA DEVICTA.

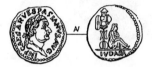 

Figure 13a   Figure 13b   Figure 14

The obverse of this coin shows the laureated bust of Vespasian sur-rounded by the inscription IMP CAESAR VESPASIANVS AVG TR P (Figure 14). Even more striking scenes are contained on the reverses of several sestertia and asses issued from 71 CE onwards. The obverse of these coins shows a portrait of Vespasian surrounded by an inscription such as IMP CAESAR VESPASIAN AVG PM TRP PP COS III (Figure 15). The reverses depict a subdued female personification of Judaea sitting beneath a palm tree, together with the figure of a Jewish male with his hands bound behind his back; typically a shield or armaments are piled up behind him. The inscription IVDAEA CAPTA surrounds the reverse scene while the letters S C stand in exergue. The reverse type exists with slight differences in how the two Jewish figures and their surrounding armaments are presented (Figure 16a, b, c, d shows four variations).[27] A related as shows just one figure, of Judaea, sitting under the tree; opposite her is a pile of armaments including a helmet and two shields (Figure 17).[28] A very similar reverse to these presents the Jewess beneath the palm tree opposite the victorious Emperor Vespasian. He stands posed in military dress, supporting a spear and a

26. *RIC* Vespasian 15-16, 34, 45, 266, 287-288.
27. *RIC* Vespasian 424-426.
28. *RIC* Vespasian 490.

Figure 15

Figure 16a-d

parazonium, his left foot resting on a helmet. The same inscription IVDAEA CAPTA surrounds the scene and the letters S C are in exergue (Figure 18).[29] Vespasian's son Titus also issued a series of coins commemorating the victory over the Jews when he came upon the throne. Typically the obverse of these shows a laureated bust of Titus, facing right, surrounded by the inscription IMP T CAES VESP AVG PM TR P P P COS VIII. (Figure 19). The reference to Titus's eighth consulship allows us to date the coins to 80 CE. The reverse of these sestertia shows the same basic scenes we noted on Vespasian's coins, although the inscription is often shortened to IVD(aea) CAP(ta), with the customary S C standing in exergue (Figure 20a, b , c, d shows four variations).[30] One final reverse type from Vespasian's reign is also worth considering. It

29. *RIC* Vespasian 427.

30. *RIC* Titus 91-92 and 141. Vespasian also issued asses with the shortened inscription (*RIC* Vespasian 393).

Figure 17   Figure 18   Figure 19

Figure 20a-d

presents the figure of the Jewess sitting under the palm tree while a winged Victory is writing on a shield which is propped against the tree. The inscription DEVICTA IVDAEA surrounds the scene and S C is in exergue (Figure 21a, b shows two examples of this reverse type, one taken from a sestertius of Vespasian[31] and the other from an aureus of Titus[32] which does not include the figure of the Jewess).

A similar reverse type is also used to commemorate Domitian's victories in Germany.[33] On these sestertia the palm tree is replaced by a trophy of arms which is flanked on the left by the figure of a German

---

31. *RIC* Vespasian 419. The Victory is writing the letters S P Q R on the shield.

32. *RIC* Vespasian 373. Here the Victory is writing IMP T CAES on the shield. Although this coin bears an obverse portrait of Titus it was issued in 69 CE during Vespasian's reign.

33. On the subject consult B.W. Jones, *The Emperor Domitian* (London: Routledge & Kegan Paul, 1992), pp. 144-49.

Figure 21a   Figure 21b

woman seated in subjection, and on the right by a German captive with his weapons stacked in surrender at his feet. The reverse inscription reads GERMANIA CAPTA. The obverse of this coin shows a laureated bust of Domitian facing right with the inscription IMP CAES DOMIT AVG GERM COS XI CENS POT P P which dates the coin to 85 CE (Figure 22).[34] Domitian's triumph over the Germans was extensively portrayed on coinage from his reign. One of the most remarkable coins of Domitian's reign is an aureus which shows as its reverse a seated figure of Germania, seated on a shield with a broken spear in the foreground, surrounded by the inscription GERMANICVS COS XIIII (Figure 23).[35] Another interesting example is an as from the same year which shows on its reverse two German shields which are set against Roman military emblems, including a vexillum, spears and trumpets (Figure 24).[36]

Figure 22   Figure 23

Figure 24

34. *RIC* Domitian 278.
35. *RIC* Domitian 127.
36. *RIC* Domitian 267.

4. *Other Public Processions*

We should not think that triumphal processions were the only public parades depicted on Imperial coinage. Other historical occasions also find their way into the domain of numismatic propaganda. For example, the Secular Games (*Ludi Saeculares*) of 26 May–3 June 17 BCE, celebration of which formed an important propaganda event during the long reign of Augustus, are represented on a number of coins which are worth noting in this regard. These games were traditionally held approximately once every hundred years[37] and there was clearly much pomp and circumstance associated with them, often involving spectacular displays of unusual animals in the public parades. Many coins minted by private moneyers depict various scenes from these public processions. A case in point is the denarius minted by M. Durmius which is dated to 18 BCE (Figure 25).[38] The obverse of the coin has the laureated head of the god Honos facing right surrounded by the inscription M. DVRMIUS III VIR HONORI. The reverse of the coin shows Augustus in a chariot being pulled by two elephants; the word AVGVSTVS stands above the scene and the word CAESAR is at the base.

Scenes from funeral processions were also a frequent motif, particularly on coins issued by an Emperor eager to honour the passing of an important family member. Thus, Tiberius issued a sestertius in 21–22 CE to honour the Divine Augustus and included an interesting scene on the reverse. It shows Augustus seated on a throne in a typical Jupiter-like pose with a sceptre in his left hand and extending his right hand

Figure 25   Figure 26

---

37. Claudius held a celebration of the Secular Games in 47 CE to mark the 800th anniversary of the foundation of Rome, and Domitian held a celebration of the Games in 88 CE.

38. *RIC* Augustus 311.

outwards as he holds a laurel branch. Augustus is in a car being pulled by a quadriga of elephants with riders upon them. The words DIVO AVGVSTO S P Q R are in the field (Figure 26).[39] Similarly, Caligula issued a sestertius (Figure 27)[40] in honour of his mother Agrippina the Elder (who died in 33 CE).[41] The reverse of the coin depicts a funeral *carpentum*, drawn by two mules, and bears the inscription MEMORIAE AGRIPPINAE together with the letters S P Q R in exergue. It is reminiscent of a sestertius issued by Tiberius in 22–23 CE which, similarly depicts a mule-drawn *carpentum*. The obverse of this coin[42] bears the inscription IVLIAE AVGVST(ae) together with the customary letters S P Q R. It probably commemorates the recovery of Livia, Tiberius's mother and the widow of Augustus whose official name was Julia Augusta, from a serious illness in 22 CE (she was not to die until 29 CE).[43]

Figure 27

5. *Paul's Triumph Imagery*

In light of this discussion what can one say about the triumph imagery which Paul alludes to via his use of the verb θριαμβεύειν? Perhaps the most important general observation to make is that the imagery would not have been at all unusual within the first-century setting in which Paul was writing. There is much to suggest that the idea of a Roman military triumph was well-known within the ancient world and, indeed, had been so for quite a long time. The triumph of Roman legions over their enemies was celebrated in various literary works, as well as a host of artistic

39. *RIC* Tiberius 56.
40. *RIC* Gaius 55.
41. S. Wood, '*Memoriae Agrippinae*', pp. 409-26, discusses the sestertius. She comments (p. 410), 'This was the first such coin ever to be devoted entirely to a deceased member of the imperial family, without images or inscriptions of the reigning emperor.'
42. *RIC* Tiberius 50-51.
43. Sutherland, *RIC*, pp. 51-53 discusses the coin.

media, including sculpture, painting, engraving and metal-working. Paul was almost certainly drawing upon this imagery in 2 Cor. 2.14, and perhaps also in Col. 2.15. In this regard the interpretation of the triumph imagery I noted as central within the work of S.J. Hafemann seems confirmed.

A second observation can also be made based upon the numismatic evidence here presented. It involves a slight, but necessary, adaptation to Hafemann's interpretation of the triumph imagery and concerns the processional *order* of the triumph itself. Specifically, I am concerned to emphasize here that the commonly accepted order within the Roman procession was to have the various slaves and conquered figures *precede* the Emperor who followed in his triumphal chariot. That is to say that the conquered peoples who were being paraded in the triumphal procession were not, as the NEB and the JB put it, 'being *led* captive' and followed 'behind the Emperor in his triumphal procession' so much as they were 'being *presented* as captives' on their way to execution. This represents a slight conceptual modification to the interpretation being offered by Hafemann. At the same time, however, the numismatic evidence does lend weight to the suggestion that the triumph imagery is intimately related to Paul's self-understanding of his apostleship as one which flourishes in the face of death for the sake of Jesus Christ. This is particularly true when it is kept in mind that the climax of the triumphal procession was the ritual sacrifice of the conquered captives on the Capitoline hill. Such an insight helps to make sense of such passages as 2 Cor. 4.8-12 and 11.23-27 where Paul interweaves thoughts of ministry and death.

> We are afflicted in every way, but not crushed; perplexed, but not driven to despair; persecuted, but not forsaken; struck down, but not destroyed; always carrying in the body the death of Jesus, so that the life of Jesus may also be manifested in our bodies. For while we live we are always being given up to death for Jesus' sake, so that the life of Jesus may be manifested in our mortal flesh. So death is at work in us, but life in you. (2 Cor. 4.8-12)

> Are they servants of Christ? I am a better one—I am talking like a madman—with far greater labors, far more imprisonments, with countless beatings, and often near death. Five times I have received at the hands of the Jews the forty lashes less one. Three times I have been beaten with rods; once I was stoned. Three times I have been shipwrecked; a night and a day I have been adrift at sea; on frequent journeys, in danger from rivers, danger from robbers, danger from my own people, danger from

Gentiles, danger in the city, danger in the wilderness, danger at sea, danger from false brethren; in toil and hardship, through many a sleepless night, in hunger and thirst, often without food, in cold and exposure. (2 Cor. 11.23-27)

Part III

THE TRAVELS OF HADRIAN

Chapter 6

THE WANDERING EMPEROR

The Imperial coinage of the Emperor Hadrian (117–138 CE) affords us an unusual opportunity to appreciate not only the extent of that Emperor's many travels, but to compose a fairly full numismatic catalogue of the constituent provinces and regions of the Empire at that time. The purpose of this chapter is to provide a brief outline of the journeys of Hadrian around the Empire as well as to introduce the Imperial sestertia which commemorate these journeys.[1] The beautifully executed sestertia, which were issued between the years of 134–138 CE at the conclusion of Hadrian's travels, stand as a lasting record of the diversity of the Roman world of the early second century and serve as a small indication of the particular themes and ideas associated with the individual provinces and regions depicted. However, there exists no single recent attempt to bring together the series as a whole and place it within a rough outline of Hadrian's travels. Here I will discuss the complete series, as well as a few related pieces, within a structured framework, and provide line-drawings for many of the coins discussed. It is in viewing the series as a whole that we can come to a greater appreciation of the magnitude of the task undertaken by Hadrian's mints in proclaiming his travels around the Empire. Let me first outline Hadrian's journeys before moving on to discuss the types of sestertia.

1. The Travels of Hadrian

The biographer Spartianus,[2] writing in the late third century, records this comment about the propensities of Hadrian: 'So fond was he of travel

---

1.   The journeys of Hadrian are not only commemorated by issues of sestertia, but by issues of other denominations as well. Most of the sestertia have matching dupondii or asses. In addition, several of the provinces or regions are represented on gold and silver issues of the Roman mint.

2.   Spartianus, the name given to the compiler of the work we now know as

that he wished to inform himself in person about all that he had read concerning all parts of the world.'[3] Cassius Dio, *Hist.* 69.9.1, similarly records, 'Hadrian travelled through one province after another, visiting the various regions and cities and inspecting all the garrisons and forts.'[4]

Within Hadrian's 21 years of rule as Emperor, a comparatively long reign considering the endless series of assassinations and political plots which served to catapult the next eager man into the purple in quick succession, a great proportion of the Emperor's time was spent away from Rome and the province of Italy. In fact, it is possible to argue that as many as 12 years out of the 21 were occupied with wide ranging journeys into the far corners of the Empire. This record of travel stands in stark contrast to Antoninus Pius, Hadrian's immediate successor, who ruled for an even longer 23 years (138–161 CE), but only made one brief foray away from the comforts surrounding him in Rome and Italy (*Life of Antoninus Pius* 7.11). Hadrian may have had a wanderlust but his travels also served a larger political end: they were a tangible expression of his aim of uniting the various nations and peoples into a single Empire in which each part was recognized and valued as an equal partner.[5]

The subject of Hadrian's various journeys has tantalized scholars of many generations as they have attempted to pin-point the exact movements of this wandering Emperor.[6] Alas, there has arisen no scholarly

the *Life of Hadrian* within the *Scriptores Historiae Augustae*, probably wrote his biography between 293 and 305 CE (hereafter I abbreviate the work as *LH*). Quite clearly the work as it now stands is made up of at least six sources, and there is considerable debate about the historical reliability of sections of it, as R. Syme, *Fictional History Old and New: Hadrian* (Oxford: Somerville College, 1984), pp. 4-8, notes. The historian Suetonius is occasionally taken to be the author of the work since he may have served as Hadrian's official scribe for a short period. See H. Lindsay, 'Suetonius as *Ab Epistulis* to Hadrian and the Early History of the Imperial Correspondence', *Historia* 43 (1994), pp. 454-68.

3.   *LH* 17.8.

4.   Both Spartianus and Cassius Dio relate that Hadrian travelled bareheaded (*LH* 23.1; *Hist.* 69.9.4), which perhaps indicates his desire to be thought of as a man of the people.

5.   M.A.K. Thornton, 'Hadrian and his Reign', *ANRW*, II.2, pp. 433-76, emphasizes this and points out how Hadrian pursued many of the policies of Augustus in so doing.

6.   See B.W. Henderson, *The Life and Principate of the Emperor Hadrian* (London: Methuen, 1923); W. Weber, 'Hadrian', *CAH*, IX, pp. 294-324; S. Perowne, *Hadrian* (Beckenham, Kent: Croom Helm Ltd, 1960); A. Garzetti *From Tiberius to*

consensus as to Hadrian's precise step-by-step movements in his journeys. The paucity of evidence renders any such attempt at precision hypothetical at best. Nevertheless, we can say with some degree of confidence that Hadrian's travels as Emperor included at least four major periods: a) August of 117 to August of 118 CE; b) spring of 121 to autumn of 125 CE; c) spring of 128 to spring of 134 CE; d) a portion of 135 CE. During the intervening periods we can assume that Hadrian was in Rome itself or at his home in Tivoli in the province of Italy.

It appears that Hadrian made it a matter of his Imperial policy to examine personally many of the constituent provinces and regions of the Empire and produced the sestertia as commemorative coins depicting that interest. Although we are unable to say precisely when he visited several of the provinces which appear in the commemorative series, it is possible to outline, in broad terms, the areas of the Empire covered in each of these four journeys. Let me now briefly sketch the itineraries of the four journeys.

a. *August of 117 CE to August of 118 CE*[7]

Hadrian was born on 24 January 76 CE and was thus 41 years old at the time of his predecessor Trajan's death in 117 CE. Trajan had been one of the guardians of Hadrian, whose own father had died when he was but ten years old. Hadrian had been appointed governor of Syria during Trajan's Parthian campaigns and was adopted as son and successor shortly before Trajan's death on 8 August.[8] Thus, we find that when Hadrian assumed the principate on 11 August 117 CE he was in the provincial capital city of Antioch in Syria. Here he remained until travelling to Rome in 118 CE via Illyricum.[9] It is possible that Hadrian stopped and visited some of the eastern provinces in Asia Minor or Greece on his way to the Imperial capital, but we do not know for certain. In any event, the arrival (*adventus*) of Hadrian in Rome on 9 July 118 CE was commemorated in a fairly extensive coin issue which includes a sestertius

---

the Antonines (London: Methuen, 1974), pp. 386-401, 684-86, 764; and R. Syme, 'The Journeys of Hadrian', *ZPE* 73 (1988), pp. 159-70.

7.   The chief sources for this journey are *LH* 5.9–7.3 and *Hist.* 69.8.1.

8.   The adoption was surrounded by rumours of its illegitimacy and so antagonized four of Trajan's generals that they raised their voices in protest, only to be executed by the Senate. See *LH* 4.8-10 and *Hist.* 69.1.1-4 for details.

9.   *LH* 4.6-7; *Hist.* 69.8.1.

(Figure 1) relevant to this study.[10] The reverse of this sestertius[11] depicts a helmeted Roma seated on a cuirass and shield, holding a spear in her left hand, while extending her right hand to Hadrian, who clasps it in a gesture of friendship and unity. Hadrian stands before Roma dressed in a toga with his head laureated and his left arm gathering the folds of his toga. The reverse inscription of the coin reads PONT MAX TR POT COS II. The abbreviation S C occurs in exergue as does the critical inscription ADVENTVS AVG. The reference to the second consulship of Hadrian allows us to date the coin precisely to 118 CE.

b. *Spring of 121 CE to Spring of 125 CE*[12]

Hadrian left Rome, probably in the spring of 121 CE, and began his first extensive journey through the Empire as the reigning Emperor. His travels took him initially through Gaul and into Germania where he inspected the German armies. He then turned to the east and examined the Rhine and Danube defence systems. We know that by spring of 122 CE he was in Britain and that by autumn of the same year he was once again in Gaul. The winter of 122–123 CE found him in Tarraco, the provincial capital of Tarraconensis in Hispania. Early in 123 CE he was engaged in military operations against rebel forces in Mauretania, and by spring of that year we know him to have been at the opposite end of the Mediterranean in Antioch of Syria. Hadrian was never again, as far as can be determined, to visit these regions of the Empire which lie west and north of Rome.

The summer of 123 CE saw him take a northwesterly journey through Galatia and Bithynia and a tour along the coast of Asia Minor to the city of Ephesus. From Ephesus Hadrian set sail for Rhodes and the Aegean islands including Samothrace. His precise movements of late 123 and early 124 CE are uncertain; perhaps they included a tour of Macedonia and Thrace. In any case, we know that by September of 124 CE he was in Athens, where he remained until March of 125 CE. During this stay Hadrian was enrolled as an initiate within the Eleusinian Mysteries (*LH* 13.1). An extensive tour of Achaea followed, including a visit to Delphi, before Hadrian departed from Nicopolis near Actium and sailed to

10.   The arrival of Hadrian prompted the offering of sacrifice *ob adventum*; i.e., for Hadrian's arrival (*Corpus Inscriptionum Latinarum* 6.2078 is a classic example).

11.   *RIC* Hadrian 547.

12.   The chief sources for this journey are *LH* 10.1–11.2; 12.1–13.4, and *Hist.* 69.9-10.

Sicily, eventually arriving again in Rome in the autumn of 125 CE.

This second period of Hadrian's travels around the Empire was highlighted by another special selection of coin types which demonstrate by their subject matter his benevolent concern for the whole of the Empire. A good example is the sestertius which proclaims Hadrian as the 'Restorer of the World'. This sestertius (Figure 2),[13] which was issued between 119 and 121 CE, has as its reverse the figure of Hadrian standing to the right and dressed in a toga, holding a scroll in his left hand. He extends his right hand toward a kneeling woman in an attempt to raise her to her feet. She is draped and wears a mural crown. Symbolically, the woman holds a globe balanced on her knee, and we deduce that she is a personification of the world. The reverse inscription reads RESTITVTORI ORBIS TERRARVM. This reverse type serves as a precursor to the later and much larger issue of sestertia which depicts some of the provincial personifications in a similar pose.

Figure 1

Figure 2

The provincial travels of Hadrian are also the subject of an additional sestertius issued between 125 and 128 CE which proclaims the 'Expeditions of Hadrian'. This sestertius[14] shows Hadrian on a prancing horse wearing full military dress with his cloak flowing behind him. The reverse inscription of COS III surrounds the scene and the inscription EXPED AVG stands in exergue. The coin was probably issued just after the completion of Hadrian's first major journey of 121–125 CE.

c. *Spring of 128 CE to Spring of 134 CE*[15]
In the spring of 128 CE the restless Hadrian once again left Rome, this time bound for Carthage in Africa, where he conducted an extensive tour of the military installations of the province, a tour which lasted through

---

13. *RIC* Hadrian 594.
14. *RIC* Hadrian 613.
15. The chief sources for this journey are *LH* 13.4–14.7; 22.14, and *Hist.* 69.11. Hadrian is specifically spoken of as returning to Rome in *Hist.* 69.16.3.

July of 128 CE. From there it was a short trip overland to Athens where he remained until March of the next year. While in Athens he was initiated into the highest grade of the Eleusinian Mysteries (Cassius Dio, *Hist.* 69.11.11).[16] The next stage of his journey was a trip to Asia, where he visited various provincial cities including Ephesus and Miletus before moving on to the province of Lycia and Pamphylia, eventually turning northward to the region of Phrygia. From here he returned to the southern coast, stopping in Cilicia before finally reaching Antioch in Syria in June of 129 CE. He was to remain in Antioch for the next year and made that city his base for excursions into neighbouring territories. It was perhaps during this time that he visited the provinces of Syria, Arabia and Judaea.

We do know that in late summer of 129 CE he set off for Cappadocia and its environs to the east, the regions of Armenia and Parthia. In all likelihood, he also visited Jerusalem in the province of Judaea in 130 CE, probably in the early spring. In July of 130 CE Hadrian set out on horseback for Egypt, and headed back to Athens via Syria, Judaea and Asia, although the precise route is a matter of conjecture. Hadrian arrived in Athens in September or October of 131 CE and spent the winter there. He left Athens in the spring of 132 CE, although his exact whereabouts for the next few years are unknown. It is known that he was back in Rome by 5 May 134 CE. Knowing his particular affinity for travelling, it is not unreasonable to suggest that the intervening period between the spring of 132 CE and the spring of 134 CE included some additional visits to various provinces of the Empire.

There is also one sestertius type which illustrates the travels of Hadrian and can be dated to the time period of this major journey. This sestertius (Figure 3)[17] depicts a Roman galley and bears a reverse inscription which proclaims the happiness or prosperity (*felicitas*) of the Empire as

16.   H.W. Pleket, 'An Aspect of the Imperial Cult: Imperial Mysteries', *HTR* 58 (1965), pp. 331-47, contains some interesting discussion of the connection between such mystery religions and the developing Emperor-cult. Interestingly, there is a late second-century papyrus fragment from Antinoopolis (founded by Hadrian in c. 132 CE, see below) which appears to be an invocational prayer from an initiation ceremony. See C.H. Roberts, *The Antinoopolis Papyri* (London: Egypt Exploration Society, 1950), pp. 39-40. For more information on the Eleusinian Mysteries, see L.J. Alderlink, 'The Eleusinian Mysteries in Roman Imperial Times', *ANRW*, II.18.2, pp. 1426-56; K. Clinton, 'The Eleusinian Mysteries: Roman Initiates and Benefactors, Second Century BC to AD 267', *ANRW*, II.18.2, pp. 1499-1539.

17,   *RIC* Hadrian 703-706 are examples.

Figure 3   Figure 4

channelled through or guaranteed by the Emperor himself. The type, which exists with a number of minor variations, shows the galley sailing over the waves with a steersman and rowers with oars. At the prow we see a mast and sail while the stern holds an acrostolium, standard and vexillum. The steersman is seated under a protective archway which rises from the stern of the ship. The inscription surrounding the galley reads FELICITATI AVG while S C stands in the field. The inscription COS III PP is in exergue. No doubt the galley motif is intended to call attention to the travels of Hadrian throughout the Empire. The coin type was probably issued just prior to the embarkation of Hadrian on this extended journey and Hadrian may be consciously borrowing from an earlier coin issued in the reign of Nero (54–68 CE). The Imperial mint in Alexandria issued a billon tetradrachma in 66–67 CE which has a similar scene on its reverse. It depicts a Roman galley under sail, with a flag at the masthead and a steersman standing at the stern. The inscription on the coin (Figure 4) is ΣΕΒΑΣΤΟΦΟΡΟΣ, signifying that the ship is 'The Bearer of Augustus' as the Emperor travelled to the eastern provinces of the Empire.[18]

d. *A Portion of 135 CE*
The final suggested journey of Hadrian is rather speculative. It is a reasonable assumption that the Bar Kochba revolt was so severe and represented such a disruption to the Pax Romana that Hadrian's personal presence in Judaea in late 134 or 135 CE was required.[19] After the trouble in Judaea was under control, the Emperor no doubt returned to

18.   M. Sadek, 'On the Billon Output of the Alexandrian Mint under Nero', *Phoenix* 20 (1966), pp. 131-47, discusses the coin.

19.   The chief sources for this hypothetical journey, which discuss the Second Jewish Revolt, are *LH* 14.2 and *Hist.* 69.12-14. Eusebius, *Hist. Eccl.* 4.6.1-4, should also be consulted.

Rome and Italy where, as far as we know, he remained until his death at Baiae near Napoli on 10th July 138 CE.[20]

2. *The Travel Sestertia of Hadrian*

The vast bulk of the sestertia of Hadrian's reign, which provide us with an opportunity to compose a catalogue of the constituent provinces and regions of the Empire, were all issued between the years 134 and 138 CE at the conclusion of the Emperor's travels. H. Mattingly comments on the subject:

> On his return from his last foreign journey…Hadrian decided to tell Rome and the world what he had hoped, planned and accomplished. The sudden burst of interest in the Roman mint can only be explained by the personal intervention of the Emperor. It was now to be made clear to every Roman that the Empire was no mere system of parts, each member sharing in the common life and contributing something to its maintenance, each enjoying the personal interest and care of the Emperor.[21]

The sestertia were issued in four major groups or types: a) province types; b) restitutor types; c) adventus types; d) exercitus types. Of the 44 constituent provinces of which the Empire was then composed, virtually all are covered within one or more of the groups or types. Some of the individual provinces are grouped together under a regional heading, such as Tarraconensis, Lusitania and Baetica under the heading of Hispania; Galatia and Lycia and Pamphylia under the heading of Phrygia; Lugdunensis, Aquitania and Narbonensis under the heading of Gallia; and Creta and Cyrenaica under the heading of Lybia. Several of the provinces which share a regional name are paired together and presented under that shared name, such as Germania Inferior and Germania Superior under the name of Germania; Moesia Inferior and Moesia Superior under the name of Moesia; Mauretania Caesariensis and Mauretania Tingitana under the name of Mauretania; and Upper Pannonia and Lower Pannonia under the name of Pannonia. Only a handful of provinces, namely Corsica, Sardinia, Belgica, Dalmatia, Cyprus and the three Alpine provinces of Alpes Maritimae, Alpes Cottiae and Alpes Poeninae, are left out of the series altogether. Two of the provinces have a special issue given over to a personification of their provincial capitals:

20. *LH* 25.5-7.
21. *CREBM*, p. clxxi.

Bithynia's capital Nicomedia and Aegyptos's capital Alexandria. Aegyptos is honoured even further via the special issue of a personification of the river-god Nilus.

Now let me describe the four groups of sestertia types in general terms before moving on to compose a full descriptive catalogue of how the various provinces and regions covered within the series are depicted.

a. *Province Types*

There are 11 provinces and regions of the Empire represented within this first major group of sestertia which consists of coins depicting personifications of the areas concerned (generally, but not always, the personifications are female figures). If we include the special issues in the name of Aelius which portray the personification of Pannonia as their reverse, then the group stands at an even dozen. The obverse of all of the coins in the group, with the exception of the Pannonia coins, shows a bust of Hadrian, variously executed, with the inscription HADRIANVS AVG COS III PP (Figure 5). It is this inscription, with its reference to the third consulship of Hadrian, which allows the series as a whole to be dated between 134 and 138 CE. The reverses of the coins in the group have the common motif of a personification of the province or region with some characteristic item of dress or native equipment which was peculiar to or identifiable with that particular geographical area.[22]

b. *Restitutor Types*

There are 13 provinces and regions of the Empire represented within this second major group of sestertia. There are two basic varieties for the reverse, both of which portray the Emperor and a personification of the area in question. Sometimes the Emperor is on the left of the scene and sometimes he is on the right, and several of the provinces and regions display both varieties. The reverses show Hadrian dressed in a toga, standing and holding a scroll in one hand while extending his other hand to the personification kneeling before him. By this gesture he appears to be raising the personification to her feet; hence the inscriptional reference to Hadrian as the 'Restorer'. The personification of the province is draped and is generally shown in characteristic provincial dress or with native attributes of her land. On some of the issues there is an item of further symbolic significance between the two figures.

---

22.   Most of the personifications are described as 'draped', meaning that they wear the Greek-style *chiton* and *himation*.

The 'Restitutor Type' is obviously an extension of the RESTITVTORI ORBIS TERRARVM issue of 119–121 CE mentioned above. The obverse of all 13 coins in this group is exactly the same as that in the 'Province Type'.

Figure 5   Figure 6

c. *Adventus Types*

There are 18 provinces and regions of the Empire represented within this third major group of sestertia. A special supplemental reverse type of the city of Alexandria is also extant. The reverses of most of the coins in the series have a common motif and style. They show Hadrian, usually standing to the left, dressed in a toga and holding a scroll in his left hand. He raises his right hand toward the female personification of the province or city (as in the case of Alexandria) which stands opposite. The female figure is draped and sacrifices out of a patera she holds in her right hand onto a lighted and garlanded altar which stands between her and the Emperor. At times there is a special object, such as a sacrificial bull or another animal, near the central altar. The inscription on the reverse usually has the words ADVENTVI AVG plus the name of the province surrounding the scene and the letters S C in exergue. No doubt the issue of this 'Adventus Type' group of coins is to commemorate the arrival (*adventus*) of the Emperor to each of the provinces and regions so honoured.

The type is also represented by an additional sestertius (Figure 6)[23] which conforms to the basic pattern of the group but shows a helmeted goddess Roma on the right, in place of the personification of the province or region. Roma brandishes a spear in her left hand and clasps right hands with the Emperor Hadrian who stands on the left. No central altar appears on this reverse type. The reverse inscription ADVENTVS AVG surrounds the scene while the customary S C stands in exergue. This Roma reverse is dated between 134–138 CE and thus stands as an integral part of the 'Adventus Type' group.

23.   *RIC* Hadrian 740.

d. *Exercitus Types*

The fourth major group of sestertia all depict scenes of Hadrian addressing the military troops serving in 10 of the provinces and regions of the Empire. Three of the provinces or regions in the 'Travel Sestertia' series are represented only by an example from within this 'Exercitus Type' group (Germania, Raetica and Syria). Because it is essentially military motifs that are used as the reverses, it is not surprising that the bulk of the provinces and regions involved lie along the sensitive Danube-Rhine defence system.[24] The coins do not rigidly conform to the pattern of using a personification of the province or region to communicate the intended association with the geographical area. Instead, the direct link with the province or region is derived from the reverse inscriptions. Usually these involve a short form of the word EXERCITVS and a shortened form of the provincial or regional name.

Several varieties of types exist in this group, often with more than one of the varieties being used for a given province or region. In spite of this variety, however, it is possible to classify the reverses into two main scenes. In the first the Emperor stands on a platform, dressed in full military gear including the long military cloak (*paludamentum*), while addressing a group of soldiers gathered around the platform. Generally he is raising his right hand in a gesture of military command and authority. In the second scene the Emperor is involved in a similar haranguing of soldiers, only this time he does so from atop a prancing horse. In both scenes there is a great variety within the presentation of the soldiers being addressed. They fluctuate in position and number and the military equipment and standards they carry differ from one provincial coin type to another.

Brief mention should be made at this point of four other reverse types which are directly connected with this essentially 'Military' category. All four of these have the same obverse as the rest of the 'Exercitus Type' group and are thus dated between 134–138 CE. The first of these is a commemorative type dedicated to the praetorian cohort. This special type comes in two varieties. The first[25] has the Emperor standing on the platform and haranguing three soldiers and an officer. The officer also

24.   The Roman army under Hadrian consisted of 30 legions distributed in 14 provinces (*LH* 15.13). See H.M.D. Parker, *The Roman Legions* (Cambridge: Heffer & Sons Ltd, 1958), pp. 160-63, for a discussion.

25.   *RIC* Hadrian 908.

faces the troops and holds a shield and sword. The inscription COH PRAETOR S C stands in exergue. The second example of this type[26] is similar except that Hadrian is joined on the platform by a high-ranking officer, possibly the praetorian prefect. The inscription COHORT PRAETOR S C stands in exergue. The second type (Figure 7)[27] shows Hadrian in a military cloak and carrying a scroll, advancing right, followed by an officer and a column of three soldiers bearing various items of military equipment. The inscription DISCIPLINA AVG stands in exergue with the letters S C in the field. The third type[28] shows Hadrian, dressed in military attire, standing to the right with his left foot upon a crocodile. With his right hand he supports an upright spear, while his left hand holds a parazonium. The letters S C again stand in the field. The fourth type[29] is very similar in form to the first general type of the 'Exercitus Type' described above. It shows Hadrian standing on a plat-form and addressing a group of soldiers. The inscription ADLOCVTIO S C stands in exergue. It is quite clear that all of these coins reflect an abiding interest on the part of the Emperor in the Roman army,[30] and the reverse type is almost certainly modelled on a reverse type common on sestertia dating to the reign of Galba (68–69 CE) which shows the Emperor addressing an assembled group of troops (Figure 8).[31] Yet it also seems clear that there is within some of the coins of Hadrian a delibe-rate association of the various armies with the provinces and regions

Figure 7

Figure 8

26. *RIC* Hadrian 911.
27. *RIC* Hadrian 746.
28. *RIC* Hadrian 782.
29. *RIC* Hadrian 739.
30. We know Hadrian to have undertaken many reforms within the military structure (*LH* 10.2–11.2; *Hist.* 69.9; M. Cornelius Fronto's letter of 165 CE to Lucius Verus entitled *Preamble to History* 10).
31. *RIC* Galba 462-68.

in which they served. Thus, we should understand the whole range of the 'Military' types to be an integral part of the 'Travel Sestertia' associated with his reign.

I shall now move through the provinces and regions in alphabetical order, incorporating within the discussion of each a consideration of coins from each of the four types which are relevant to that province or region. The specialized coins of Nicomedia, Alexandria and the Nile will be discussed under the appropriate provinces of Bithynia and Aegyptos.

3. *The 'Travel Sestertia' Catalogue*

1. *Achaia*—represented by a single example from the 'Restitutor Type' which conforms to the pattern of that type. On the reverse of this coin (Figure 9)[32] we have depicted the female personification of the province, draped and kneeling on the left before the standing figure of Hadrian on the right. The Emperor is dressed in a toga and extends his right hand to the personification of Achaia in a gesture of goodwill, intending to raise her to her feet. Between the figures of Hadrian and Achaia is a Greek-style vase or amphora which contains a palm branch. The inscription RESTITVTORI ACHAIAE surrounds the scene and S C stands in exergue.

Hadrian visited the province of Achaia on both of his major journeys to the east.[33] A bronze coin issued by the province to commemorate Hadrian's visits is, also worth noting (Figure 10). It depicts the god Mercury, standing naked and holding a caduceus in his left hand, while a cloak is casually draped over his right arm. In front of him is a pedestal

Figure 9   Figure 10

with a bust on it. Hadrian was particularly fond of the city of Athens within the province of Achaia and lavished innumerable gifts upon it,

---

32.   *RIC* Hadrian 938.

33.   Cassius Dio, *Hist.* 69.16.1, records only one of these visits, while Spartianus *LH* 13.1, 6 records both.

including a variety of extensive building projects.[34] We know that he spent the winter months of 124–125 CE and 128–129 CE within that 'Queen' of cultural cities, described by S. Perowne as 'the city of his soul'.[35]

2. *Aegyptos*—represented by a single example of the 'Province Type'. The reverse of this coin (Figure 11) [36] depicts the female personification of Aegyptos, draped in a long, flowing gown, reclining left. She is resting her left elbow on a basket of fruit while extending her right arm in which she holds a sistrum of Isis. At her feet is a small ibis, a native Egyptian bird, standing on a column. The inscription AEGYPTOS surrounds the top of the scene while S C stands in exergue.

Although there was trouble in Egypt at the beginning of Hadrian's reign which might have occasioned his visiting the province (*LH* 5.2; *Hist.* 69.8.1),[37] it appears that his only confirmed visit to the province came during his second great journey to the east between 128 and 134 CE. More specifically, his tour of the province lasted from the summer of 130 CE to the spring of 131 CE. While on this tour he may have visited the II Traiana legion which was stationed near Alexandria.

34.   *Hist.* 69.16.1-2; *LH* 13.1, 6; 19.2-3. Also note the discussion in J.H. Oliver, 'Documents concerning the Emperor Hadrian', *Hesperia* 10 (1941), pp. 361-70.

35.   *Hadrian,* p. 100.

36.   *RIC* Hadrian 838.

37.   A further riot within Alexandria is mentioned in *LH* 12.1. The trouble in Egypt is also mentioned in passing by Appian, *The Civil Wars* 2.90. The subject of the Jewish Revolt in Egypt, particularly the trouble in Alexandria, has received a great deal of scholarly attention. For some interesting papyrus fragments detailing a debate between Alexandrian Jews and Greeks in the presence of Hadrian, see P.J. Alexander, 'Letters and Speeches of the Emperor Hadrian', *HSCP* 49 (1938), pp. 156-58; V. Tcherikover and A. Fuchs (eds.), *Corpus Papyrorum Judaicarum,* II (London: Harvard University Press, 1960), pp. 87-99. The debate probably takes place early in Hadrian's reign, perhaps about 119 or 120 CE, and deals with domestic matters to be settled following the revolt in the province under Trajan in 115–117 CE. Also worth noting on the subject are V. Tcherikover, 'The Decline of the Jewish Diaspora in Egypt in the Roman Period', *JJS* 14 (1963), pp. 1-32; A. Kasher, 'Some Comments on the Jewish Uprising in Egypt in the Time of Trajan', *JJS* 27 (1976), pp. 147-58; and M.P. ben Ze'ev, 'Greek Attacks against Alexandrian Jews during Emperor Trajan's Reign', *JSJ* 20 (1989), pp. 31-48.

| Figure 11 | Figure 12 |

3. *Nilus*—also represented by a single example of the 'Province Type'. The reverse of this coin (Figure 12)[38] is a good artistic complement to the Aegyptos reverse. It depicts a male personification of Nilus, this time reclining right. He is naked to the waist and leans with his right elbow on a rock, possibly a symbol of the pyramids. In his right hand he holds some reeds, a plant reminiscent of the papyrus, while his left hand supports a cornucopia. Two children are playing around the cornucopia. In the field at the right is a hippopotamus surrounded by additional reeds. Native wildlife of the Nile is further represented in the form of a crocodile which rests in the waters in the foreground. The inscription NILVS surrounds the top of the coin while S C stands in exergue. Incidentally, the Nile is specifically mentioned in *LH* 14.5 and is connected with the report of the death of Antinous: 'During a journey on the Nile he [Hadrian] lost Antinous, his favourite, and for this youth he wept like a woman.' The incident is also discussed in *Hist.* 69.11.2-4 where it is somewhat scandalously reported that Antinous was sacrificed for the life of the Emperor.[39] Hadrian had Antinous deified, and established temples for the cultic worship of him.[40] The city of Antinoopolis

38.   *RIC* Hadrian 863.

39.   M. Yourcenar, in her highly praised fictional retelling of the life of the Emperor entitled *Memoirs of Hadrian* (London: Secker and Warburg, 1955), builds much upon the love that Hadrian had for Antinous. R. Lambert, *Beloved and God* (London: Weidenfeld & Nicolson, 1984), has made a detailed study of the relationship between the two based on all of the available historical evidence.

40.   Hadrian founded the city of Antinoopolis in Egypt in Antinous's honour. Also worth considering on the subject are W. den Boer, 'Religion and Literature in Hadrian's Policy', *Mnemosyne* 8 (1955), pp. 123-44, and P.J. Sijpesteijn, 'A New Document concerning Hadrian's Visit to Egypt', *Historia* 18 (1969), pp. 109-18. The fact that Hadrian had Antinous proclaimed a god and erected temples in his honour was a cause of some caustic comment among Christians of the day, as Justin Martyr, *Apology* 29.4, demonstrates.

was founded in Egypt in his honour[41] and many cities of the eastern provinces struck commemorative coins bearing an idealized likeness of him as their obverse. A good example is the bronze coin issued by the city of Smyrna in Ionia. This coin (Figure 13) [42] has a bare-headed Antinous facing left surrounded by the Greek inscription ANTINOOC HPWC. It is perhaps this association with the beloved Antinous which is responsible for the Nile being honoured with a special issue within the series.

4. *Alexandria*—represented by three examples, one of the 'Province Type' and two of the 'Adventus Type'. The first of these coins[43] is similar in design to the Aegyptos sestertius reverse. Alexandria is also draped and reclining left, while holding corn-ears in her right hand and a vine-branch in her left. She rests her left arm on a basket of fruit and at her feet are some growing corn-ears. The inscription ALEXANDRIA surrounds the scene and S C stands in exergue. The second example[44] conforms in large part to the standard pattern of the 'Adventus Type' group described above. The one distinguishing feature of the

Figure 13

Figure 14

personification is that she holds a purse[45] in her left hand. This may be to emphasize the economic power of the city within the Roman world, since it was through her ports that the vital grain harvests were

41. H.I. Bell, 'Antinoopolis: A Hadrianic Foundation in Egypt', JRS 30 (1940), pp. 133-47, and M. Zahrnt, 'Antinoopolis in Agypten: die hadrianische Gründung und ihre Priviligien in der neueren Forschung', *ANRW*, II.10.1, pp. 669-706, give details.

42. Sear, *Greek Imperial*, p. 123, lists this coin as 1331.

43. *RIC* Hadrian 876.

44. *RIC* Hadrian 877.

45. J.M.C. Toynbee, *The Hadrianic School* (Cambridge: Cambridge University Press, 1934), p. 42, argues that the object is a situla, a vessel for carrying sacred Nile water. See Juvenal, *Satires* 6.527-41, for an interesting comment on this.

channelled to the hungry Empire.[46] The reverse inscription reads ADVENTVI AVG ALEXANDRIAE with the letters S C in exergue. The third example[47] bears the exact same inscription as the previous coin but displays a remarkable scene which is unparalleled within the series. The reverse shows Hadrian and his wife Sabina standing on the right and offering their hands to Serapis and Isis who stand on the left. These two Egyptian cultic deities, both of whom had a long association with the city of Alexandria stretching back for several hundred years,[48] are identifiable by their headdresses. Serapis is shown with a modius on his head while Isis bears a lotus on hers. The figure of Isis also carries a sistrum in her hand. Between the two pairs of figures stands an altar surmounted by a pine-cone. This reverse depicting Sabina is the only numismatic evidence within the series which chronicles her accompanying Hadrian on his journeys. It is possible that she was with him throughout the whole of his second journey to the east, but it is much more likely that she joined the Imperial party for the tour of Egypt itself. Certainly she was with him on the fateful journey up the Nile during which Antinous died since the inscription on the base of the Colossus of Memnon tells of her waiting impatiently at Thebes for the miraculous voice of Memnon to speak at sunrise. The inscription carved at the base of that Colossus can be precisely dated to 21 November 130 CE.

The mint at Alexandria issued quite an extensive series of billon tetradrachmas and bronze coins during Hadrian's reign which depicted various reverse scenes, including some bearing Egyptian motifs. For example there is a tetradrachma which portrays the Emperor seated in

46.   See E.G. Huzar, 'Alexandria and Aegyptos in the Julio-Claudian Age', *ANRW*, II.10.1, pp. 619-68.

47.   *RIC* Hadrian 843.

48.   See D. Magie, 'Egyptian Deities in Asia Minor in Inscriptions and on Coins', *AJA* 57 (1953), pp. 163-87; H.C. Youtie, 'The *Kline* of Sarapis', *HTR* 41 (1948), pp. 9-29; R. Stiehl, 'The Origin of the Cult of Sarapis', *HR* 3 (1963–64), pp. 21-33; and T.T. Tinh, 'Sarapis and Isis', in B.F. Meyer and E.P. Sanders (eds.), *Jewish and Christian Self-Definition. III. Self-Definition in the Graeco-Roman World* (London: SCM Press, 1982), pp. 101-17, for more on the Egyptian cults. There is strong evidence of a flourishing cult of Serapis and Isis in the city of Corinth in the mid-second century CE. See T.A. Bradley, 'A Head of Sarapis from Corinth', *HSCP* 51 (1940), pp. 61-69; D.E. Smith, 'The Egyptian Cults at Corinth', *HTR* 70 (1977), pp. 201-31, for more on this. The Egyptian cult also held a prominent position in Athens, another metropolis dear to Hadrian's heart. On this see S. Dow, 'The Egyptian Cults in Athens', *HTR* 30 (1937), pp. 183-232.

the prow of a galley with his imperial staff held crooked in the left arm and his right hand raised in greeting (Figure 14). The field of the tetradrachma has the inscription L IE which dates the coin to the 15th year of Hadrian's rule (130–131 CE); clearly it was minted in Alexandria to commemorate the arrival of the Emperor in the province. The goddess Isis is featured on a related bronze coin (Figure 15).[49] She is seated on a throne facing to the right and holds a small figure of her son Horus on her lap. An ibis stands on a pedestal in front of them and the letters L and B in the field of the coin serve to date it to the 2nd year of Hadrian's rule (117–118 CE). Another tetradrachma has as its reverse

Figure 15   Figure 16

the figure of Hadrian being greeted by the personification of Alexandria, presumably on the occasion of his arrival in the city (Figure 16).[50] Hadrian is on the right and holds an imperial staff in his left hand. He extends his right hand to the figure of Alexandria, on the left, who offers it a kiss. She bears in her left hand two ears of corn, symbol of the importance of the province as provider of grain for the Empire. Another of the more interesting coins (Figure 17)[51] has as its obverse a portrait of Sabina, wearing a diadem and facing right; around her is the Greek inscription CABINA CEBACTH (meaning 'Sabina Augusta'). The reverse of the coin depicts one of Alexandria's most famous landmarks, the legendary Pharos lighthouse with a standing figure at its top, accompanied by two tritons on either side.[52] Surrounding the lighthouse is the inscription L ENNEA KD, which dates the coin to the 19th year

49.   G. Askew, *A Catalogue of Roman Coins* (London: Seaby, 1948), p. 49, lists this coin as 761.

50.   Sear, *Roman Coins*, p. 140, lists this coin as 1073.

51.   Askew, *Catalogue,* p. 49, lists this coin as 774.

52.   S. Handler, 'Architecture on the Roman Coins of Egypt', *AJA* 75 (1971), pp. 57-74 + Plates 11-12, gives details of numismatic representations of several sites in Alexandria, including the Pharos and the Serapium.

Figure 17

of Hadrian's rule (134–135 CE). Hadrian and Sabina may have visited the famous Museum of Alexandria, as there is a fleeting reference in *LH* 20.2 to Hadrian's debating with resident scholars there.

5. *Africa*—represented by three examples, one of the 'Province Type', one of the 'Restitutor Type', and one of the 'Adventus Type'. The first of these examples[53] shows the female personification wearing a headdress in the shape of an elephant's head with the elephant's trunk extending upwards and the ear flaps of the animal covering the side of her head. She rests her elbow on a rock and supports a cornucopia with her left arm while holding a scorpion in her extended right hand. At her feet stands a basket containing some corn ears. The inscription AFRICA surrounds the top of the scene while S C stands in exergue (Figure 18). The second example (Figure 19)[54] shows the personification draped, wearing the same headgear, and in some examples holding corn-ears in her left hand. The corn-ears also feature within the central space between the figures of Africa and Hadrian, where we see three corn-ears springing from the ground. The inscription RESTITVTORI AFRICAE surrounds the top of the scene while S C stands in exergue. The third example[55] shows the personification similarly draped and dressed. In her left arm she cradles a cornucopia and, as in the 'Province Type' reverse, she holds a scorpion in her extended right hand. The inscription ADVENTVI AVG AFRICAE surrounds the scene and S C stands in exergue. There also exists a variant of this reverse in which the personification holds a vexillum in place of the cornucopia.

Hadrian's visit to Africa took place in spring-summer of 128 CE and his arrival was accompanied by a fortuitous rainstorm which ended a

---

53.   *RIC* Hadrian 840.
54.   *RIC* Hadrian 943.
55.   *RIC* Hadrian 872.

Figure 18   Figure 19

five-year drought and won him the affections of the Africans (*LH* 22.14).[56] It was during this visit that he delivered the famous speech to the legionary troops of III Augusta at Lambaesis on the Kalends of July (1 July).[57] The occasion was marked by the erection of a monument which bore the text of the speech. The ruins of this column are still visible today.[58] It was these events, illustrative of Hadrian's interest in the military affairs of the province, which probably occasioned the use of the vexillum as a variation of the 'Adventus Type' reverse.

6. *Arabia*—represented by two examples, one of the 'Restitutor Type' and one of the 'Adventus Type'.[59] Within both the personification is draped and holds a long, straight object in her left hand. It is in the identification of this object that we have a hint of a product charac-teristic of Arabia. J.M.C. Toynbee suggests[60] that it is a bundle of sweet cane, a product known to have been associated with Arabia throughout the Roman world.[61] The characteristic features of the province of Arabia are further emphasized in the 'Restitutor Type' reverse by the repre-sentation of a dromedary which stands between the Emperor and the personification. The inscriptions for the reverses are ADVENTVI AVG ARABIA and RESTITVTORI ARABIAE respectively. The letters S C stand in exergue in both.

Hadrian is mentioned as visiting the province only once (*LH* 14.4). The visit occurred as the Emperor was on his way to Egypt from Syria

---

56.   R.H. Chowen, 'The Problem of Hadrian's Visits to North Africa', *CJ* 65 (1969–70), pp. 323-24.

57.   See Alexander, 'Letters', pp. 147-49, for details.

58.   See Grant, *Army*, pp. 239-40, for a translation of the reconstructed text.

59.   *RIC* Hadrian 943 and 878 respectively.

60.   *Hadrianic School*, p. 48.

61.   Pliny, *Natural History* 12.104, mentions this.

in 129 or 130 CE. He probably inspected the troops of III Cyrenaica stationed within the province at Bosra as part of this visit.[62]

7. *Asia*—represented by two examples, one of the 'Restitutor Type' and one of the 'Adventus Type' (Figure 20). Both conform to the standard pattern of their respective groups. The distinguishing feature on each is the headdress of the personification of Asia. We can see quite clearly that in both she wears a turretted crown, a well-known symbol of Asia. We also see that within both reverses the personification holds a sceptre in her left hand. The sceptre probably stands as a symbol of the wealthy and influential cities of Asia, notably Ephesus, and their dominating influence in the life of the province. Hadrian was particularly fond of Ephesus and this affinity is partially evidenced by the extensive indigenous cistophori of the city, minted under Imperial authority, which includes types depicting the famous Temple of Diana. In one example the cultic figure from the Temple of Diana appears, along with the inscription DIANA EPHESIA (Figure 21).[63] To return to the sestertia under discussion, the inscription on the first example[64] is RESTITVTORI ASIAE, while that of the second coin[65] is ADVENTVI AVG ASIAE. The letters S C stand in exergue in both coins. Hadrian visited the province on at least two occasions, once for an extended period in 123–124 CE and once in early 129 CE (*LH* 13.1, 6).

Figure 20   Figure 21

8. *Bithynia*—the province of Bithynia, or as it more technically named, Bithynia and Pontus, is represented by two examples, one of the

62.   For a discussion of the Roman legionary forces in Arabia, see G.W. Bowersock, 'A Report on Arabia Provincia', *JRS* 61 (1971), pp. 219-42.

63.   *RIC* Hadrian 525. See also *RIC* Hadrian 474-76 and 526-27. Some of the cistophori struck in Asia Minor during the reign of Hadrian also contain motifs associated with the Temple of Diana at Ephesus. See W.E. Metcalf, 'Hadrian, IOVIS OLYMPIVS', *Mnemosyne* 27 (1974), pp. 59-66.

64.   *RIC* Hadrian 845.

65.   *RIC* Hadrian 880.

'Restitutor Type' and one of the 'Adventus Type'. Both conform to the standard pattern of their respective groups. The first coin[66] depicts the female personification draped, wearing a mural crown, and resting a rudder on her shoulder. She stands with her foot placed on the prow of a ship. In some specimens of this coin the rudder is replaced by an acrostolium. The reverse inscription is RESTITVTORI BITHYNIAE with the letters S C in exergue.

The second example[67] again depicts the personification with the same features, a mural crown on her head and a rudder balanced over her shoulder. Both of these attributes emphasize the essentially naval character of this province, which bordered the Black Sea and thus had a long coastline. The inscription for this second coin is ADVENTVI AVG BITHYNIAE with the letters S C in exergue.

Bithynia is best remembered as far as Hadrian is concerned as the birthplace of his beloved Antinous. Hadrian made one recorded visit to Bithynia and Pontus in 123 or 124 CE as part of his first extended tour of the east. Included in his journey were visits to the cities of Nicomedia and Nicaea.

9. *Nicomedia*—represented by a single example of the 'Restitutor Type'. The reverse of this coin[68] is virtually a carbon-copy of the 'Restitutor Type' reverse of Bithynia, the only difference being the altered inscription reading RESTITVTORI NICOMEDIAE with the letters S C in exergue. Even the characteristic mural crown and rudder are repeated to emphasize the maritime nature of the city. There is some debate as to why a coin of Nicomedia was included in the series. This might be due to the fact that both Nicomedia and Nicaea were severely damaged by earthquakes in 123 CE, shortly before the Emperor's visit there (*LH* 21.5). Hadrian took a major part in funding the rebuilding of the city following this calamity and it is perhaps in commemoration of this Imperial benevolence that the 'Restitutor Type' coin was issued. An alternative answer may lie in the fact that Nicomedia was the capital city of Antinous's home province.

10. *Britannia*—represented by four examples, one of the 'Province Type', one of the 'Adventus Type' and two of the 'Exercitus Type'.

66.   *RIC* Hadrian 948.
67.   *RIC* Hadrian 881.
68.   *RIC* Hadrian 961.

The first of these coins (Figure 22)[69] depicts the female personification draped and seated slightly to the right while facing head-on. She rests her right foot on a pile of rocks, an obvious visual reference to Hadrian's defensive wall within the province (*LH* 11.2). Britannia rests her head on her right hand while cradling a spear within the crook of her left arm. To the right and leaning against her body is a full-length body shield with boss and spike. The inscription BRITANNIA surrounds the border and the standard S C is in exergue.

This coin is the only one of the 'Province Type' series which has a direct type precursor in an earlier issue of Hadrian's mints. There exists quite a rare as from 119 CE which bears as its reverse the exact same figure of Britannia as the sestertius.[70] This earlier bronze issue was probably connected with the suppression of a rebellion within the province early in Hadrian's reign (*LH* 5.2). Hadrian's visit to Britannia, including the likely possibility that he personally commanded troops in the quelling of this revolt within the province, occurred in the early part of 122 CE (*LH* 11.2; 12.1-5).[71] It is not surprising, given the military history of Britannia, that the armed and vigilant personification of the province was chosen as the reverse for this 'Province Type' reverse.

In the second example (Figure 23)[72] a different image of the personified Britannia is presented. Here we note a return to the standard characterization of provincial personification within the group, for she wears the conventional Greek-style dress. She sacrifices onto the altar which stands between her and the Emperor. At the base of the altar is an animal, perhaps a wild boar. The inscription ADVENTVI AVG BRITANNIAE surrounds the scene with the letters S C standing in exergue.

Britannia is also represented by two examples of the 'Exercitus Type' which correspond to the two main scenes of that group outlined above. The first[73] has Hadrian standing left on a platform and addressing three soldiers standing to the right. The first soldier holds an aquila, the second a standard, the third a shield. A vexillum stands in the background. The inscription EXERC BRIT S C stands in exergue. The second has Hadrian

69. *RIC* Hadrian 845.

70. *RIC* Hadrian 577.

71. The Ninth Hispania legion was destroyed during this rebellion of 119–122 CE. M. Cornelius Fronto alluded to this in his letter of 162 CE entitled *On the Parthian War* 2.

72. *RIC* Hadrian 882.

73. *RIC* Hadrian 913.

on horseback with his right hand raised, addressing five soldiers (Figure 24)[74] The first soldier holds a vexillum while the other four all hold standards. The inscription EXER BRITANNICVS S C stands in exergue. Both of these 'Exercitus Type' reverses testify to the strategic importance of the province within the Empire. This importance is underlined by the degree of military strength committed to the area. There were three legions stationed in Britannia following the revolt of 119–122 CE, II Augusta stationed in Isca Silurum, VI Victrix stationed in Eboracum and XX Valeria Victrix stationed in Deva.

Figure 22

Figure 23

11. *Cappadocia*—represented by two examples, one of the 'Province Type' and one of the 'Exercitus Type'. The first of these coins[75] depicts the personification standing and wearing a short military tunic and an animal-skin cloak. She also sports high hunting boots and a turretted crown. With her left hand she supports a vexillum while in her extended right hand is a small pile of stones. The stones are probably a visual representation of Mount Argaeus near the provincial capital of Caesarea. The inscription CAPPADOCIA surrounds the scene while the letters S C stand in the field on either side of the personification. We can see in the attributes of the personification some indication of the military importance of Cappadocia in the Roman Empire. This is brought out even further by the second example[76] which emphasizes the Roman military presence within the province. The reverse has Hadrian on horseback addressing three soldiers; the first soldier holds an aquila, and the other two support military standards. The inscription EXER CAPPADOCICVS S C stands in exergue.

There were two legions stationed in Cappadocia, both along the sensitive border with Armenia. The first, the XV Apollinaris, had its headquarters in Setela, while the second, the XII Fulminata, had its

74.   *RIC* Hadrian 912.
75.   *RIC* Hadrian 847.
76.   *RIC* Hadrian 914.

headquarters in Mekitene. Hadrian visited the province in the summer of 129 CE as part of his second journey to the East (*LH* 13.7).

12. *Cilicia*—represented by a single example of the 'Adventus Type'. This coin[77] shows Hadrian dressed in a short military tunic and wearing high boots. The personification of Cilicia, on the other hand, is draped and wears a crested helmet on her head. In her left hand she holds a vexillum. The inscription ADVENTVI AVG CILICIA surrounds the scene and the letters S C stand in exergue.

   None of the known historical sources specifically record the arrival of Hadrian in this province; indeed, the numismatic evidence is our sole authority for such a visit. However, the visit most probably occurred in spring of 129 CE as Hadrian worked his way eastwards from Ephesus toward Antioch in Syria.

Figure 24

Figure 25

13. *Dacia*—represented by three examples, one of the 'Province Type' and two of the 'Exercitus Type'. The first of these coins (Figure 25)[78] is reminiscent of the Britannia 'Province Type' reverse discussed above and shows the personification sitting on a pile of rocks and facing left. Dacia wears a tunic and cloak and has on high-topped hunting boots. In her arm is cradled a curved sword, the characteristic weapon of the soldiers of the province, while in her right hand she hold a vexillum. Her right foot rests upon a rock. The inscription DACIA stands in exergue with the letters S C in the field to the left and right of the personification.

   The two examples from the 'Exercitus Type' group correspond to the two main scenes of that group outlined above. The first of these coins[79] has Hadrian standing on a platform to the left while addressing an officer and three soldiers who stand to the right. The officer faces the

77.   *RIC* Hadrian 883.
78.   *RIC* Hadrian 849.
79.   *RIC* Hadrian 917.

troops, as does Hadrian, while holding a spear and shield. The three soldiers face the Emperor and hold an aquila, a standard and a spear respectively. The inscription EXERC DACICVS stands in exergue, while the letters S C are in the field on either side of the scene. The second of these coins[80] has Hadrian on horseback addressing three soldiers. The first soldier holds an aquila and the other two support standards. The inscription EXERC DACICVS S C stands in exergue.

We know that Hadrian accompanied Trajan on both of his Dacian campaigns of 101–102 CE and 105–106 CE (*LH* 13.2, 6). During the second campaign Hadrian was appointed to command the First Legion and distinguished himself in battle. We have no record of a further visit by Hadrian as Emperor to this province, although he did judge it strategic enough to assign one of his most trusted commanders, Marcius Turbo, as prefect of the province before setting off to Rome in 118 CE (*LH* 6.7; 7.3).[81] In any case, its strategic location on the eastern perimeter of the Roman world was enough to guarantee its abiding importance within the military defence network of the Empire. The province had a legion, XIII Gemina, garrisoned at Apulum.

14. *Gallia*—represented by two examples, one of the 'Restitutor Type' and one of the 'Adventus Type'. The first of these coins (Figure 26)[82] shows the personification draped and kneeling in accordance with the pattern of the type outlined above. There is no distinguishing feature or native attribute for the personification of Gallia immediately recognizable on the coin. The inscription RESTITVTORI GALLIAE surrounds the scene with the letters S C taking their customary place in exergue.

The second example (Figure 27)[83] of the 'Adventus Type' conforms very much to the standard of the type and the personification is likewise void of any distinguishing characteristic. Toynbee attempts an explanation for this fact when she says, 'It is as if the artist had sought, by the very absence of distinctive attributes, to emphasize the complete absorption of

---

80. *RIC* Hadrian 915.

81. This was quite an unusual appointment since Marcius Turbo was only a member of the equestrian order at the time. Turbo had already been instrumental in helping to curb the revolts in Judaea and Mauretania (*LH* 5.2, 8; Eusebius, *Hist. Eccl.* 4.2.3-4). On the subject of Roman provincial administration, see the excellent article by P.A. Brunt, 'The Administrators of Roman Egypt', *JRS* 65 (1975), pp. 124-47.

82. *RIC* Hadrian 950.

83. *RIC* Hadrian 884.

the Gallic provinces into the common Graeco-Roman civilisation.'[84] Here, once again the inscription is predictable: ADVENTVI AVG GALLIAE surrounds the scene with the letters S C in exergue.

Figure 26   Figure 27

Hadrian is said to have begun his first journey of 121–125 CE with a visit to the province of Gaul (*LH* 10.1), where he reputedly demonstrated his generosity by the relief aid given to various cities there. It may be in commemoration of this act of Imperial benevolence that the Gallia 'Restitutor Type' was issued.

15. *Germania*—represented by a single example of the 'Exercitus Type'. This sestertius (Figure 28)[85] shows Hadrian on horseback with his right arm raised. He addresses a group of three soldiers, the first of whom carries an aquila while the other two carry military standards. The inscription EXERCITVS GERMANICVS stands in exergue.

Hadrian is mentioned as visiting the region of Germania early in 121 CE at the beginning of his first extensive tour of the Empire. No doubt his visit was also an occasion to inspect the military legions stationed in Germania. He was, in a sense, returning to familiar territory for we know that earlier in his own military career Hadrian had been in Upper Germania as tribune in the XXII Primigenia legion (*LH* 2.5). Owing to the sensitive location of the provinces of Germania Superior and Germania Inferior along the Rhine frontier, we find a heavy military presence there. Two legions defended Germania Superior, XXII Primigenia stationed in Moguntiacum and VIII Augusta stationed in Argertoratum. Two legions also defended Germania Inferior, I Minerva stationed in Bonna and XXX Ulpia Victrix stationed in Vetera.

16. *Hispania*—the only province or region within the series which enjoys at least one example from each of the four types. This might be due to the fact that there is a close association between the Emperor and the city of Italica in Baetica, one of the constituent provinces of

84.   *Hadrianic School*, p. 85.
85.   *RIC* Hadrian 920.

Hispania.[86] The first example (Figure 29),[87] of the 'Province Type', is reminiscent of the examples of Aegyptos, Alexandria and Africa I have already discussed within that group. It shows a reclining figure of Hispania holding an olive-branch in her extended right hand. She rests

Figure 28   Figure 29

her left arm on a rock, possibly an allusion to Alpe, the Rock of Gibraltar, located within the province of Baetica. At the personification's feet is a rabbit. The inscription HISPANIA surrounds the scene with the letters S C in exergue. The region of Hispania was renowned both for its excellent oil, derived from olive groves, and its rabbits, hence their use as provincial attributes in the coin reverse.[88] The second example (Figure 30) [89] is of the 'Restitutor Type' and employs the same two attributes within its reverse; the olive branch is resting on the left shoulder of the personification of Hispania, while the rabbit appears crouching at her feet between her and the Emperor. The inscription RESTITVTORI HISPANIAE surrounds the scene while S C stands in exergue.

The third example,[90] of the 'Adventus Type', retains the olive-branch motif, the branch being held in Hispania's left hand, but drops the rabbit from its presentation. There is, however, a bull at the base of the sacrificial altar which stands between the Emperor and the personification.

There are two examples of the 'Exercitus Type' corresponding to the two main scenes characteristic of that group. The first of these[91] shows

86.   Indeed, Cassius, Dio *Hist.* 69.1.1, presents Italica as the birthplace of Hadrian. However, he is more likely to have been born in Rome as Spartianus *LH* 1.3 suggests, although his family certainly lived in Italica (*LH* 2.1-2; 19.1). R. Syme, 'Hadrian and Italica', *JRS* 54 (1964), pp. 142-49 discusses the matter.

87.   *RIC* Hadrian 851.

88.   Toynbee, *Hadrianic School*, pp. 103-105, gives details and classical references to support this. She also calls attention to the Latin term for rabbit (*cuniculus*) which can also be translated as 'burrow' or 'mine', and suggests that this could be a veiled reference to the mineral wealth of the region.

89.   *RIC* Hadrian 952.

90.   *RIC* Hadrian 886.

91.   *RIC* Hadrian 922.

Hadrian standing on a platform addressing an officer and three soldiers. The officer faces the other soldiers and carries a sword. The three soldiers hold an aquila, a vexillum and a standard respectively. The inscription EXERC HISPAN S C is in exergue. The second example[92] again conforms to the pattern type and shows Hadrian on horseback addressing three soldiers, all of whom carry shields. The first soldier also carries a vexillum while the other two carry standards. The inscription EXERC HISPANICVS S C stands in exergue.

Hadrian visited Hispania in 122–123 CE on his first tour around the Empire and wintered in Tarragona in Tarraconensis where Spartianus tells us that he restored the temple of Augustus and successfully avoided an assassination attempt by an insane slave (*LH* 12.4–5). There was only one legion stationed in this largely pacified region. This was the VII Gemina stationed in Legio in Tarraconensis.

Figure 30					Figure 31

17. *Italia*—represented by two examples, one of the 'Restitutor Type' (Figure 31)[93] and one of the 'Adventus Type'.[94] In both sestertia the personification is draped and holds a cornucopia in her left hand. The cornucopia may stand as a symbol of the rich blessings which the province provided for the Empire. The surrounding inscriptions for the two examples are RESTITVTORI ITALIAE and ADVENTVI AVG ITALIAE respectively. The letters S C stand in exergue in both reverses.

The Emperor made a journey through Italia to Campania early in his reign in 119 CE in the course of which he channelled Imperial gifts and benefits to many cities within the province (*LH* 9.6). It is perhaps this visit which is commemorated on both of these coin reverses.

18. *Judaea*—represented by three distinct examples, two of the 'Province Type' and one of the 'Adventus Type'. The two examples of

92.	*RIC* Hadrian 923.
93.	*RIC* Hadrian 956.
94.	*RIC* Hadrian 888.

the 'Province Type' are slightly unusual in that they do not conform wholly to the pattern of the type, but have a representation of the Emperor as well as that of the provincial personification on their reverses. In this way, both are very similar to the 'Adventus Type' or the 'Restitutor Type' patterns. The third example, that of the 'Adventus Type',[95] conforms more closely to the pattern of its type; I shall reserve discussion of this particular coin until Chapter eight below.

The first of these 'Province Type' reverses (Figure 32)[96] shows Hadrian in a toga, standing to the left while raising his right hand. Opposite him stands the female personification of Judaea, wearing a full-length robe. Between the two figures are two smaller children, holding palm branches, as if presenting them to the Emperor.[97] Behind the figure of Judaea stands a third child. Toynbee comments on the children thus:

> The centre of the design is occupied by two plump little naked boys, standing one behind the other, who hold tall palm-branches and advance, unabashed, to meet the Emperor; but a third and yet smaller boy, over-awed, it seems, by the Imperial presence, has taken refuge behind *Iudaea* and clings for protection to the skirts of her *chiton*.[98]

The inscription IVDAEA stands in exergue while the letters S C are in the field on either side of the scene. The second example (Figure 33)[99] has exactly the same inscriptions as the coin just discussed. Its scene is very reminiscent of the 'Restitutor Type' reverses in that it depicts the Emperor dressed in a toga and extending his right hand to the kneeling personification of Judaea. The same three children are present, all in position as before.

Hadrian visited the province, and Jerusalem, in 130 CE while on his second tour of the east. In addition, as I noted, he probably visited the province again sometime in 135 CE when he helped to quell the

95.   *RIC* Hadrian 890.

96.   *RIC* Hadrian 853.

97.   Perhaps as an evocative image by which Hadrian calls for the Jewish people to submit to the kingly authority of the Roman Emperor? I cannot help but recall the ironic words of Jn 19.15 when seeing this reverse type, or remembering that palm branches were cut from the trees by the populace and placed before Jesus at the triumphal entry into Jerusalem (Jn 12.13).

98.   *Hadrianic School*, p. 120.

99.   This coin is not listed in *RIC* but an example of this type is found in the National Museum of Naples. For a brief discussion and photograph of the rare piece, see Breglia, *Roman*, pp. 140-41.

Figure 32   Figure 33

rebellion. It appears that two legions were stationed in the province from 132 CE onwards. In addition to the X Fretensis, which had been stationed in Jerusalem since it helped to suppress the First Jewish Revolt of 66–70 CE, Hadrian felt it necessary to move other forces into the area, possibly the VI Ferrata from Syria to Caparcotna near Jerusalem in 132 CE.[100] In addition, there is some debate about whether the II Traiana was also stationed in Judaea, perhaps as early as 120 CE,[101] and occasionally on the basis of numismatic evidence it has been suggested that the V Macedonia was responsible for the reconquering of Jerusalem.[102] What we do know with some certainty is that the XXII Deiotariana, originally stationed in Alexandria, was destroyed in the war.[103]

100.   See B. Lifschitz, 'Sur la Date du transfert de la legion VI Ferrata en Palestine', *Latomus* 19 (1960), pp. 109-111.

101.   See B. Isaac and I. Roll, 'Legio II Traiana in Judaea', *ZPE* 33 (1979), pp. 149-56; J.R. Rea, 'The Legio II Traiana in Judaea?', *ZPE* 38 (1980), pp. 220-22; B. Isaac and I. Roll, 'Legio II Traiana in Judaea—A Reply', *ZPE* 47 (1982), pp. 131-32; P. Schäfer, 'Hadrian's Policy in Judaea and the Bar Kokhba Revolt: A Reassessment', in P.R. Davies and R.T. White (eds.), *A Tribute to Geza Vermes: Essays on Jewish and Christian Literature and History* (JSOTSup, 100; Sheffield: JSOT Press, 1990), pp. 281-303.

102.   J. Meyshan, 'The Legion which Reconquered Jerusalem in the War of Bar Kochba (AD 132–135)', *PEQ* (January–June 1958), pp. 19-26.

103.   M. Cornelius Fronto alludes to this in his letter of 162 CE to Antoninus entitled *On the Parthian War* 2. On the subject of the placement of legionary forces within Judaea, see L.J.F. Keppie, 'The Legionary Garrison of Judaea under Hadrian', *Latomus* 32 (1973), pp. 859-64; B. Isaac and I. Roll, 'Judaea in the Early Years of Hadrian's Reign', *Latomus* 38 (1979), pp. 54-66; G.W. Bowersock, 'A Roman Perspective on the Bar Kochba War', in W.S. Green (ed), *Approaches to Ancient Judaism*, III (BJS, 9; Chico, CA: Scholars Press, 1980), pp. 131-41. Bowersock does not believe that the XXII Deiotariana was destroyed in the revolt of 132–135 CE and challenges several other assumptions about the events surrounding the Bar Kochba war.

19. *Libya*—represented by a single example of the 'Restitutor Type'. This sestertius[104] is exceedingly rare and most of the extant specimens are in such poor condition that it is very difficult to determine precisely how the personification of Libya was presented. We do know that a common feature of artistic representations of the personified Libya at the time was long, curled ringlets of hair. Perhaps this feature also appeared on the coin reverse. The inscription is RESTITVTORI LIBYAE with the letters S C in exergue. We have no definite record of a visit by Hadrian to either of the provinces of Cyrenaica or Creta which constituted the region known as Libya. However, there is mention of a disturbance in the region early in Hadrian's rule (*LH* 5.2) which may have occasioned an Imperial visit.[105] There are also indications of a reconstruction programme in the region under Hadrian which may help to explain the 'Restitutor Type' reverse of Libya.[106]

20. *Macedonia*—represented by two examples, one of the 'Restitutor Type' and one of the 'Adventus Type'. Both conform closely to the standard pattern of each group. In the first example[107] the female personification of Macedonia appears in a short chiton and boots and is characterized by her wearing a *kausia*, the national headdress. In addition she holds a whip in her hand which may point to the essentially pastoral or agricultural nature of the province. The reverse inscription RESTITVTORI MACEDONIAE surrounds the scene with S C standing

---

104. *RIC* Hadrian 958.

105. No doubt this is a continuation of the trouble which erupted in Cyrenaica at the end of Trajan's rule in 115 CE and spread to Egypt, Cyprus and Mesopotamia. Cassius Dio, *Hist.* 68.32.1-2, and Eusebius, *Hist. Eccl.* 4.2.1-5, both allude to this. For a survey of the Jewish Revolt of 115–117 CE under Trajan's rule, see S. Applebaum, 'Notes on the Jewish Revolt under Trajan', *JSJ* 2 (1950), pp. 26-30, and A. Fuks, 'Aspects of the Jewish Revolt in AD 115–117', *JRS* 51 (1961), pp. 98-104. E.M. Smallwood, 'Palestine c. AD 115–118', *Historia* 11 (1962), pp. 500-10, argues that the revolt even spread to Palestine and that allusions to it are embedded within many rabbinic sources.

106. On this see P.M. Fraser, 'Hadrian and Cyrene', *JRS* 40 (1950), pp. 77-90; S. Applebaum, 'The Jewish Revolt in Cyrene in 115–117 and the Subsequent Recolonization', *JJS* 2 (1951), pp. 177-86; M.E. Smallwood, 'The Hadrianic Inscription from the Caesareum at Cyrene', *JRS* 42 (1952), pp. 37-38; S. Applebaum, 'Cyrenensia Judaica', *JRS* 12 (1962), pp. 31-43.

107. *RIC* Hadrian 959.

in exergue. The second example[108] shows exactly the same attributes within its presentation of the provincial personification. The inscription on this reverse is ADVENTVI AVG MACEDONIAE with the letters S C in exergue. We have no written record of a visit to the province by Hadrian, but it appears likely that he included a short stay in Macedonia in late 123 CE or early 124 CE while on his way from Samothrace to Athens.

21. *Mauretania*—represented by three examples, one of the 'Province Type', one of the 'Adventus Type' and one of the 'Exercitus Type'. The first of these types (Figure 34)[109] was minted with slight variations of detail. It shows the female personification of Mauretania dressed in a short tunic with a chlamys and wearing boots. She leads a horse by the reins which she holds in her left hand as she looks back over her shoulder to the horse. In her right hand she supports a javelin. Another coin,[110] a variation of the 'Province Type' group, similarly shows the personification and the horse, only this time the personification stands well in front of the horse and carries two javelins in her hand. The inscription MAVRETANIA surrounds both scenes with SC in exergue in both reverses.

The second example (Figure 35)[111] again depicts the female personification wearing the short tunic while holding a vexillum in her left hand.[112] There is an altar with a small bull at its base between her and the Emperor who stands on the left of the scene. The inscription ADVENTVI AVG MAVRETANIAE surrounds the scene while S C stands in exergue. The third example[113] shows Hadrian standing on a platform addressing three soldiers who carry two standards and a spear respectively. The inscription EXERCITVS is at the top of the scene while MAVRETANICVS S C is in exergue.

The military motif is unquestionably emphasized within these issues depicting the provinces of Mauretania. We see it clearly in the military dress of the personification as well as in the selection of attributes which surround her. The Mauretanians were well known for both their

108. *RIC* Hadrian 895.
109. *RIC* Hadrian 855.
110. *RIC* Hadrian 858.
111. *RIC* Hadrian 897.
112. In some examples this vexillum is replaced by corn-ears.
113. *RIC* Hadrian 924.

spearsmanship and their use within the legionary armies as cavalry auxiliaries.[114] Cassius Dio, *Hist.* 68.32.4, mentions Trajan's use of Mauretanian cavalry within his Dacian campaigns. It is perhaps this critical role that such auxiliary troops played within the Roman army[115] that is directly responsible for the 'Exercitus Type' issue, since there was no legion permanently stationed within the region of Mauretania during Hadrian's rule. Or it may be that detachments of III Augusta, stationed nearby at Lambaesis, served in Mauretania and that they were the

Figure 34   Figure 35

honoured recipients of the issue. We do know that there were disturbances within the region at the beginning of Hadrian's reign (*LH* 5.2, 8; 6.7; 7.3) which required the Emperor's appointment of his trusted commander Marcius Turbo to the region.[116] It is also probable that Hadrian visited the region in connection with the repression of these revolts (*LH* 12.7). It is perhaps this visit, which took place early in 123 CE, which occasioned the 'Adventus Type' issue described above.

22. *Moesia*—represented by two examples, one of the 'Adventus Type' and one of the 'Exercitus Type'. The first of these coins (Figure 36)[117] shows Hadrian in short tunic and boots greeting the female personification who also wears a short tunic. She has her hair gathered into a knot at the nape of her neck. In some examples it appears that she holds

114. Strabo, *Geography* 17.3.7; Horace, *Odes* 1.22.2.
115. See the discussion in M. Roxan, 'The Auxilia of Mauretania Tingitana', *Latomus* 32 (1973), pp. 838-55.
116. Marcius Turbo was encountered in my discussion of Dacia above. Cassius Dio, *Hist.* 69.18.1-4, gives us an account of the capable commander who had a long service record as an Imperial 'trouble-shooter'. Eusebius, *Hist. Eccl.* 4.2.3-4, relates Marcius Turbo's role in helping to suppress the Jewish Revolt in Egypt and Cyrene during the final years of the reign of Trajan. Also note R. Syme, 'The Wrong Marcius Turbo', *JRS* 52 (1962), pp. 87-96, and his discussion of Turbo in 'Guard Prefects in Trajan and Hadrian', *JRS* (1980), pp. 64-80.
117. *RIC* Hadrian 903.

a bow in her left hand among the folds of her tunic, a quiver of arrows standing ready by her side. The surrounding inscription is ADVENTVI AVG MOESIAE with the letters S C in exergue. The Moesians were known as excellent archers and held a valuable position within the auxiliary forces supporting the Roman legions on this basis.[118] The essentially military character of the region is also highlighted by the 'Exercitus Type' reverse. This coin (Figure 37)[119] shows Hadrian on the left, with his right arm raised, addressing an officer and three soldiers. The officer faces the other soldiers and holds a sword and spear. The three soldiers face the Emperor and carry an aquila and standards. The inscription EXER MOESIACVS S C is in exergue.

Figure 36   Figure 37

We have no record of an Imperial visit by Hadrian to the region of Moesia, but we do know that earlier in his military career, at the end of Domitian's reign (81–96 CE), he was posted to Lower Moesia as tribune of the legion V Macedonia which was stationed there (*LH* 2.3). Perhaps it was this visit which occasioned the 'Adventus Type' issue. On the other hand, it seems more likely that Hadrian would have visited Moesia on his tour of the Rhine-Danube defence system in 121 or 122 CE and that this is the visit commemorated within the issue. A third possibility is the visit implied by *LH* 6.6 which took place in 118 CE shortly after Hadrian came to power. Because of its strategic location, the region of Moesia was heavily fortified with a Roman military presence. In addition to the V Macedonia garrisoned at Tromesmis, Lower Moesia had two other legions serving within its provincial boundaries, I Italica located in Novae, and XI Claudia located at Ducortorum. The province of Upper Moesia also contained two legions, IV Flavia located at Singudunum and VII Claudia located at Viminacium.

118. Pliny, *Natural History* 3.149.
119. *RIC* Hadrian 926.

23. *Noricum*—represented by two examples, one of the 'Adventus Type' and one of the 'Exercitus Type'. The first of these[120] again shows Hadrian wearing the short military tunic and boots. The female personification also wears the military tunic and supports a vexillum with her left hand. Both of her characteristic features serve to emphasize the military importance of the province. The inscription ADVENTVI AVG NORICI surrounds the scene with S C in exergue. The military theme is further emphasized by the 'Exercitus Type' issue (Figure 38).[121] On this reverse the Emperor stands on a platform, along with the praetorian prefect, and addresses an officer and three soldiers, one atop a horse. The officer faces the other troops and holds a sword. The four soldiers hold a shield, a standard, an aquila and a standard respectively. The fourth soldier sits on the horse. A further standard is sometimes depicted in the background. The inscription EXERC NORICVS SC stands in exergue.

We have no mention of a visit by Hadrian to the province, but he could have passed through Noricum on his way to Moesia in 118 CE (*LH* 6.6). Alternatively, he could easily have visited the province as part of his inspection of the Rhine-Danube defence system in 121–122 CE. Noricum had no legions permanently stationed within her borders, but many detachments from the neighbouring areas of Upper and Lower Pannonia would have seen service there. In addition, we should not forget the importance of Noricum as a recruiting ground for auxiliary troops, particularly cavalry. The 'Exercitus Type' is thus well-suited to this province as a military centre.

| Figure 38 | Figure 39a | Figure 39b |

24. *Pannonia*—represented by a single example of the 'Province Type'. It is slightly irregular compared to the rest of the coins in the series in that it was issued under the name of Lucius Aelius Caesar and not the Emperor Hadrian himself. Thus the obverse of the coin (Figure 39a)[122] is

120. *RIC* Hadrian 904.
121. *RIC* Hadrian 927.
122. *RIC* Aelius 1059.

different from the one normally found in the series and shows a bust of Aelius with a surrounding inscription of L AELIVS CAESAR. The reverse of the coin (Figure 39b) shows the female personification of Pannonia, wearing a mural crown, with her head turned to one side. She is draped in a long, flowing gown which she gathers up in her left hand. In her right hand she holds a vexillum. The inscription TR POT COS II surrounds the scene, while PANNONIA and S C stand in the field on either side of the personification. The reference to the second consulship of Aelius allows us to date the coin precisely to 137 CE.

We know that Aelius was adopted by Hadrian as son and heir in 136 CE (*LH* 23.11-12; *Life of Aelius* 1.2; 2.1-2, 6). We also know that in 137 CE Hadrian placed Aelius in charge of the two provinces of Pannonia (*LH* 23.13; *Life of Aelius* 3.2, 5-6), where he enjoyed some military success. It was in connection with this appointment that Aelius received

Figure 40   Figure 41

his second consulship. Unfortunately, the young Caesar appears never to have had robust health. He returned to Rome from Pannonia just prior to his untimely and mysterious death by poison (*Life of Aelius* 3.7–4.8; 6.1-7).

Hadrian had himself served as Trajan's praetorian legate to II Adiutrix in Lower Pannonia in 107 CE (*LH* 3.9), so he was familiar with the region and the requirements of the governorship there.

We can assume that since no other examples of the 'Travel Sestertia' are given over to the region of Pannonia, Hadrian intended this issue of Aelius to serve as the region's contribution to the series. It speaks of the special regard in which Aelius was held, and we should not be overly concerned that the coin falls rather late (137 CE) within the possible time range of the series (134–138 CE). No doubt the specialized issue was intended both to highlight the successor to the Imperial throne and to magnify the important role of Pannonia within the military structure of the Empire by showing the personification holding a vexillum. The region of Pannonia had four legions stationed within its borders, X

Gemina at Vindobona, XIV at Carnuntum, I Adiutrix at Brigetioni and II Adiutrix at Aquincum.

25. *Phrygia*—represented by two examples, one of the 'Restitutor Type' and one of the 'Adventus Type'. I have already suggested that by the region 'Phrygia' is meant the provinces of Galatia and Lycia and Pamphylia.[123] The first of these coins depicting Phrygia[124] shows the personification of the region wearing a short tunic, a chlamys and boots. On her head is the identifying Phrygian cap. In her left hand she carries a pedum, a shepherd's throwing stick. The inscription RESTITVTORI PHRYGIAE surrounds the scene with the letters S C in exergue. It is these two characteristic features of Phrygia, the cap and the pedum, that we see repeated in the presentation of the personification in the second example from the 'Adventus Type' (Figure 40).[125] The inscription ADVENTVI AVG PHRYGIAE surrounds the scene with the letters S C again in exergue. Toynbee stresses the use of the pedum within the presentation, 'for it reveals at once that the 'province' is here represented as contributing to the Empire the cult of Cybele and of her youthful lover, the Phrygian shepherd Attis'.[126] Hadrian probably visited the region of Phrygia in the summer of 123 CE as part of his tour through Asia Minor while on his first extended journey to the east.

26. *Raetia*—represented by two examples of the 'Exercitus Type' corresponding to the two main scenes from that group (there is some variation in the details). The first example[127] depicts Hadrian standing on the customary platform as he addresses three soldiers, all of whom carry shields and standards. The inscription EXERCITVS surrounds the scene with the letters S C in exergue. The second example (Figure 41)[128] shows Hadrian on horseback addressing four soldiers. The first soldier holds an aquila while two others hold standards and a vexillum. The inscription EXERCITVS is at the top of the scene while RAETICVS is in exergue.

---

123. Occasionally the province of Lycia and Pamphylia (it was a single unit in terms of Roman administration) is associated with Cilicia.

124. *RIC* Hadrian 962.

125. *RIC* Hadrian 905.

126. *Hadrianic School*, p. 127.

127. *RIC* Hadrian 930.

128. *RIC* Hadrian 929.

As in the case of the neighbouring province of Noricum, we have no confirmed record of a visit by Hadrian to this province. He may have visited the area on his tour of inspection of the Rhine-Danube frontier in 121–122 CE. Certainly this issue was to honour the importance of Noricum as a military centre within that sensitive region. As with Noricum, there was no legionary force permanently stationed within the province, although detachments of nearby forces would have been present.

27. *Sicilia*—represented by three examples, one of the 'Province Type', one of the 'Restitutor Type' and one of the 'Adventus Type'. The first example[129] is very rare and details of the reverse are extremely sketchy, based on a poorly preserved specimen in Paris. However, we do know that there is a dupondius type which is similar in many of its features and appears to have been issued as a companion to the sestertius.[130] It shows a triskelis with a Medusa-head as its central motif. The image is firmly associated with Sicily as being a three-cornered island.[131] The inscription SICILIA surrounds the figure and the letters S C stand in exergue.

The second example[132] shows the Emperor draped and raising the female personification of Sicilia who wears the triskelis on her head. In her left hand she holds some corn-ears; Sicilia was one of the most important centres for grain within the Roman world. The inscription RESTITVTORI SICILIAE surrounds the scene with S C in exergue. The third example[133] shows the Emperor in a short military tunic and boots hailing the personification of Sicilia who, once again, wears the triskelis on her head and carries corn-ears in her left hand. The inscription ADVENTVI AVG SILICIAE surrounds the scene and the letters S C stand in exergue.

Hadrian is mentioned in *LH* 13.3 as visiting Sicilia in the summer of 125 CE at the end of his first extended tour of the Empire. Spartianus tells us he climbed Mount Etna while there in order to see the beautiful sunrise. From Sicilia he returned to Rome, thereby concluding his first journey around the Empire.

129. *RIC* Hadrian 871.
130. The dupondius is *RIC* Hadrian 966.
131. Lucretius, *On the Nature of the Universe* 1.716-717, mentions this tradition.
132. *RIC* Hadrian 965.
133. *RIC* Hadrian 906.

28. *Syria*—represented by two examples of the 'Exercitus Type' corresponding to the two major scenes within that group. There are many varieties of these two main scenes for the province of Syria.[134] The first example[135] shows Hadrian on horseback with his arm raised while addressing three soldiers. The first soldier carries an aquila while the other two support standards. The inscription EXERCITVS is at the top of the scene with SYRIACVS S C in exergue. The second example[136] depicts the Emperor on a platform in military tunic and cloak with a sceptre in his left hand. He addresses three soldiers, all of whom carry shields and standards. The inscription EXERCITVS is at the top of the scene with SYRIACVS in exergue. The letters S C stand in the field on either side of the scene.

The Emperor Hadrian was well-acquainted with the province of Syria, having been appointed its governor by Trajan in 114 CE (*LH* 4.1; *Hist.* 69.2.1) and remaining such until Trajan's death (*LH* 4.6).[137] There are hints of 'bad blood' between Hadrian and the residents of Antioch (*LH* 14.1). Perhaps the Emperor's experiences as governor had soured his opinion of the province, and that is why it enjoys no issue within the 'Province Type' or the 'Adventus Type' of sestertia. Instead its place within the 'Exercitus Type' was virtually imperative since Syria was so vital militarily. It was among the most heavily fortified of Rome's provinces and protected the eastern flank of the Empire from the Parthians. A total of three legions were stationed within the province, XVI Flavia in Samosata, and IV Scythia and III Gallica both stationed near Antioch.

29. *Thracia*—represented by a single example of the 'Adventus Type'. This sestertius[138] shows the Emperor wearing a toga and greeting the personification in accordance with the standard pattern of the type. The female personification of Thracia is undistinguished in her costume, a short tunic, and does not carry any characteristic attribute associated with her province. Her left arm is by her side. This lack of identifiable features may reflect the fact that Thracia had only recently been

---

134. *RIC* lists seven varieties, more than any other province or region within the group.

135. *RIC* Hadrian 933.

136. *RIC* Hadrian 936.

137. Cassius, Dio *Hist.* 2.1-2, tells of a portent of Hadrian's succession to the throne while he was governor of Syria. Apparently he was offering sacrifice on Mount Casius near Antioch when lightning struck. See also *LH* 14.3.

138. *RIC* Hadrian 907.

elevated to provincial status by Trajan and had yet to make her contribution to the Empire's diversity in a way recognizable by a visual symbol. Hadrian probably visited the province early in 124 CE on his way to Athens from Samothrace. While in the province he probably founded the city of Hadrianopolis (*Life of Elagabalus* 7).

Summary

I have attempted to show how the series of 'Travel Sestertia' are reflective of the Emperor Hadrian's interest in the various provinces and regions which made up the Empire at that time. As a coin series they stand as a unique record of the Roman world as it was during the reign of Hadrian. In the end, we have a better grasp not only of this wandering Emperor himself, but also of the world that he ruled for over twenty years. In the next two chapters I shall move to consider specific topics relevant to New Testament studies which make use of this survey of the life and movements of Hadrian.

Chapter 7

HADRIAN AND THE NERO *REDIVIVUS* MYTH

The Nero *redivivus* myth is a standard interpretative feature in most commentaries on Revelation. Virtually every major commentary on Revelation mentions the myth to some degree, where it has most often been applied to cryptic passages in chs. 13 and 17.[1] For instance, in 13.3 we find that the Nero myth is alluded to in order to explain the curious description of the seven-headed beast as having one of its heads slain and remarkably revived. This description of a fatal wound to one of the heads which is later healed is continued in two other verses of the chapter (13.12, 14). The identification of the beast as a symbol of Nero is confirmed via the use of *gematria* in the form of the number 666 in 13.18.[2] It is highly probable that underlying the beast imagery is the Imperial cultus as it was practised in Asia Minor.[3]

We also find use of the Nero *redivivus* myth in 17.8-11 where the creature of seven heads and ten horns is described as the beast (το θηρίον)[4] which 'was and is not and is about to rise out the abyss' (ἦν

1.   H.B. Swete, *The Apocalypse of St John* (London: Macmillan, 1909), p. 164, notes that Victorinus of Petau (died 303 CE) was the first commentator on the book of Revelation to discuss the Nero *redivivus* myth in connection with the cryptic passages in chs. 13 and 17.

2.   This is if we take the cryptic number to have the Greek characters of ΝΕΡΩΝ ΚΑΙΣΑΡΩΝ in mind. This suggestion is well supported by the fact that Irenaeus, *Haer.* 5.28.2, mentions a variant reading of 616 in Rev. 13.18 within some Latin manuscripts. In the Latinized spelling of ΚΑΙΣΑΡΩΝ the final N would be dropped and yield the altered number. On the whole issue see A.Y. Collins, 'Numerical Symbolism in Jewish and early Christian Apocalyptic Literature', *ANRW*, II.21.2, pp. 1221-87.

3.   As suggested by S.J. Sherrer, 'Signs and Wonders in the Imperial Cult', *JBL* 103 (1974), pp. 599-610.

4.   Philostratus, *Life of Apollonius of Tyana* 4.38, also calls Nero a θηρίον. Also note the description in *Sib. Or.* 8.157 where Nero is called a great beast (θὴρ μέγα).

καὶ οὐκ ἔστιν καὶ μέλλει). The beast is certainly a symbol of the Roman Empire, personified in the Roman Emperor himself.[5] The unusual three-fold temporal description (past/present/future) stands as an echo of the Nero *redivivus* myth in which Nero is both the Emperor who was (that is, in his own historical reign from 54–68 CE), and the Emperor who is about to return from the abyss (in the form of a future ruler, the Nero *redivivus*). Such an interpretation is supported by the references to the kings in Rev. 17.10 in which five of the kings are said to have already fallen, one presently rules, and the seventh is yet to reign. Following these seven rulers there shall arise an eighth who is described as also being one of the previous seven. It is this link between the eighth ruler and the other seven which is strongly suggestive that the Nero *redivivus* myth underlies the passage in Rev. 17.6.[6] Let us examine this interesting section of Rev. 17.8-11 more closely.

Various attempts to ground the passage in Roman Imperial history have been made. A listing of three possible suggestions will serve to

5.   R.H. Charles, *Revelation*, II (ICC; repr.; Edinburgh: T. & T. Clark, 1976 [1920]), pp. 58-62, offers a suggestion as to how the dual description of the beast as representing both Roman Empire and Emperor arises. He sees this as due to the author's use of two different apocalyptic sources (17.1-10 and 17.11-18) which originally identified the beast as the Empire and Emperor respectively. We should not take the sources to be necessarily at variance with each other, however. It would be very easy and natural for a shift in understanding to be made between the two. The author of Revelation is simply stating that the Empire's policies and attitudes are personified in its leader.

6.   The political upheaval following Nero's death is certainly responsible for helping to create an atmosphere of eager expectation and excitement concerning what the future held in store. As far as can be determined, Nero committed suicide on the night of 8 June 68 CE (although note the alternative suggested by B. Reece, 'The Date of Nero's Death', *AJP* 90 [1969], pp. 72-74). His reign was followed by a quick succession of three Emperors within the span of 18 months. Galba reigned from June of 68 to January of 69 CE; Otho reigned from January to April of 69 CE; Vitellius reigned from April to December of 69 CE. Only when Vespasian came upon the scene in December of 69 CE was stability returned and confidence in the Emperor restored. On this traumatic year of 68–69 CE see G.E.F. Chilver, 'The Army in Politics, AD 68–70', *JRS* 47 (1957), pp. 29-35; P.A. Brunt, 'The Revolt of Vindex and the Fall of Nero', *Latomus* 18 (1959), pp. 531-59; J.B. Hainsworth, 'Verginius and Vindex', *Historia* 11 (1962), pp. 86-96; P.A.L. Greenhalgh, *The Year of the Four Emperors* (London: Weidenfeld & Nicolson, 1974); D.C.A. Shotter, 'A Time-Table for the *Bellum Neronis*', *Historia* 24 (1975), pp. 59-74; L. Daly, 'Verginius at Vesontio: The Incongruity of the *Bellum Neronis*', *Historia* 24 (1975), pp. 75-100; K. Wellesley, *The Long Year AD 69* (London: Paul Elek, 1975).

demonstrate the difficulties involved.[7] One attractive possibility is to begin reckoning the Emperors, as symbolized by the heads of the beast, from Nero, Galba, Otho, Vitellius and Vespasian. This reckoning places Titus on the throne at the time of the writing ('the one who is') and Domitian assumes his place as the one who will soon appear and rule for a short while. Perhaps the succession of Titus by Domitian was already foreseen by the politically astute. After Titus's reign the stage is then set for the anti-Christ, Domitian, as the Nero *redivivus*,[8] whose appearance will usher in the eschatological events which bring the world to an end.

A second possible reckoning,[9] which is a slight variation on the first, is to begin counting the Emperors from Caligula and count the five who have already passed as Caligula, Claudius, Nero, Vespasian and Titus. Domitian thereby becomes the Emperor alive at the time of the writing of Revelation and the seventh and eighth rulers are to appear soon in connection with the eschatological events which bring the world to an end. As will readily be noticed, this reckoning omits Galba, Otho and Vitellius from the calculations, no doubt due to their short periods of rule.[10] This suggested interpretation has the additional feature of conformity to the tradition mentioned by Irenaeus[11] about the composition of the Revelation by John during the reign of Domitian.[12]

A third possibility is mentioned by J. Bishop. He suggests that the five fallen Emperors might be those of the Julio-Claudian line: Augustus, Tiberius, Caligula, Claudius and Nero. The present ruling Emperor then

7. For an excellent introduction to this issue see A.Y. Collins, 'Myth and History in the Book of Revelation: The Problem of its Date', in B. Halpern and J.D. Levenson (eds.), *Traditions in Transformation: Turning Points in Biblical Faith* (Winona Lake, IN: Eisenbrauns, 1982), pp. 377-403. Also worth noting is J.M. Court, *Myth and History in the Book of Revelation* (Atlanta: John Knox, 1979), pp. 122-53.

8. Domitian is called a second Nero in Juvenal, *Satires* 4.38.

9. As is argued in L. Brun, 'Die romischen Kaiser in der Apokalypse', *ZNW* 26 (1927), pp. 128-51, and A. Strobel, 'Abfassung und Geschichtstheologie der Apokalypse nach Kap. XVII. 9-12', *NTS* 10 (1963–64), pp. 433-45.

10. It is questionable whether any attempt to calculate the Emperors which overlooks the three of the year of Civil War is a viable option, especially in light of the fact that Josephus, *War* 9.9.2; Suetonius, *The Twelve Caesars; 4 Ez.* 11–12; and *Sib. Or.* 5.12-51 all include them in their historical listings.

11. *Haer.* 5.30.3. The tradition is also quoted by Eusebius, *Hist. Eccl.* 3.18.3.

12. A date during Domitian's reign is a debated point. For discussion see A.Y. Collins, 'Myth and History', pp. 379-81, and B. Newman, 'The Fallacy of the Domitian Hypothesis', *NTS* 10 (1963–64), pp. 133-39.

becomes Galba, with the one who will shortly appear and reign a little while being Otho. It is following the brief reign of Otho that the stage is set for the return of Nero and the *redivivus* myth becomes operative. Such an interpretation means that an early date for the writing of Revelation can also be suggested. As Bishop says, 'the author is perhaps writing in 69 during the brief reign of Galba as Galba's power is tottering and Otho is talked of as his successor'.[13] The use of the Nero *redivivus* myth by the author of Revelation does not necessarily demand an early date for Revelation, however. Bishop himself goes on to say that a later date is also possible, in many ways even more probable:

> [The author] was writing in the early second century, a refugee from a later wave of persecutions, and using the events of 64 to 69 in Rome as a cloak for his view of his own times... To the author of Revelation the cheap and nasty legend of the risen Nero would seem the perfect legend for the anti-Christ, ever opposed to the truly and gloriously Risen Lord of his own faith.[14]

Regardless of how we calculate the Emperors and the symbolic heads, and the permutations are virtually endless, it appears that the Nero *redivivus* myth is set within a schematization of history and is being used by the author of Revelation to proclaim to his intended audience the nearness of eschatological events.[15]

The fact that ancient Jewish and Christian authors were able to find new and creative means of applying the Nero *redivivus* mythology to their own situations is particularly interesting. Are we able to detect any further influence of the myth within apocalyptic texts of the second century? In particular, is there any evidence for the association of the Emperor Hadrian with the figure of Nero *redivivus* within documents generally dated to Hadrian's reign? Is there any evidence to suggest that Hadrian himself was ever thought of as Nero *redivivus*? These questions demand a fuller investigation and yield some interesting results. Let me begin by taking note of the origin and extent of the Nero *redivivus* myth as it occurs in ancient sources. We will also want to pay particular atten-

13. *Nero: The Man and the Legend* (London: Robert Hale, 1964), p. 173. A.A. Bell, 'The Date of John's Apocalypse: The Evidence of Some Roman Historians Reconsidered', *NTS* 25 (1978–79), pp. 93-102, similarly argues for a composition date of around 68–69 CE during the reign of Galba.

14. *Nero*, p. 174.

15. As J.J. Collins, 'Pseudonymity, Historical Reviews and the Genre of the Revelation of John', *CBQ* 39 (1977), pp. 329-43, notes.

tion to the ways in which the myth is developed in subsequent literature and applied to new historical contexts and situations, including the early second-century reign of Hadrian.

1. *Origin and Development of the Nero Redivivus Myth*

M.P. Charlesworth[16] suggested a generation ago that there were three conditions necessary for belief in the 'return' of a deceased historical figure to develop. These three conditions were 1) a widespread popular affection for the figure by people who regarded the deceased as their benefactor or defender; 2) a general feeling that the figure concerned died leaving his work incomplete; 3) mysterious or suspicious circumstances surrounding the figure's death. As Charlesworth powerfully argues, each of these conditions was fulfilled in the case of Nero, hence the rise of the *redivivus* myth. In the beginning, immediately after Nero's death, the rumours were that Nero had not really died but merely escaped to the east. Eventually the expectations took on a different emphasis and began to focus on Nero's resurrection from the dead and his coming return with a violent and powerful army. In effect, it seems clear that the expectations of Nero's 'return' became progressively distanced from the historical Nero and developed into an elaborate and complex mythology. This development raises some very interesting questions about the application of these Nero *redivivus* myths to later historical figures. How do the myths remain relevant to a later generation? In what ways can they be re-applied to a subsequent historical figure, such as Hadrian? Are we able to trace any of that re-application process?

One of the most extensive treatments of the complex Nero *redivivus* myths is that of J.J. Collins.[17] Collins enters into discussion of the myth by way of extended passages in *Sib. Or.* 5. There the Nero myth, in various forms, occurs in five passages, 5.28-34; 5.93-110; 5.137-61; 5.214-27 and 5.361-80. The importance of *Sib. Or.* 5 for our understanding of the myth cannot be overestimated since it contains much of the most significant material of the myth. However, we are not wholly dependent upon it for our knowledge of the legend as it existed in antiquity. We also find reference to the Nero *redivivus* legends in Tacitus, *Histories* 2.8-9; Cassius Dio, *Hist.* 64.9; and Suetonius, *Nero* 57. In

16. 'Nero: Some Aspects', *JRS* 40 (1950), pp. 69-76.
17. *The Sibylline Oracles of Egyptian Judaism* (SBLDS, 13; Missoula, MT: Scholars Press, 1974).

addition, important material is also contained within several other sections
of the *Sib. Or.,* including 3.63-74; 4.119-24, 137-39; 8.65-72, 139-59;
and 12.78-93.[18] Finally, mention must be made of both the *Asc. Isa.* 4.1-
2 and John Chrysostom, *Orations* 21.10, since both of these Christian
writers apply the Nero *redivivus* myth to the prevailing expectations of a
mythical anti-Christ/Belial figure.[19]

However, it is on the passages in *Sib. Or.* 5 that I focus my discussion, and I shall turn to Collins's work to help to guide us in our understanding of the Nero myth and its development. Collins has sought to
demonstrate the various stages of the development of the Nero *redivivus*
myth from its original focus on the historical figure of Nero to its full-
blown mythical and legendary dimensions. In other words, Collins seeks
to demonstrate how the Nero *redivivus* myth moves from one which
emphasizes the historical return of an Emperor whose death was
surrounded by unusual circumstances and shrouded in mystery, to one
in which the figure of Nero is intimately tied up with the mythical,
eschatological adversary of God. The former, which emphasizes the
historical dimension, Collins calls the 'non-Jewish' or 'pagan' legend. The
latter, which emphasizes the cosmic and eschatological dimension and
has little concern for the historical facts about Nero, Collins describes as
'Jewish' or 'mythological'. Basically Collins suggests three stages of
development of the Nero *redivivus* myth and groups the sources
accordingly: 1) pagan expectations about the historical return of Nero

---

18. Collins does not specifically discuss *Sibylline Oracles* 12 in his monograph
but does within his contribution on 'The Sibylline Oracles', in *OTP*, pp. 443-52. I
shall be reliant upon this work for my translations of the Oracles.

19. This is not the place to discuss these sources at length. That work has already
been admirably done by J. Lawrence, 'Nero Redivivus', *Fides et Historia* 11 (1978),
pp. 54-66, who collates all of the ancient sources which reflect the Nero myth up to
the fifth century. Lawrence's central contribution is the presentation of the relevant
primary sources. He does not deal at length with how the Nero myth becomes re-
applied and re-interpreted by various writers as time goes on. One interesting point
he does discuss is that there is some discrepancy within the sources as to whether
there were two or three original historical figures who claimed to be Nero *redivivus*.
On this issue, see A. Momigliano's article on 'Nero' in *CAH*, X, pp. 702-780;
A.E. Pappano, 'The False Neros', *CP* 32 (1937), pp. 385-92; S.J. Bastomsky, 'The
Emperor Nero in Talmudic Legend', *JQR* 59 (1969), pp. 321-25; P. Gallivan, 'The
False Neros: A Reexamination', *Historia* 22 (1973), pp. 364-65. The most thorough
recent discussion of the various texts is G.C. Jenks, *The Origins and Early
Development of The Antichrist Myth* (BZNW, 59; Berlin: de Gruyter, 1991).

(Tacitus, *Histories* 2.8-9; Cassius Dio, *Hist.* 64.9; Suetonius, *Nero* 57; *Sib. Or.* 4.119-24, 137-39; 5.28-34; 8.70-72, 138-59); 2) quasi-mythological expectations based on pagan legends of Nero's return but assimilated to Jewish apocalyptic forms (*Sib. Or.* 5.93-110, 137-61, 214-27, 361-80); 3) wholly mythological associations of Nero with Beliar, the eschatological adversary of God (*Asc. Isa.* 4.1-2; John Chrysostom, *Orations* 21.10; *Sib. Or.* 3.63-74).

Collins's own work based on *Sib. Or.* 5 is thus an investigation into the second stage of the development of the Nero *redivivus* myth. He dates *Sib. Or.* 5 between 70 and 132 CE and argues strongly for their Egyptian provenance.[20] The former date is provided by the frequent references to the destruction of the Jewish temple in Jerusalem and the latter is provided by the favourable references to Hadrian in verses 46-50 which seem to indicate that they were written before the bitter experiences of the Second Revolt.[21] For myself, I accept a date during the reign of Hadrian (117–138 CE) for several sections of *Sib. Or.* 5, for reasons which will soon become apparent.

There are several significant features within these five passages from *Sib. Or.* 5 which help us to identify the portrayal of Nero. These are 1) his part in the destruction of Jerusalem (5.107, 150-51);[22] 2) his murder of his mother Agrippina (5.30, 142, 224, 363);[23] 3) his claim to be God

20. 'The Provenance of the Third Sibylline Oracle', *BIJS* 2 (1974), pp. 1-18.

21. Collins, *OTP*, p. 390, detaches v. 51 from the body of the *Oracles*. This verse refers to Marcus Aurelius and was probably added to the extended section dealing with Hadrian after Aurelius had ascended the Imperial throne in 138 CE.

22. Although the destruction of the Second Temple did not in fact occur during Nero's reign, the First Jewish Revolt which precipitated it did break out while he was Emperor and the bulk of the war was fought while Nero was on the throne. This caused the Revolt and its aftermath to be forever linked with the memory of Nero. The destruction of Jerusalem is also described in 5.397-402 and 408-413 but it is quite clear in these passages that Titus is the culprit. A similar section is found in *Sib. Or.* 4.115-26. This is followed immediately by a passage which alludes to the eruption of Vesuvius which took place on 23-24 August 79 CE during Titus's reign and was thought by the author to be punishment upon Rome for its destruction of the city of Jerusalem (4.130-36).

23. See also Suetonius, *Nero* 34; Tacitus, *Annals* 14.1-13; Cassius Dio, *Hist.* 62.11-14. The reference to Nero's matricide is also retained in *Asc. Isa.* 4.2. The play *Octavia*, sometimes attributed to Seneca, has the matricide as one of its themes (especially lines 310-376), and contains much important information from a near-contemporary source. On this play see C.J. Herington, '*Octavia Praetexta*: A Survey', *CQ* 11 (1961), pp. 18-30; R.W. Garson, 'The Pseudo-Senecan Octavia: A

(5.34); 4) his favour in the East[24] and close association with Parthia (5.99-101, 147-49, 363);[25] 5) his construction of the canal at the isthmus of Corinth (5.32, 138-39, 217-18).[26]

Accepting that Collins's suggestion of three stages in the development

Plea for Nero?', *Latomus* 34 (1975), pp. 754-56; M. Carbone, 'The *Octavia*: Structure, Date, and Authenticity', *Phoenix* 31 (1977), pp. 48-67; T.D. Barnes, 'The Date of the Octavia', *Museum Helveticum* 39 (1982), pp. 215-17. The matricide itself, which took place in 59 CE, is the subject of much scholarly discussion. See W. Alexander, 'The Communique to the Senate on Agrippina's Death', *CP* 49 (1954), pp. 94-97; R. Katzoff, 'Where Was Agrippina Murdered?', *Historia* 22 (1973), pp. 72-78; R.D. Scott, 'The Death of Nero's Mother (Tacitus, Annals, XIV, 1-13)', *Latomus* 33 (1974), pp. 105-15; B. Baldwin, 'Nero and his Mother's Corpse', *Mnemosyne* 32 (1979), pp. 380-81. P. Gallivan, 'Suetonius and Chronology in the "de vita Neronis"', *Historia* 23 (1974), p. 312, places the murder between 23 March and 5 April.

24. Nero was particularly benevolent to the province of Asia. E.M. Sandford, 'Nero and the East', *HSCP* 48 (1937), pp. 75-103, stresses Nero's preoccupation with the east and his underlying desire to present himself as a successor to Alexander the Great.

25. The contrast between east and west is the subject of an extended passage in *Sib. Or.* 3.350-80. This section outlines the revenge of Asia (representing the East) upon Rome (representing the West). What is interesting is that this attack upon the west by the east is led by a woman (in Greek δέσποινα), generally taken to be a Cleopatra *rediviva* figure. Horace, *Odes* 1.37, is an important passage discussing the mythical development of the Cleopatra figure. On the subject see W.W. Tarn, 'Alexander Helios and the Golden Age', *JRS* 22 (1932), pp. 135-60; K.W. Meiklejohn, 'Alexander Helios and Caesarion', *JRS* 24 (1934), pp. 191-95; T.C. Skeat, 'The Last Days of Cleopatra', *JRS* 43 (1953), pp. 98-100; S. Commager, 'Horace, *Carmina* I.37', *Phoenix* 12 (1958), pp. 47-57; E. Kocsis, 'Ost-West Gegensatz in den Judischen Sibyllinen', *NovT* 5 (1962), pp. 105-110; J.V. Luce, 'Cleopatra as *Fatale Monstrum* (Hor., *Carm.* I.37.21)', *CQ* 57 (1963), pp. 251-57; A.T. Davis, 'Cleopatra Rediviva', *Greece and Rome* 16 (1969), pp. 91-94; J. Lindsay, *Cleopatra* (London: Constable & Company Ltd, 1971), pp. 355-80; J.J. Collins, *OTP*, p. 358; M. Wyke, 'Augustan Cleopatras: Female Power and Poetic Authority', in A. Powell (ed.), *Roman Poetry and Propaganda in the Age of Augustus* (London: Bristol Classical Press, 1992), pp. 98-140. It may well be that the Cleopatra *rediviva* mythology helped to pave the way for a similar evaluation of what might be expected from the philhellenic Nero.

26. The Corinthian canal of Nero is also mentioned by Philostratus, *The Life of Apollonius of Tyana* 4.24; Cassius Dio, *Hist.* 62.17; Pausanius, *Guide to Greece* 2.1.5; Josephus, *War* 3.540; Suetonius, *Nero* 19.2; Pliny, *Natural History* 4.9-11. Suetonius specifically mentions Nero's part in the opening ceremony of the construction of the canal.

of the Nero *redivivus* myth is correct, it is interesting to note how each of these features also appears in earlier sections of the *Sibylline Oracles* which Collins says reflect the 'non-Jewish' or 'pagan' stage of the Nero legend. Note these references: 1) his part in the destruction of Jerusalem (4.115-18, 125-27); 2) his matricide (4.121; 8.71; 12.81-82); 3) his claim to be God (12.86); 4) his favour in the East and close association with Parthia (4.145-48; 8.72); 5) his construction of the canal at the isthmus of Corinth (8.155; 12.84). In short, it appears that the themes were an integral part of the Nero *redivivus* myth, at least within its first two stages, and became part of its standard features as it developed. They served to identify Nero as the subject of the Oracle concerned by appealing to historical facts surrounding his life as Emperor. What has not yet been fully appreciated is the way in which several of these identifying historical features of the Nero *redivivus* myth, notably the first, third and fourth, have close parallels with the description of the Emperor Hadrian contained in several passages of the *Sibylline Oracles*. Let me examine this more closely. In so doing we will begin to appreciate that the *redivivus* myths become re-applied to a later Emperor in such a way that Hadrian was thought by the author or redactor of those sections to be Nero *redivivus*.

2. *Hadrian as Nero Redivivus*

Hadrian is associated in the Sibylline literature with the Nero *redivivus* legends we find deposited there in two ways. First of all, note the close redactional relationship that there is between sections describing Hadrian and sections describing Nero *redivivus*. That is to say that several of the descriptions of the Nero *redivivus* figure follow immediately after, or at least are proximal to, an extended description of Hadrian. Secondly, we also see hints of how several of the historical features which identified Nero within the myths themselves are adapted, transferred and re-applied to Hadrian. Both of these ways suggest that Hadrian himself was at one time understood by an author or redactor of several of the books of the Oracles to be Nero *redivivus*, or at least to be closely connected with the rise of the Nero *redivivus* figure. Both of these two means of association are worthy of further investigation.

Hadrian is specifically mentioned in four major sections of the *Sibylline Oracles*: 1) 5.46b-50; 2) 8.50-64; 3) 8.131-138; 4) 12.163b-175. In light of their literary nature it is very difficult to date precisely any of the *Sibylline Oracles*. Generally we can only suggest a date for the final redaction of a Sibylline book based upon the last identifiable historical reference recorded within the book concerned. If we apply this principle to those Oracles which speak of Hadrian, what dates suggest themselves for the final redaction of the three books concerned? Let me examine each of these three books on that basis, while at the same time paying particular attention to the redactional connection between the Hadrian passages and the Nero *redivivus* passages. The tone of the presentation of the Hadrianic passages is also a very important consideration.

a. *Sibylline Oracles 5: An Early Indirect Association*

As mentioned above, *Sib. Or.* 5 is to be dated no later than 130 CE, since the last clear historical reference is to Hadrian himself. Hadrian is positively presented and this would seem to indicate a date before the outbreak of the Second Revolt after which any Jewish presentation of Hadrian would almost certainly have been much more negative. I have already had occasion to note the extensive treatment of the Nero *redivivus* figure within *Sib. Or.* 5. At this point I simply call attention to the fact that those legends of eschatological judgment and destruction which involve Nero *redivivus* are set within a book of Oracles which was probably composed during Hadrian's reign. I also note that the Hadrian passage in 5.46b-50 is both preceded and followed by sections which speak of Nero *redivivus*.

5.28-34 (*Nero Redivivus*)[27]

> One who has fifty as an initial will be commander,
> a terrible snake, breathing out grievous war, who one day
> will lay hands on his own family and slay them, and throw everything
>   into confusion,
> athlete, charioteer, murderer, one who dares ten thousand things.
> He will also cut the mountain between two seas and defile it with gore.
> But even when he disappears he will be destructive. Then he will return
> declaring himself equal to God. But he will prove that he is not.

27. This section dealing with Nero falls within a historical survey of Roman rulers from the time of Julius Caesar up to Nero (5.12-50), and thus focuses primarily upon the historical reign of Nero as opposed to the Nero *redivivus* figure. However, the legend of Nero's return cannot be rigidly separated from statements about the historical Nero, as vv. 33-34 indicate.

5.46b-50 (*Hadrian*)

> After him another will reign,
> a silver-headed man. He will have the name of a sea.
> He will also be a most excellent man and he will consider everything.
> And in your time, most excellent, outstanding, dark-haired one,
> and in the days of your descendants, all these days will come to pass.

5.93-110 (*Nero Redivivus*)

> For the Persian will come onto your soil like hail,
> and he will destroy your land and evil-despising men
> with blood and corpses, by terrible altars,
> a savage-minded mighty man, much bloodied, raving nonsense,
> with a full host numerous as sand, bringing destruction on you.
> And then, most prosperous of cities, you will be in great distress.
> All Asia, falling to the ground, will lament for the gifts she enjoyed from
> you when she wore a crown on her head.

There are two intervening sections, namely 5.35-46a and 5.52-92, which break up the direct redactional connection between the Hadrian passage and the Nero *redivivus* passages. The former of these is a description of Roman Emperors from Galba to Trajan and serves to tie together Nero and Hadrian within a historical review of Roman Imperial successions. The second is an extended prophecy of eschatological judgment and doom which will fall upon Egypt. This description of coming destruction upon the nation of Egypt, which we must remember is the provenance of *Sib. Or.* 5, was probably part of the author's understanding of how the coming of Nero *redivivus* would adversely affect Egypt itself. The placing of 5.52-92 between the descriptions of Nero *redivivus* and Hadrian can probably be explained in that light. Note that in many of the manuscripts of *Sib. Or.* 5 there is a gap following line 91, and in some manuscripts a gap following line 92. This may indicate that 5.52-92 is indeed an insertion into the Oracles, which otherwise would have run directly from 5.50 to 5.93ff., thus connecting Hadrian and Nero *redivivus*. We can also catch a glimpse of how 5.52-92 may have come to be inserted into the Oracles in its present position if we note the concluding phrase of line 91, 'and the day of return (καὶ νόστιμον ἦμαρ)', which sets up the description of the return of Nero *redivivus* which follows in vv. 93-110.

What is not quite so clear is why Hadrian is presented so positively by the author of *Sib. Or.* 5 and yet, at the same time, why he is surrounded

by the descriptions of the evil Nero *redivivus*. Clearly Hadrian himself
was not thought by the author to be Nero *redivivus*. But in the mind of
the author of *Sib. Or.* 5 is Hadrian in some way connected with or
associated with the rise of the Nero *redivivus* figure? Perhaps the
answer to this question is to be found when considering more closely the
date of composition of the *Oracle*. Let us assume that the positive description of Hadrian is decisive in correctly determining that *Sib. Or.* 5
was written before the outbreak of the Second Revolt. What other hints
are to be found in the historical review of 5.12-50 which help us to
understand the historical situation in which the author or redactor was
working? Note that all three of the Flavian Emperors, Vespasian, Titus
and Domitian, are presented in 5.36-40a as evil and wicked rulers:

5.36-40a (*Flavian Emperors*)

> Then will come a certain great destroyer of pious men,
> who shows a clear initial of seven times ten.
> His son, with a first initial of three hundred, will get the better of him
> and take away his power. After him will be a commander,
> with an initial of four, a cursed man.

No doubt the memory of the debacle of the First Revolt is largely
responsible for this very negative presentation of the Flavians. In
contrast, Nerva is described in 40b-41a as 'a revered man' and is thus
positively presented. In a similar manner, Trajan is, for the most part,
positively presented in 41b-46a. At least there is no outright indictment
of either Nerva or Trajan as Emperors who stand against God and
pursue policies which persecute his people.[28] Perhaps it is the memory of
how an Emperor *could* act which sensitized the author to the future
appearance of another Emperor in the tradition of the Flavians or, for
that matter, Nero. The author perhaps looked to the Roman throne with
fear lest another Emperor rise to power and rule with the same cruelty
and viciousness as did Nero and the Flavians. Every new or future ruler
was viewed with suspicion and potentially represented Nero *redivivus*.
Hadrian himself might be worthy of praise, but what of his successor? It

---

28. There is a reference to Trajan's 'hastening to an Eastern war' in 5.43. It is
possible that this is an oblique reference to the Jewish Revolt which took place in
115–117 CE while he was Emperor, but it is more likely that it refers either to his
Dacian campaigns of 101–102 CE and 105–106 CE or the Parthian campaign of 114–
116 CE. On the subject see R.P. Longden, 'Notes on the Parthian Campaign of
Trajan', *JRS* 21 (1931), pp. 1-35.

is perhaps this dynamic which is in operation and helps to explain how Hadrian can be so positively presented himself while at the same time standing as a constant reminder of a force utterly opposed to God. Thus, the sheer fact of Hadrian's position as Emperor, with all the attendant associations and historical memories, means that Hadrian and the Nero *redivivus* have an indirect relationship. It is this connection which helps us to understand 5.49-50: 'and in your time, most excellent, outstanding, dark-haired one, *and in the days of your descendants*, all these days will come to pass'. It is no wonder that the narrative passes directly at this point to a description of the appearance of Nero *redivivus* and the effects upon Egypt of his rise (5.52-110).

The final three sections of *Sib. Or.* 5 which discuss the Nero *redivivus* figure (5.137-61, 5.214-27 and 5.361-80) do not refer back to Hadrian in any direct way but appear to follow the lead of 5.28-34 and 5.93-110 in suggesting that Nero *redivivus* was shortly to arrive on the political scene. Perhaps the author felt some of the tensions between the Roman Imperial structure and the province of Judaea, and could see that a clash was inevitable. Nero *redivivus* was bound to appear soon. All of the political and religious indicators seemed to point in that direction.

Thus we have in *Sib. Or.* 5 the presentation of Hadrian and Nero *redivivus* in such a way that the author or redactor is able to speak of the eschatological events which are signalled by the rise of the Nero *redivivus* figure as being on the horizon and intimately tied up with the Imperial throne itself. There is no direct assertion that Hadrian is himself Nero *redivivus* although an indirect association is set up between Hadrian, the present ruling Emperor, and the Nero figure.

b. *Sibylline Oracles 8: A Direct Association*

With regard to *Sib. Or.* 8, note that as it now stands the book probably dates to about 175 CE because of the reference to Marcus Aurelius (reigned 161–180 CE) contained in vv. 65-72. Yet in spite of the fact that Hadrian does not figure as the last identifiable figure in the Oracle, the description of the return of Nero follows on very closely from an extended discussion of Hadrian as the 15th king of Egypt in 8.50-64. Indeed, we only have to take vv. 65-70a to be a later update added in the time of Aurelius[29] to have the description of Hadrian given in 8.50-64. At the same time we note that the description of Hadrian in 8.131-

---

29. Collins has similarly argued that *Sib. Or.* 5.51 is a later update. See footnote 21 above.

38 is already immediately followed by an extended description of the return of Nero in 8.139-59.[30]

8.50-64 (*Hadrian*)

But when, luxurious one, you have had fifteen kings
who enslaved the world from east to west,
there will be a gray-haired prince with the name of a nearby sea,
inspecting the world with polluted foot, giving gifts.
Having abundant gold, he will also gather more
silver from his enemies and strip and undo them.
He will participate in all the mysteries of magic shrines.
He will display a child as god, and undo all objects of reverence.
From the beginning he will open the mysteries of error to all.
Then will be a woeful time, because 'the woeful' himself will perish.
One day the people will say, 'Your great power, O city, will fall,'
knowing that the fated evil day is immediately at hand.
Then fathers and infant children will mourn together,
regarding your most piteous fate.
Mournful, they will raise dirges by the banks of the Tiber.

8.70b-72 (*Nero Redivivus*)

So that when the blazing
matricidal exile returns from the ends of the earth
he will give these things to all and award great wealth to Asia.

8.131-38 (*Hadrian*)

Then the sixth generation of Latin kings
will complete its last life and abandon scepters.
Another king of the same race will reign
who will rule the whole earth and gain sway over dominions.

---

30. It is worth noting that line 139, which connects the Hadrian passage and the Nero *redivivus* passage, does not form a smooth transition from one subject to the other, but it does include an interesting linking motif. Collins, *OTP*, p. 421, renders it, 'Then when comes the time of the Phoenix, of the fifth period...' The reference to the phoenix is of great interest considering that the bird was commonly believed to return resurrected from its own ashes. Thus the phoenix might have served as a symbolic representation of the Nero *redivivus* passage which follows in 8.140-59. We do know that later Christian writers fasten on the symbolic myth of the phoenix as a means of expressing the Christian resurrectionfrom the dead. See S.M. McDonald, 'Phoenix *Redivivus*', *Phoenix* 14 (1960), pp. 187-206, for full details of the phoenix legend within ancient sources.

He will rule by the counsels of the great God without contamination,
his children and the race of his unshaken children.
For thus it is prophesied, in the cyclic course of time,
whenever there will have been fifteen kings of Egypt.

8.139-159 (*Nero Redivivus*)

Then when comes the time of the Phoenix, of the fifth period...
he will come to ravage the race of peoples, undistinguished tribes,
the nation of the Hebrews. Then Ares will take Ares captive.
He himself will destroy the overbearing threat of the Romans.
For the empire of Rome, which then flourished, has perished,
the ancient queen over the surrounding cities.
No longer will the plain of luxuriant Rome be victorious
when he comes from Asia, conquering with Ares.
Having done all these things, he will come to the trampled town.
You will fulfil thrice three hundred and forty-eight
years when an evil violent fate
will come upon you fulfilling your name.
Alas for me, thrice-wretched one, when will I see that day,
destructive indeed to you, Rome, and especially to all Latins?
Celebrate, if you wish, the man of secret birth,
riding a Trojan chariot from the land of Asia
with the spirit of fire. But when he cuts through the isthmus
glancing about, going against everyone, having crossed the sea,
then dark blood will pursue the great beast.
The hound pursued the lion that was destroying the herdsmen.
They will take away dominion, and he will pass over to Hades.

The intervening section (8.73-130) is an extended discussion of the eschatological judgment which will shortly fall upon Rome, and is similar to the section in *Sib. Or.* 5.52-92. It too details the doom and judgment which is part of the generalized worldwide calamity which accompanies the rise of the Nero *redivivus* figure.

In place of the historical review which I noted in *Sib. Or.* 5.12-50, there is in *Sib. Or.* 8 a description of Hadrian as the 15th king (8.50, 138). He is also noted to be the sixth generation of Latin kings (8.131), an interesting description in light of the fact that Hadrian was the sixth Emperor after Nero (providing we omit the brief reigns of Galba, Otho and Vitellius). In contrast to the positive presentation of Hadrian in *Sib. Or.* 5, here we note that the Emperor is presented in a very negative light. This suggests that the work may have been written after the beginning of the Second Revolt and Hadrian's measures to crush the rebellion have soured the evaluation of the Emperor by the author or redactor of the book. Perhaps it is this repressive policy toward the Jewish revolt which prompts the author's identification of Hadrian with the Nero *redivivus* figure. This identification helps to explain the close redactional relationship between those passages which describe Nero *redivivus* and the passage which describes Hadrian. Thus, we have in *Sib. Or.* 8 a direct association between Hadrian and the Nero *redivivus,* and his attitude and actions toward the people of God confirm this identification.

The transition points from the descriptions of Nero *redivivus* and the description of Hadrian are not very smooth and reflect the oracular nature of the material. The roughness of transition is also caused by the competing traditions that the Nero *redivivus* figure will come from the East, namely Parthia, and march against Rome. This is not an easy juxtaposition to make especially in light of the fact that Rome thereby has a dual function in the legends. As Collins has commented on this point as it occurs in *Sib. Or.* 5, this

> is merely part of the eschatological confusion... Nero appears both as
> king of Rome and its destroyer. The confusion was a natural combination
> of the view that Nero would return to destroy Rome with the view which
> saw Rome, like Nero, as an anti-Messiah.[31]

It is interesting to note how Hadrian is presented in 8.50-64. There are several descriptions which serve to identify Hadrian historically by referring to specific actions during his reign as Emperor. For instance, a reference to Hadrian's extensive journeys around the Empire occurs in v. 53. His admission to the Eleusinian Mysteries is alluded to in v. 56 and his attempt to propagate the cult of Antinous is mentioned in v. 57. Each of these three items is worthy of further comment for together they contribute to an understanding of Hadrian as another Nero-like Emperor and thus are supportive of the outright identification of Hadrian with Nero *redivivus* which I am suggesting that the author intended within his book of Oracles.

First of all, note that Hadrian's many travels around the Empire are mentioned in 8.53. I discussed his journeys in detail in Chapter 6 above, noting that he made at least two major journeys to the eastern half of the Empire. The first of these lasted from spring of 121 CE to autumn of 125 CE while the second lasted from spring of 128 CE to spring of

---

31. *Egyptian Judaism*, pp. 83-84.

134 CE. Most importantly for my consideration of *Sib. Or.* 8 is the fact that Hadrian visited the province of Judaea, including Jerusalem, in 130 CE while on his way to Egypt.[32] He so disrupted the life of the province of Judaea, which after all was never an easy one to govern, that he sowed the seeds of future dissatisfaction and rebellion. The full harvest was to be gathered in the Jewish Revolt of 132–135 CE. What was it precisely that Hadrian did to so antagonize the Jewish population that they responded in open rebellion? Spartianus tells us that the revolt was precipitated by Hadrian's ban on the practice of circumcision.[33] Cassius Dio, however, associates the revolt more firmly with this decision to found a new city, Aelia Capitolina, on the ravaged site of Jerusalem and erect a temple to Jupiter on the site of the Jewish temple there.[34] Several interesting colonial coins issued during the reign of Hadrian provide intriguing insights into Hadrian's official policy with regard to the city. These bronze coins, produced in the newly founded city and probably datable to 136 CE, have survived in small numbers. Because the coins are bronze it is difficult to find copies whose detail is clear and sharp (the metal is softer and oxidizes much more quickly than silver when it is buried in the ground). However, a fairly accurate composite picture can be reconstructed from the examples which have survived. Several examples are worth noting briefly. The reverse of one coin has a portrait bust of Hadrian, laureated and draped, surrounded by the inscription IMP CAES TRAIANO HADRIANO. The reverse depicts a team of oxen ploughing the first furrow in a new field, under the control of the Emperor Hadrian, who stands behind them (sometimes just off the field of the coin). A vexillum is planted in the background, and illustrates the

32. See W.F. Stinespring, 'Hadrian in Palestine, 129–130 AD', *JAOS* 59 (1939), pp. 360-65.

33. *LH* 14.2. See also R. Harris, 'Hadrian's Decree of Expulsion of the Jews from Jerusalem', *HTR* 19 (1926), pp. 199-206; S. Klein, 'The Hadrianic Persecution and the Rabbinic Law of Sale', *JQR* 23 (1932–33), pp. 211-31; E.M. Smallwood, 'The Legislation of Hadrian and Antoninus Pius against Circumcision', *Latomus* 18 (1959), pp. 334-47, and her 'Addendum', *Latomus* 20 (1961), pp. 93-96; H. Mantel, 'The Causes of the Bar Kokba Revolt', *JQR* 58 (1967–68), pp. 224-42 and 274-96; L.W. Barnard, 'Hadrian and Judaism', *JRS* 5 (1968–69), pp. 285-98; M. Gichon, 'New Insight into the Bar Kokhba War and a Reappraisal of Dio Cassius 69.12-13', *JQR* 77 (1986–87), pp. 15-43; A.M. Rabello, 'The Legal Condition of the Jews of the Roman Empire', *ANRW*, II.13, pp. 662-762; D. Golan, 'Hadrian's Decision to Supplant "Jerusalem" by "Aelia Capitolina"', *Historia* 35 (1986), pp. 226-39.

34. *Hist.* 69.12.1

Roman military presence. The reverse inscription reads COL AEL
KAPIT, declaring the Colony of Aelia Capitolina, while the word COND
in exergue proclaims Hadrian as the Founder (*conditor*) of the new site
(Figure 1 gives the obverse of the coin together with two views of the
reverse).[35] Another coin of the same date similarly presents an obverse
portrait of the bearded Emperor Hadrian, laureated and facing right,
surrounded by the inscription IMP CAES TRAI HADRIAN AVG. The
reverse of the coin shows the god Jupiter Capitolinus seated on a throne
which is placed within a temple; on either side of him are figures holding
spears. Surrounding the coin is the inscription COL AEL CAP, again
denoting the Colony of Aelia Capitolina (Figure 2). A third example
shows on its reverse another temple, slightly different in style, which has
a figure of a turreted god standing left and holding a globe in his right
hand and a spear in his left. The letters COND appear on the left of the
scene and CO AE CAP appears in exergue (Figure 3). A final example
is a coin issued by Hadrian's successor Antoninus Pius (138–161 CE).
The obverse of the coin shows a bust of Antoninus, laureated and facing
right, with a surrounding inscription which reads IMP AEL HAD ANT.
The reverse shows a bust of the Egyptian god Serapis wearing a modius

Figure 1   Figure 2

on his head, while the inscription surrounding the bust reads COL AE
CAP (Figure 4). The coin illustrates how Hadrian's policy of reforming
the life of the city, including the introduction of other religions, was
carried on by the Roman Emperors who succeeded him.

In any event, the journeys of Hadrian to the east would have been
remembered by the Jewish people as particularly ominous, and we see
something of the memory helping to shape the negative assessment of
the Emperor in these verses from *Sib. Or.* 8. Hadrian was primarily
remembered as the Emperor who commanded the forces responsible for
the destruction of Jerusalem. I noted above that this is precisely one of
the features which occurs in the Nero *redivivus* legends and reflects the

35. Sear, *Greek Imperial*, p. 114, lists this coin as 1249.

memory that the First Revolt began in Nero's reign. Thus it appears that here we have an understandable link between Nero and the presentation of Hadrian as Nero *redivivus*.

What about other points of comparison? Note that Hadrian's generosity to the eastern provinces, particularly Greece, is well documented and is reflected in 8.53b-55.[36] Not since the time of Nero had such care and attention been showered on the east. As C.E. Manning has commented,

> Though he was considerably older, there was much about Hadrian that was reminiscent of Nero. There was the same philhellenism, the same lavish generosity in giving shows and building theatres, the same interest in unorthodox innovation in architecture and engineering. Like Nero, his literary studies and in particular his poetic ambitions were of an extent and type that the senate considered unsuitable for the princeps.[37]

Nero himself visited Greece from autumn of 66 CE to December of 67 CE, staying in Corinth for most of his time in the province.[38] He did, however, make excursions to various sites, including Olympia and Delphi,

Figure 3

Figure 4

primarily to participate in the various festival games which were specially arranged in his honour. Thus it appears that Hadrian's attitude of benevolence and generosity to Greece and the East may well have

36. Hadrian visited the province of Achaia on both of his two major journeys to the east. He was particularly fond of the city of Athens within the province and lavished innumerable gifts upon the city, including a variety of extensive building projects. Perowne, *Hadrian*, p. 100, describes Athens as 'the city of his soul'. See *LH* 13.1, 6; 19.2-3, and Cassius Dio, *Hist.* 69.16.1-2. The subject is also discussed by Oliver, 'Documents', pp. 361-70.

37. 'Acting and Nero's Conception of the Principate', *Greece and Rome* 22 (1975), p. 173.

38. See K.R. Bradley, 'The Chronology of Nero's Visit to Greece AD 66/67', *Latomus* 37 (1978), pp. 61-72; P. Gallivan, 'Nero's Liberation of Greece', *Hermes* 101 (1973), pp. 230-34. The major sources for Nero's trip to Greece are Cassius Dio, *Hist.* 63; Suetonius, *Nero* 22-24; and *LH* 5.7.

brought to mind the similar policy of Nero a generation earlier. It may be that the author of *Sib. Or.* 8 is deliberately referring to Hadrian's eastern benevolence as a means of emphasizing his conformity to the pattern of Nero. In effect, this reflects that the author is portraying Hadrian as Nero *redivivus*.

With regard to Hadrian's entrance into the Eleusinian Mysteries, alluded to in 8.56, Spartianus tells us that Hadrian was enrolled as an initiate during an extended stay in Athens between September of 124 CE and March of 125 CE.[39] This occurred during Hadrian's first extensive journey to the East. Cassius Dio relates that Hadrian was also enrolled into the highest grade of the Mysteries during a second stay in Athens between August of 128 CE and March of 129 CE.[40] This occurred during Hadrian's second extensive journey to the East. It is noteworthy that the reference to Hadrian's own participation in the Eleusinian Mysteries in 8.56 is immediately followed by a reference to his propagation of the cult of Antinous in 8.57-58. Antinous was, of course, Hadrian's beloved heir who died tragically by drowning in the Nile in 130 CE during the Emperor's second tour of the East.[41] Hadrian sought to honour his deceased lover by enrolling him among the gods and setting up temples dedicated to his name. We mentioned above that one of the historical features used to identify the Emperor Nero was his claim to be god (as in *Sib. Or.* 5.34 and 12.86). In all likelihood this is a veiled reference to Nero's construction of the *Domus Aureus* and the huge 120-foot high bronze statue of himself that adorned its entrance. We know that the statue caused quite a stir when it was erected in Rome itself and it is usually pointed to as evidence of Nero's increasing megalomania (Suetonius, *Nero* 31.1). M.T. Griffin has commented that 'There had long been statues of the Emperor and members of his family set up in Rome, but the size of this monument clearly made a different impact, for colossal statues were traditionally reserved for the gods.'[42] Could it be that Hadrian's attempt to propagate a cult of Antinous is being deliberately mentioned by the Jewish author of *Sib. Or.* 8 with that

---

39. *LH* 13.1.

40. *Hist.* 69.11.1

41. *Hist.* 69.11.2-4 and *LH* 14.5. See the discussion above on pp. 160-61.

42. Griffin, *Nero*, p. 131. It is open to question whether a religiously sensitive Jew, such as the author of *Sib. Or.* 8, would have maintained this distinction between human portrait/representation of a god. To his mind, the whole episode would probably have smacked of blasphemy.

memory of Nero's religious arrogance in mind?[43] After all, Spartianus mentions that Hadrian re-erected the Colossus of Nero, moved it to another site and re-dedicated it to the Sun god.[44] It may well be that the attempt to propagate a cult of Antinous by Hadrian was seen as an extension of a similar move by Nero a generation earlier.[45] If so, we have once again an instance where the author of *Sib. Or.* 8 is re-applying aspects of the Nero *redivivus* myth to Hadrian, based on historical parallels between Hadrian's and Nero's reigns, and is thus speaking to his own historical situation.

Are there any other relevant sources of information which would help us to understand how Hadrian could come to be understood as Nero *redivivus*? There is one important source which is often overlooked: numismatic evidence. For example, there is a series of Imperial asses relevant to the matter which were issued by the mints at both Rome and Lugdunum from 62–68 CE. These coins have as their reverse a representation of Nero as the god Apollo, draped and advancing right, playing the lyre which he holds in his left hand (Figure 5) [46]. The same scene is also picked up by Hadrian's mints in Ephesus, Sardis and Smyrna within the province of Asia Minor and used as a reverse within the extensive cistophori coinage issued throughout most of Hadrian's reign. The reverse on this coin (Figure 6)[47] bears the inscription COS III in the field on either side of the representation of Apollo. Such coins provide indirect supportive evidence of just how closely Hadrian and Nero were associated at the beginning of the second century, and illustrate how Hadrian might have come to be viewed as a second Nero by the population at large. They demonstrate some very striking parallels between the coinage of

43. It may well be that ultimately the religious arrogance of Nero is itself a historical reapplication of sentiment originally focusing on the actions of Caligula in 40–41 CE in attempting to set up an image of himself as a Roman god in the temple of Jerusalem. P. Bilde, 'The Roman Emperor Gaius (Caligula)'s Attempt to Erect his Statue in the Temple of Jerusalem', *ST* 32 (1978), pp. 67-93, discusses the episode.

44. *LH* 19.12-13.

45. Or it could be that Hadrian's own association with the god Jupiter following his second journey to the east helped to prepare the way for a hatred of him as a blasphemous megalomaniac in the tradition of Nero. We know that in 129 CE the city of Ephesus produced a vast issue of cistophori which bore an obverse portrait of Hadrian and a reverse type of Jupiter. On this see Metcalf, 'Hadrian', pp. 59-66.

46. The series includes *RIC* Nero 73-82, 121-23, 205-212, 380-81, 384-85, 414-17, 451-55. The inscriptions on the reverses differ depending on their year of issue.

47. *RIC* Hadrian 482.

Nero and Hadrian, showing that a deliberate identification of the two Emperors was being made by Hadrian's moneyers.

Figure 5   Figure 6

What shall we conclude from this? It suggests that Hadrian may have deliberately styled himself after Nero, at least as far as the advertisement of his eastern policies on his coins is concerned. Hadrian's use of this Apollo reverse type is a convenient means of political propaganda to that end and certainly stands as indirect evidence for an understanding of Hadrian as a second Nero. It thus contributes to an overall atmosphere of identification of the two Emperors which I am suggesting is operative in *Sib. Or.* 8 since the author or final redactor of that book presents Hadrian as Nero *redivivus*.

Thus in *Sib. Or.* 8 we have a direct association, even identification, between Hadrian and Nero *redivivus* made by the author or redactor of the book. This is evidenced, first of all, by the way in which source material is presented, with descriptions of Nero *redivivus* surrounding the description of Hadrian. The outright identification of Hadrian with Nero *redivivus* is also suggested by the way in which the author has selected certain historical facts about Hadrian and recast them in such a way that the conformity of Hadrian to the pattern of Nero is emphasized. The association of Hadrian with Nero also appears to be a deliberate policy within the Imperial mint of Hadrian, and I have noted several examples of Neronic reverse types being used to that end with great effect. In light of this *Sib. Or.* 8 should be dated to the period immediately following the outbreak of the Second Jewish Revolt in 132 CE. It is the heightened atmosphere of tension and excitement which that Revolt inevitably brought which is responsible for the eschatological fervour capable of interpreting the distress and persecution suffered by the Jews, including the author, as confirmation that the end of the world had come. Nero *redivivus* had arrived in the person of the Emperor Hadrian.

c. *Sibylline Oracles 12: A Later Dissociation*

With regard to *Sib. Or.* 12 note that the book as it now stands probably dates to 235 CE because of the reference to Alexander Severus (reigned

222–235 CE) in verse 288. Unlike *Sib. Or.* 8 the description of Hadrian in 12.163b-175 is not followed by a description of the return of Nero. Indeed, *Sib. Or.* 12 contains no clear description of the Nero *redivivus* myth at all. Even v. 85, which speaks of the lingering influence of Nero after his death, does so not in terms which seem to reflect the Nero *redivivus* myth itself but in terms of the political upheaval of the years 68–69 CE. The description of Hadrian is clearly dependent upon *Sib. Or.* 8.50-64 and actually corrects that earlier passage at several points. It is an obvious attempt to portray Hadrian in a positive light, and reflects redactional forces to that end. Note, for instance, how Hadrian's travels are described in 12.167-68 as compared to 8.53b-55 and how the description of Hadrian's entry into the Eleusinian Mysteries and the propagation of Antinous's cult in 12.166, 169-70 compares to 8.56-58.

12.163b-175 (*Hadrian*)

> After him another will be prince,
> a silver-headed man. He will have the name of a sea,
> presenting the beginning of the alphabet, an Ares of four syllables.
> He will also dedicate temples in all cities,
> inspecting the world on his own foot, bringing gifts.
> Gold and much alloy he will give to many.
> He will also master all the mysteries of
> the magic shrines. Indeed the thunderbolt
> will give a much better ruler to men.
> There will be a long peace when this prince
> will be. He will also be a singer of splendid voice,
> sharer in lawful things, and a just legislator.
> He will fall, undone by his own fate.

The section which outlines Nero (12.78-94) falls within a generalized historical outline and focuses on the historical person of Nero and his reign as Emperor in 54–68 CE. In this context it retains several of the historical features mentioned above, including the description of Nero as a matricide (v. 82), the Corinthian canal episode (v. 84) and the claim to be god (v. 86).

12.78-94

> Another man of the number fifty will come again,
> terrible and frightful. He will destroy many
> who are outstanding in wealth from all the cities,
> a terrible snake, breathing grievous war, who one day

will lay hands on his own family and kill them and perform many things
as athlete, charioteer, murderer, one who dares ten thousand things.
He will also cut the mountain between two seas
and will defile it with gore.
But he will be destructive to the Italians, even when he has disappeared.
Making himself equal to God, he will convince a willing people.
There will be a deep peace when this man rules
and quaking of men. Cleaving the tide under the Ausonians,
he will reach the strange water from the stream of Oceanus.
Glancing about him, he will set up many contests for peoples,
and he himself will compete as a contestant
with voice and lyre, singing a song accompanied by strings.
Later he will flee, abandoning the royal dominion.
Perishing wretchedly, he will make amends for what he did.

Thus it appears that in *Sib. Or.* 12 both Nero and Hadrian are presented as historical figures and the mythological relationship between the two is no longer maintained.[48] That is to say, there is no indication that Hadrian was understood as Nero *redivivus* by the final author or redactor of *Sib. Or.* 12 in the same way as I observed was the case in *Sib. Or.* 8. Nor is Hadrian indirectly associated with the Nero *redivivus* figure as I noted in *Sib. Or.* 5. Perhaps the simplest conclusion that we can draw from these observations is that by the time that *Sib. Or.* 12 was composed in the mid-third century, enough time had elapsed to render meaningless any direct association of the Nero *redivivus* myths with Hadrian. He had been dead too long to allow any such association to be of any value for either the Emperor, or prospective Emperor, who was the redactor's contemporary and who directly affected the lives of him and his audience. Thus *Sib. Or.* 12 reflects a later dissociation of the Emperor Hadrian from the Nero *redivivus* figure.

Summary

I began this chapter by noting that the Nero *redivivus* myth underlies the description of the beast in Revelation 13 and 17. By using the myth the author of the Revelation addressed his own contemporary situation in such a way that the nearness of eschatological events was proclaimed and Roman Imperial history updated to his own time. This creative use

48. Yet it is worth mentioning that both Hadrian and Nero are described as having fine singing voices (vv. 12.173 and 12.92 respectively), recalling the mention above of the Apollo-type reverses on coinage of both Emperors.

of mythological material prompted me to consider whether the Nero *redivivus* myth is similarly re-applied in other literature dealing with eschatological matters. I examined *Sib. Or.* 5, 8 and 12 to that end and traced a progressive development of the use of the *redivivus* myth in its application to the Emperor Hadrian.

I noted that *Sib. Or.* 5 indirectly associates Hadrian with the expected rise of the *redivivus* figure and appears to identify the Nero *redivivus* with one of Hadrian's successors to the Imperial throne. *Sibylline Oracles* 5 was probably written about 130 CE prior to the outbreak of the Bar Kochba rebellion. *Sibylline Oracles* 8, however, goes a step further and actually identifies Hadrian as Nero *redivivus*, probably under the impact of the Second Jewish Revolt which was then raging. This outright identification is achieved in two ways, by redactional juxtaposition of material and by the selection and presentation of historical features of the two Emperors, Hadrian and Nero. *Sibylline Oracles* 12 appears completely to dissociate Hadrian and the Nero *redivivus* figure and break any mythological connection between the two. This dissociation is reflective of the third-century date of the book.

An important implication of this study is the apparent need of the Nero *redivivus* myth to have a degree of contemporary applicability— that is to say, that an author would use the mythology when it in some way enabled his audience to place themselves within the historical schematization that the myth implies. Myths, after all, if they are to retain their power, need to be relevant to the people using them. It goes without saying that a mythology focusing on Nero *redivivus* also implies that an atmosphere of hostility and persecution prevails. Nero was primarily remembered as an evil and wicked ruler by both Jews and Christians alike. It is no wonder that the outright identification of Hadrian and Nero *redivivus* occurs within a document which was written by a Jew during a time when Hadrian was engaged in an armed struggle with the Jewish people.

Chapter 8

THE ROMAN IMPERIAL *ADVENTUS* COINAGE OF HADRIAN
AND THE PAROUSIA OF CHRIST

> But when, luxurious one, you have had fifteen kings who enslaved the
> world from east to west, there will be a gray-haired prince with the name
> of a nearby sea, inspecting the world with polluted foot, giving gifts.
>
> (*Sib. Or.* 8.50-53)

So begins a passage from the *Sibylline Oracles* describing the Emperor
Hadrian (117–138 CE). In Chapter 7 I argued that within sections of
the *Sibylline Oracles* it is possible to trace an association between the
Emperor Hadrian and some prevailing eschatological myths of the day;
that is to say, those myths surrounding the shadowy and elusive figure
of Nero *redivivus*. It appears that the Jewish author(s) of the *Sibylline
Oracles* developed in his (their?) opinion of Hadrian, presenting a progressively more negative assessment of the Emperor, probably under
the influence of the bitterly contested Second Jewish Revolt of 132–135
CE, a conflict which was brutally crushed by Hadrian's legions. This
association of the Emperor Hadrian with the Nero legends, as seen
within the *Sibylline Oracles*, builds upon the fact that Hadrian pursued
an official Imperial policy in which he sought to portray himself as an
Emperor in the revived spirit of Nero. In particular, it seems clear that
Hadrian consciously adopted many of Nero's benevolent policies toward
the eastern half of the Empire.

One of the important secondary sources of evidence for Hadrian's
preoccupation with the Emperor Nero is the numismatic evidence of the
Imperial Roman mints. The fact the Hadrian borrowed some of Nero's
coin types for his official imperial mint issues, and used them as a means
of popular propaganda, is indisputable. In Chapter 7 I suggested that
Hadrian deliberately borrowed an image from coinage issued during
Nero's reign which presents the Emperor as the god Apollo playing the
lyre. Another particular coin type, initially used by Nero and later adopted

by Hadrian, is also of special interest for studies on Second Temple Judaism and Christian origins because it demonstrates a striking linguistic parallel to a very important term contained therein—παρουσία. There are coins minted at Corinth in 67 CE during Nero's reign which have a particular bearing on this point. These coins were local issues, struck in bronze by the officials of Corinth working under Roman auspices. Two of the reverse types depict a Roman galley as a symbol of Nero's travels in the East and carry the Latin inscription ADVEN(tus) AVG(usti) (Figure 1)[1] and ADLO(cutio) AVG(usti) respectively. They were obviously commemorative of Nero's visit to Corinth and his speech of liberation proclaiming the freedom of the city.[2] Hadrian adopts precisely these same two inscriptions within his own extensive official coinage commemorating his travels around the Empire. As I noted in Chapter 6, in the concluding years of his reign (from 134–138 CE), Hadrian produced a large and fairly comprehensive series of coins, gold, silver and bronze, which all bore the reverse inscription *Adventus Augusti* in some form.[3] These *Adventus* coins celebrated the arrival of the Emperor in the various provinces and bear inscriptions to that effect, usually accompanied by an additional inscription of the name of the province concerned.[4]

Figure 1

This numismatic evidence is often alluded to by scholars as they give background information about the term παρουσία itself. For instance, note the following three examples in which the Hadrianic coinage, along with the earlier Neronic types, is mentioned in passing. All three come from authoritative sources within New Testament research; indeed, the sources are often appealed to as foundational research tools illustrating

1.   Sear, *Greek Imperial*, p. 52, lists this coin as 555.
2.   The speech is preserved in an inscription from Acraephis in Boeotia. A translation is offered by Braund, *Augustus*, pp. 102-103.
3.   The *Adlocutio* type also occurs in a single issue of Hadrian's reign (*RIC* Hadrian 739); the reverse type was extensively used on Nero's Imperial coinage as well. Sestertia were issued between 63–67 CE with the same basic motif of an adlocution scene. See *RIC* Nero 95-97, 130-36, 371, 386-88, 429, 489-92, 564-65.
4.   *RIC* Hadrian 224-27, 315-20, 374, 740-42, 793-94, 872-907.

the milieu from which the idea of the parousia of Christ was to arise, grow and flourish. The first comes from the pen of no less an authority of the ancient world than A. Deissman:

> In memory of the visit of the Emperor Nero, in whose reign St. Paul wrote his letters to Corinth, the cities of Corinth and Patras struck advent coins. *Adventus Aug(usti) Cor(inthi)* is the legend on one, *Adventus Augusti* on the other. Here we have corresponding to the Greek *parusia* the Latin word *advent*, which the Latin Christians afterwards simply took over, and which is to-day familiar to every child among us. How graphically it must have appealed to the Christians of Thessalonica, with their living conception of the parusiae of the rulers of this world, when they read in St. Paul's second letter of the Satanic 'parusia' of Antichrist, who was to be destroyed by 'the manifestation of the parusia' of the Lord Jesus! A whole host of advent-coins resulted from the numerous journeyings of the Emperor Hadrian; we have specimens, I suppose, from most of the Imperial provinces, and these, it may be remarked, were official coinages of the Empire.[5]

The second example comes from G. Kittel's *TDNT*:

> The imperial period with its world ruler or members of his household... certainly invested the parousia of the ruler with even greater magnificence. This could be done by the inauguration of a new era...or by buildings... or by the minting of advent coins, e.g., in Corinth on the coming of Nero: *Adventus Augusti*, or the like. Hadrian's travels produced such coins in most provinces.[6]

The third example comes from Brown's *NIDNTT*:

> Technically the noun is used for the arrival of a ruler, a king, emperor or even troops from the Ptolemaic period to the 2nd century AD. Special payments in kind and taxes were exacted to defray the costs. In Greece a new era was reckoned from the *parousia* of Hadrian, and special advent coins were struck in various places to commemorate the *parousia* of an emperor. The corresponding Lat. term is *adventus*.[7]

---

5.   *Light from the Ancient East* (New York: Harper & Brothers, 1922, 4th edn), p. 371.

6.   A. Oepke, 'παρουσία', *TDNT*, V, p. 860.

7.   G. Braumann, 'παρουσία', *NIDNTT*, II, p. 898. Also note the discussion in E. Schürer, *The History of the Jewish People in the Age of Jesus Christ*, I (rev. and ed. G. Vermes, F. Millar and M. Black; Edinburgh: T. & T. Clark, 1973), pp. 541-42, and C. Spicq, *Theological Lexicon of the New Testament*, III (3 vols.; Peabody, MA: Hendrickson, 1994), pp. 53-55.

It seems clear that the inscription of the *Adventus Augusti* coinage provides a tantalizing linguistic link to the term παρουσία, as well as to the conceptually related ἀπάντησις.[8] I have already discussed some of these coins above in Chapter 6, noting the artistic representation on the reverses of a number of sestertia, as well as the range of inscriptions contained on them.[9] Within this short chapter my aims are two-fold. First, I shall build upon the historical framework of Hadrian's travels presented in Chapter 6 and give due attention to one particular issue within the 'Travel Sestertia' series; namely the *Adventus Augusti* coin associated with the province of Judaea. Second, I shall suggest some ways in which this numismatic evidence might help us to appreciate some later Christian understandings of the *parousia* of Christ, particularly as they were expressed in the interpretation of the Apocalypse of John.

1. *The Adventus Augusti Coin Series: The Judaea Sestertius*

Included within the 'Adventus Type' coins issued by Hadrian's imperial mints to commemorate his travels around the Empire was one proclaiming his arrival in Judaea. This sestertius[10] (Figure 2) conforms closely to the general pattern of coins within its type. It shows the figure of Judaea draped, with her head covered by part of her gown, sacrificing over an altar. She has one child in front of her and one behind her. Both children carry palm branches in their hands. The inscription ADVENTVI AVG IVDAEAE surrounds the scene with S C in exergue.

The presentation of the personification of Judaea is particularly worth noting. She appears draped in standard Graeco-Roman dress, with any reference to her provincial dress conspicuously absent. This may be a deliberate attempt to downplay any nationalistic tendencies or associations that provincial dress might have fostered in favour of presenting a provincial image more in keeping with Imperial interests. The emphasis

8.   Some argue that Paul's use of ἀπάντησις in the apocalyptic passage of 1 Thess. 4.17 also has as its background the civic custom of giving a public welcome to rulers upon their arrival in a city or district.

9.   The provinces in question are Africa, Arabia, Asia, Bithynia, Britannia, Cilicia, Gallia, Hispania, Italia, Judaea, Macedonia, Mauretania, Moesia, Noricum, Phrygia, Sicilia and Thrace. There is also an Adventus issue for the city of Alexandria. Note also that there are aurei of this reverse type for the provinces of Africa, Hispania and Italia as well as for the city of Alexandria. Denarii are extant for the provinces of Africa and Hispania.

10.   *RIC* Hadrian 890.

on the children highlights this concern, by visually presenting the idea of a new generation growing up under the advantages of Imperial rule. No

Figure 2

doubt the recent events of the Second Jewish Revolt of 132–135 CE were largely responsible for this obvious attempt to refashion the provincial image away from a militaristic one to a more domesticated one. The revolt of Bar Kochba was, after all, the only serious breach of the *Pax Romana* which characterized Hadrian's rule.[11] At the same time, it is easy to see how the portrayal of the personification of Judaea within the Hadrianic coinage must have been particularly galling to the Jewish nation.

2. *The Implications of the Adventus Augusti Coinage for a Study of the Parousia of Jesus Christ*

This is not the place to discuss the complex question about how a doctrine of the Second Advent of Christ arose within the Christian church. That ground is well trodden and the major pathways through its terrain seem clear, even though many important matters are still contested.[12] It

11. L. Mildenberg, 'Bar Kochba Coins and Documents', *HSCP* 84 (1980), p. 317, comments, 'For Hadrian [this revolt was] a personal affront to be avenged quickly and erased from memory. Apparently the Emperor considered neither the revolt itself nor even an allusion to the subduing of the rebels worthy of mention on his proclamatory coinage.' The precise historical details of the Second Jewish Revolt of 132–135 CE remain a matter of considerable scholarly debate. For an introduction to this issue see B. Isaac and A. Oppenheimer, 'The Revolt of Bar Kokhba: Ideology and Modern Scholarship', *JJS* 36 (1985), pp. 33-60. Recent studies also worth noting include S. Freyne, *Galilee from Alexander the Great to Hadrian, 323 BCE—135 CE: A Study of Second Temple Judaism* (Wilmington, DE: Michael Glazier, 1980); M. Mor, 'The Bar-Kokhba Revolt and Non-Jewish Participants', *JJS* 36 (1985), pp. 200-209.

12. I have discussed this subject at some length within my *Jesus and God in Paul's Eschatology* (JSNTSup, 19; Sheffield: JSOT Press, 1987), pp. 100-102.

is certainly true that the phrase 'the second advent (or coming)' appears for the first time in the writing of Justin Martyr,[13] immediately after Hadrian passed from the scene. But is that to say that the idea of the παρουσία (*adventus*) of the Roman Emperor, whether he be Nero or Hadrian or someone else, has no real relevance to our understanding of the New Testament documents, such as the Apocalypse of John, which clearly wrestle with this theme? It is true that the term παρουσία does not occur in the Apocalypse of John, but the idea of Christ's victorious triumph over the powers of evil at the end of history is foundational to the work as a whole and the theological idea of the παρουσία of Jesus Christ cannot be dismissed so easily from the work. Yet how does the Hadrian *Adventus Augusti* coinage help us to understand the concept?

Let me attempt to fit the pieces together. If we are correct in assuming that the Nero *redivivus* mythology does indeed underlie the descriptions of the beast from the sea in Revelation 13 and 17, and if we are correct in seeing that there was a strong tradition within Jewish apocalyptic writing (such as the *Sibylline Oracles*) which associated the Emperor Hadrian with that *redivivus* mythology, might we realistically expect that it is possible to draw a connection between the two ideas? Is this possibility not even more likely when we consider that a number of Jewish apocalyptic writings, in addition to the obvious Christian example of the genre we have in the New Testament, were being produced at around the same time; that is, around the time of Hadrian's reign as Emperor? The two most important examples, *4 Ezra* and *2 Baruch*, are sometimes dated, at least in their final edited forms, to the first part of the second century CE—that is, within Hadrian's reign. In other words, does the possibility that Hadrian might be the beast of Revelation 13 (the Nero *redivivus*) aid us in our understanding of the life situation of the church in Asia Minor when the Apocalypse of John was being copied, read and distributed by Christians in the province? It seems clear that, given the circumstantial evidence, we must at least entertain this as a real possibility.

However, one point of clarification needs to be interjected here. This is not to suggest that the Apocalypse of John should itself be dated as late as Hadrian's reign. The difficulties raised by such a suggestion seem to me insurmountable, and given the very nature of apocalyptic mythology are in the end unnecessary. Apocalyptic mythology is continually in need of reinterpretation in the light of fresh settings and

---

13. *Dialogue with Trypho*, 14.3 and 52.1. Note also *Apologia* 52.3. On this subject, see L.W. Barnard, 'Justin Martyr's Eschatology', *VC* 19 (1965), pp. 86-98.

circumstances (we noted above how this occurs in the *Sibylline Oracles* with regard to the Nero *redivivus* myth); this is natural and understandable. Thus, I see no reason for not accepting the traditional date of c. 90 CE for the Apocalypse of John. But that is not to deny that the Apocalypse of John could have been re-interpreted by Christians living in Asia Minor a generation later as referring to a subsequent setting and relating to a different historical figure, for it seems clear that the Apocalypse became a subject of some discussion among Christians around the very time of Hadrian's repression of the Second Jewish Revolt. The best example of this is Justin Martyr, who specifically mentions that his *Dialogue with Trypho* was written either while the war with Hadrian was still raging, or immediately after it was concluded (see 1.3; 9.3). In one place Justin goes so far as to describe Jerusalem as already destroyed by the Roman forces (108.3). In fact, he also goes on to describe the heavenly Jerusalem, which will replace the earthly one now destroyed, and appeals to the Apocalypse of John 20 as proof of God's promise to this effect (80.3–81.3). In short, we see the 'coming' of Jesus Christ contrasted with the 'coming' of Hadrian (and his armies) to Jerusalem.

Indeed we might go so far as to suggest that it is natural that the Apocalypse of John should be reinterpreted by the next generation of Christians (including such a figure as Justin Martyr) in light of these historical events and that Hadrian should be seen in light of the Nero *redivivus* mythologies which we know were current at the time. The veiled allusions to the Roman Imperial system we find in Revelation 13 and 17 clearly seem to be a reflection of an impending clash which the original author of the Apocalypse of John saw as being between the beast of the visions and Jesus Christ himself.[14] Might not the readers of the Apocalypse, and those listening to it being read to them in the churches of Asia Minor, be expected to think of Hadrian as the fulfilment of this prophetic vision? Might not his very arrival (*adventus*) in the province be seen as an antitype to Christ's glorious arrival which was eagerly and expectantly awaited? The answer may be in the affirmative if we remember that Hadrian visited the province of Asia on at least two occasions, once for an extended time in 123–124 CE, and once for a shorter visit in 129 CE (*LH* 13.1, 6) with the result of his visits to the East being that the Second Jewish Revolt broke out a few short years later. Almost certainly Hadrian stayed in Ephesus during his visit to Asia Minor, and given the strong tradition associating John the Elder with

14. Sherrer, 'Signs', pp. 599-610.

that city,[15] it is perhaps not too farfetched to see the Imperial visit as contributing to the heightening of eschatological expectation in the church that John left behind, an expectation which we see manifested in the way that they interpreted the Apocalypse of John. Given that the *Adventus Augusti* coinage began to appear at the very time that the Second Jewish Revolt was being hotly contested by Jewish nationalist forces and Roman Imperial armies, it is not difficult to imagine that some Christians would have interpreted the events of the day as heralding the end of the age and thought that the parousia of the Lord Jesus was imminent.[16]

15. Eusebius, *Hist. Eccl.* 3.18.1; 3.20.9; 3.23.4, relates that the Evangelist (and Elder) John returned to Ephesus after his banishment in Patmos and lived there until the reign of Trajan. This means that the imprisonment of John to Patmos was understood to have taken place during Domitian's reign. However, there are many problems with the Domitian dating as proving the confrontational setting of the book of Revelation itself. See Newman, 'Fallacy', pp. 133-39, for details. The matter is also discussed in P. Keresztes, 'The Jews, the Christians, and the Emperor Domitian', *VC* 27 (1973), pp. 1-23.

16. S. MacCormack, 'Change and Continuity in Late Antiquity: The Ceremony of *Adventus*', *Historia* 21 (1972), pp. 721-52, discusses how the Christian Church developed the idea of the *adventus* of Christ, particularly in art in the 4th and 5th centuries.

CONCLUSION

All coins are the product of three decisions. It is the economist or state treasurer who normally decides an issue of coinage is required; it is the politician or ruler who decides what designs are placed on the coins; and it is an artist who carries out those designs. Each of these stages involves the discussion of quite different problems, and the resolution of each is bound closely to the time and place of the issue. Coins are thus inseparable from the history of the state that issued them, and at the same time they provide a sequence of miniature pictures that trace the history of art from the seventh century BC to the present day.[1]

In various ways each of the three areas described in this paragraph has been addressed in the course of this volume. Economic, political and artistic considerations have all had their part to play within the discussion; at times they have been so intertwined that it would be impossible to separate one from the others.

I began this study by noting the way in which coins can serve as a bridge linking the twentieth century with the first. They can fire our imaginations and make history come to life in a way that written texts alone cannot. Coins are concrete, tangible reminders of peoples and places far removed from our contemporary world, and as such they fascinate us. There is a great deal that numismatics can offer to the student of the New Testament world when it is carefully investigated and properly applied. Not only can coins provide remarkable portraits of many of the key figures of the time, but they can also serve as a way to understand better the social and economic dynamics which prevailed. In short, we neglect the study of coinage at our own peril for they represent one of the best historical resources at our disposal.

In this volume I have concentrated on Roman Imperial coinage and the contribution that it can make to certain key passages and themes contained within the New Testament. Thus, I examined specific New Testament passages in light of the numismatic evidence: the 'Q' saying

1. Price, 'Foreword', p. 7.

of Mt. 24.28/Lk. 17.37; the passage in Acts 19.23-41 describing Paul's part in the riot of Demetrius and the silversmiths in Ephesus; and the triumph imagery alluded to by Paul in 2 Cor. 2.14 and Col. 2.15, are all cases in point. I also addressed several thematic topics, including the question of the apotheosis of the Roman Emperor as a backdrop for early christological thought, and the development of a doctrine of the parousia of Jesus Christ in light of the common understanding of the arrival (*adventus*) of the Roman Emperor to a given province in his various travels around the Empire. I even took a couple of numismatic tours of the New Testament world, one to Rome courtesy of coinage issued during Nero's reign and one around the constituent provinces of the Empire courtesy of coinage issued during Hadrian's reign. In each instance I suggested that coinage affords a new slant, a fresh angle, a different perspective on the issue under discussion.

All of this means that numismatics does have a valued, if overlooked, place in historical research in general, and within New Testament studies in particular. It is hoped that the study here presented will inspire others to discover other ways in which coins can enhance our appreciation and understanding of the New Testament and its world.

AN ANNOTATED RESOURCE LIST ON NUMISMATICS
AND NEW TESTAMENT STUDIES

I. *Books, Articles and Essays on Numismatics*
and the New Testament World

Abel, E.L., 'Who Wrote Matthew?', *NTS* 17 (1970–71), pp. 138-52: Mentions in passing the reference to the temple tax in Mt. 17.24-27 as part of a larger discussion about the dating and provenance of Matthew's Gospel. Partly based on the fact that the 'stater' (στατήρ) of 17.27 was most likely a didrachma (as mentioned in 17.24), and that it was valued as such only in Antioch and Damascus, the association of the Matthean community with the city of Antioch is argued. The debate about paying a temple tax is taken to reflect the Jewish-Christian community's concern over such matters in a pre-70 CE period (*contra* G.D. Kilpatrick, *The Origins of the Gospel according to St Matthew* (1946), pp. 41-42, 129, who takes it to reflect the period of 70–96 CE when the tax was being levied for the Temple of Jupiter Capitolinus).

Bauckham, R., 'Coin in the Fish's Mouth', in D. Wenham and C. Blomberg (eds.), *Gospel Perpectives*. VI. *The Miracles of Jesus* (Sheffield: JSOT Press, 1986), pp. 219-52: Essentially this is a full-bodied interpretation of the miracle passage recorded in Mt. 17.24-27. The main contribution to numismatic discussion revolves around the value of the didrachma mentioned in the passage and the level of taxation required (the half-shekel levy). Some discussion is also given to Nerva's *fiscus Iudaicus* as a means of dating Matthew's gospel.

—*The Bible in Politics: How to Read the Bible Politically* (London: SPCK, 1989), pp. 73-84: Discusses two passages which focus tangentially on numismatic issues: the question of the temple tax (Mt. 17.24-27) and the question of tribute to Caesar (Mk 12.13-17). The discussion here is primarily concerned with Jesus' attitudes to crucial political issues of his day.

Black, M., 'ΕΦΦΑΘΑ (Mk 7.34), [TA] ΠΑΣΧΑ (Mt. 26.18W), [TA] ΣΑΒΒΑΤΑ (*passim*), [TA] ΔΙΔΡΑΧΜΑ (Mt. 17.24 bis)', in A. Descamps and R.P.A. de Halleux (eds.), *Mélanges Bibliques en hommage au R.P. Béda Rigaux* (Gembloux: Duculot, 1970), pp. 57-62: Discusses the use of the term τὰ δίδραχμα which occurs twice in Mt. 17.24. Black suggests that the plural form is probably an 'Aramaized' form of the singular δίδραχμα which was regarded as a plural and treated as such. Black suggests that τὰ δίδραχμα be translated in the passage by a singular, '*the* tetradrachma'.

Bruce, F.F., 'Render to Caesar', in E. Bammel and C.F.D. Moule (eds.), *Jesus and the Politics of his Day* (Cambridge: Cambridge University Press, 1984), pp. 249-63: Makes passing reference to coins within its discussion, most of which deals with historical issues. Bruce notes that taxes to Rome were paid in Imperial coinage and follows the suggestion of J.D.M. Derrett that the temple tax was usually paid in Tyrian silver.

Cassidy, R., 'Matthew 17.24-27—A Word on Civil Taxes', *CBQ* 41 (1979), pp. 571-80: Offers an interpretation which takes the story recorded in Matthew to refer to civil taxes (as opposed to a tax for the temple in Jerusalem). Much of the discussion concentrates on the meaning of key words in the passage. Some helpful background to Roman taxation practices is also provided.

Derrett, J.D.M., 'Peter's Penny', in *Law in the New Testament* (London: Darton, Longman & Todd, 1978), pp. 248-49 [an earlier version of this study first appeared in *NovT* 6 (1963), pp. 1-15]: This study offers an interpretation of Mt. 17.24-27. Derrett discusses several suggestions about the identification of the coin that was found in the fish's mouth and concludes that it was a Tyrian shekel. The study contains a good discussion of the various Mishnaic sources which deal with the matter of the temple tax. There is also some discussion of Nerva's revocation of the *fiscus Iudaicus*.

—'Render to Caesar...', in *Law in the New Testament* (London: Darton, Longman & Todd, 1978), pp. 313-38: This is a wide-ranging study of the passage contained in Mk 12.13-17 and parallels. Background discussion of Roman taxation practices is offered and many relevant passages from the Mishnah which deal with monetary matters are treated. Derrett suggests that cultic worship, considered idolatrous to Jews, lies beneath the story, especially given Jesus' words about the 'image of the Emperor' which is found on the obverse of the coin brought to him within the passage. The coin which is at issue in the story is identified as a denarius of either Augustus or Tiberius. The obverse inscription, TI CAESAR DIVI AVG F AVGVSTVS, is cited once in the discussion which suggests that Derrett has the denarius of Tiberius, traditionally described as the 'tribute penny', in mind.

—'Luke's Perspective on Tribute to Caesar', in R.J. Cassidy and P.J. Scharper (eds.), *Political Issues in Luke–Acts* (Maryknoll, NY: Orbis Books, 1983), pp. 38-48: Concentrates on the interpretation of the critical passage without much recourse to the numismatic evidence. The main consideration which is relevant for my concerns revolves around the question of whether any Jews of Jesus' day (such as the Zealots) refused to use coinage which bore the Emperor's image. However, Derrett rightly concludes that the question of tribute to Caesar assumes that such coinage was in use at the time. He suggests (p. 42) that for the Zealots this would not have been an issue; the question probably never occurred to them.

Donaldson, T.L., *Ancient Architecture on Greek and Roman Coins and Medals* (Chicago: Argonaut, 1965): A classic reference work first published in 1859 by the distinguished British architect Thomas Leverton Donaldson (1795–1885). The chief contribution of the volume to numismatic studies is its numerous plates. These depict various buildings, temples, triumphal arches, monuments, altars and so on, which appear on Greek and Roman coins and medals of the ancient world. A total of 92 such coins are illustrated in large line-drawings (most approximately 3-4 inches in diameter). Included are representations of the Pharos of Alexandria, the Temple of Artemis in Ephesus, the Temple of Mars the Avenger in Rome, the Altar of Augustus at Lugdunum, Trajan's Column in Rome, the Triumphal Arch of Nero in Rome, the Colosseum in Rome, the Port of Ostia and many others. There is also quite an extensive discussion of each architectural monument listed.

Hamburger, H., 'Money, Coins', in *IDB*, III, pp. 423-35: A fairly helpful survey article which offers a basic introduction to the use of money/ coins from Old Testament times through to the New Testament period.

There is also a section on Jewish numismatics which is worth consulting for those interested in this specialized topic. The article does contain a photograph of the much discussed Yehud coin from Gaza which is housed in the British Museum collection (see the article by E.L. Sukenik [1934] below). Perhaps the most useful feature of the article is the line-drawings of some 43 different coins mentioned or alluded to within the biblical text. Incidentally, vol. I of *IDB* makes some errors in its use of photographs of coins to illustrate the portraits of Roman Emperors. Thus, on page 489 the coin used to provide a portrait of Caligula (37–41 CE) is actually a denarius from the reign of Vitellius (68 CE), while on page 640 the coin used to provide a portrait of Claudius (41–54 CE) is actually a denarius of Tiberius (14–37 CE).

Hart, H.St.J., 'The Crown of Thorns in John 19.2-5 (with 2 Plates)', *JTS* 3 (1952), pp. 66-75: Several Greek and Roman coins form the basis of this study which explores the presentation of obverse portraits of figures wearing radiate crowns. The suggestion is that these coins help us understand the curious reference to the 'thorny crown' of Jesus' passion. Eight coins are reproduced in the plates along with photographs of the particular palm branch (*Phoenix dactylifera*) out of which the crown was probably fashioned.

—'Judaea and Rome: The Official Commentary', *JTS* 3 (1952), pp. 172-98 and plates I-VI: This is a thorough and detailed article which surveys how the victory over Judaea in the various clashes it had with the Roman world was handled within the various propaganda media of the day. Numismatic evidence figures prominently within the discussion. Special attention is given to the various sestertia issued by the Flavian Emperors and by Hadrian which depict a personification of Judaea in various poses of subjection. An excellent place to begin a study of the Judaea Capta coinage and one which is frequently cited. Photographs of a total of 59 coins are included in the plates, as are some interesting views of relevant statues of the winged victory (the Brescia statue) and the triumphant Emperor in a cuirass. Some of the rarest reverse types are included in the photographs.

—'The coin of "Render unto Caesar..." (A Note on Some Aspects of Mark 12.13-17; Matt. 22.15-22; Luke 20.20-26)', in E. Bammel and C.F.D. Moule (eds.), *Jesus and the Politics of his Day* (Cambridge: Cambridge University Press, 1984), pp. 241-48: This study gives technical details of the various denarii issues of Tiberius, and argues that the 'tribute penny' brought to Jesus in the Gospel story was an example of one of these coins. The possibilities of other silver coins being identified as the 'tribute penny' are discussed. Photographs of seven coins are included in the essay, including various Roman denarii of Augustus and Tiberius, a billon tetradrachma of Augustus from Alexandria and the shekel of Tyre. Hart mentions in passing the textual variant ἐπικεφάλαιον which appears in D and other authorities for Mk 12.14, a reading which suggests that the question posed by the Pharisees and Herodians was one involving the payment of poll-tax rather than indirect taxation.

Horbury, W., 'The Temple Tax', in E. Bammel and C.F.D. Moule (eds.), *Jesus and the Politics of his Day* (Cambridge: Cambridge University Press, 1984), pp. 265-86: The focus in this essay is on the history of Roman and Jewish taxation practices and on the interpretation of Mt. 17.24-27. Numismatics figures only tangentially within the discussion.

Janzen, E.P., 'The Jesus of the Apocalypse Wears the Emperor's Clothes', in E.H. Lovering, Jr (ed.), *Society of Biblical Literature 1994 Seminar Papers* (Atlanta: Scholars Press, 1994), pp. 637-61 (with 4 plates): This study concentrates on the DIVVS issues of the various Emperors as a means of exploring how Jesus is presented within the Apocalypse. Special attention is given to coins from the Flavian dynasty, notably those minted during the reign of Domitian (the ruler probably on the Imperial throne when the Apocalypse of John was written). The article also contains a wide-ranging discussion of numismatic issues within the footnotes, including some interesting remarks on the tribute-penny episode recorded in Mk 12.13-17 and parallels. Twenty coins are reproduced in the plates.

Kadman, L., 'Temple Dues and Currency in Ancient Palestine in the Light of Recent Discovered Coin-Hoards', *INB* 1 (1962), pp. 9-11: Discusses a large hoard of coins found in 1960 at Isfiya on Mount Carmel. The hoard consisted of 3400 Tyrian shekels, 1000 half-shekels and 160 Roman denarii of Augustus (including at least thirty of Tiberius, as noted in H.St.J. Hart's essay from 1984 discussed above). Kadman suggests that the hoard represents a cache of temple dues in accordance with the tradition recorded in Mt. 17.24-27.

Kennard, J.S., Jr., *Render to God: A Study of the Tribute Passage* (1950): Does not agree with the standard identification of the 'tribute penny' as a denarius of Tiberius, but suggests instead that another silver coin more native to Palestine is meant.

Kraybill, N., *Imperial Cult and Commerce in John's Apocalypse* (JSNTSup, 132; Sheffield: Sheffield Academic Press, 1996): The basic thesis of this book is that the author of the Apocalypse believed the Imperial cult to be a monstrous evil which permeated the whole of the Roman Empire and because of this he warns his readers to sever all economic and political ties with Rome. Attention is focused on ch. 18 of the Apocalypse where maritime trade with Rome is mentioned at several points. In the course of discussion Kraybill makes use of several Imperial coin types which illustrate various aspects of commercial life. Two are discussed in particular, the famous Port of Ostia sestertius issued by Nero in 64 CE, and the sestertia issued by Domitian in connection with the Secular Games of 88 CE. Photographs of the two coins are provided.

Liver, J., 'The Half-Shekel Offering in Biblical and Post-Biblical Literature', *HTR* 56 (1963), pp. 173-98: A survey article exploring the half-shekel offering first introduced in Exod. 30.11-16. The article concentrates on the place that the offering had within Jewish religious practices and, although it does not deal explicitly with coins themselves, it does provide an important background to the story contained in Mt. 17.24-27. Some discussion of coin sizes and coin types is pursued in the footnotes.

McEleney, N.J., 'Mt. 17.24-27—Who Paid the Temple Tax?', *CBQ* 38 (1976), pp. 178-92: This study is primarily concerned with attempting to place the miracle story of the 'coin in the fish's mouth' within a proper historical setting (does it tell us of Jesus' own attitude to the question of taxation, or that of the early community, or that of Matthew the Gospel writer?). Numismatics *per se* does not figure prominently within the discussion. However, the article also contains a survey of scholarly debate concerning the Jewish background to the temple tax as well as a discussion of the size, weight and provenance of the possible coins used to pay it.

Montefiore, H., 'Jesus and the Temple Tax', *NTS* 11 (1964–65), pp. 60-71: The major contribution of this article is that it sets the story in Mt. 17.24-27 within a post-70 CE context, attempting to show how an earlier saying arising out of the ministry of Jesus is adapted to a new situation; the assumption throughout is that the temple tax was a secular rather than a religious obligation. The study contains some interesting discussion of Roman military protection for the conveyance of money to Jerusalem, the *fiscus Iudaicus*, and miracle stories from rabbinic folk-tales that are similar to the one recorded in Mt. 17.24-27 wherein a coin is found in a fish's mouth. There is some discussion of the relative weights and values of coinage connected with the temple tax.

Roth, C., 'The Historical Implications of the Jewish Coinage of the First Revolt', *IEJ* 12 (1962), pp. 33-46: The focus of this study is on the history of the First Jewish Revolt as gained from a consideration of the Jewish coins issued at the time. There are some interesting comments about particular coins, notably shekels bearing an inscription marking the fifth year of the revolt, and the Tyrian shekel, the preferred coin used in paying the temple tax. In this connection Roth mentions in a footnote the famous Isfiya hoard from Mount Carmel (4650 Tyrian shekels) as well as a hoard of some 500 specimens found in Qumran.

Scott, J.M., 'The Triumph of God in 2 Cor. 2.14: Additional Evidence on Merkabah Mysticism in Paul', *NTS* 42 (forthcoming): This article essentially deals with christological issues, particularly those arising from such 'throne' passages as 2 Cor. 5.10 and Rom. 14.10 which may be viewed against the backdrop of Merkabah Mysticism. Scott extends the discussion of Merkabah Mysticism to include 2 Cor. 2.14, the famous passage containing triumph imagery, and 2 Cor. 12.2-4, the passage describing Paul's heavenly ascent. His basic point is to suggest that the triumph imagery drawn from Roman military ceremonies invites an interpretation of 2 Cor. 2.14 in which God is the victorious conqueror who rides in his throne-chariot and leads the apostle Paul captive. Scott points to one particular coin type (RIC Nero 6-7), which appeared in 55 CE during Nero's reign, to support his interpretation (the type was issued in both aurei and denarii). The coins show on their reverse an image of a triumphal chariot being drawn by elephants. In the chariot are two figures on thrones representing the deified Emperors Augustus and Claudius (who sits at his right hand). Scott suggests that a comparison with the figures of God and Jesus Christ (who sits at his right hand) naturally invites itself. One illustration of the relevant coin type accompanies the study.

Sperber, D., 'Mark xii 42 and Its Metrological Background: A Study in Ancient Syriac Versions', *NovT* 9 (1967), pp. 178-90: This article attempts to use the various textual versions of the story of the widow's mite, notably the Peshitta, and the way in which the coin denomination is described in these versions, to arrive at a clearer understanding of the relative weights and values of coinage in the New Testament and rabbinic periods. Some interesting suggestions are made about the various synoptic interrelationships on this basis. A chart setting out the linguistic and denominational evidence accompanies the article.

Stauffer, E., 'The Story of the Tribute Money', in *idem, Christ and the Caesars: Historical Sketches* (London: SCM Press, 1955), pp. 112-37: This study focuses on the story contained in Mk 12.13-17 (and parallels). Stauffer discusses the story as an illustration of the clash between church and state which (he feels) runs through the New Testament. He identifies the 'tribute penny' as the common denarius of Tiberius with the Maxim Pontiff reverse. The chapter includes two enlarged black-and-white plates of the Tiberius denarius. Some interesting remarks about Pontius Pilate's minting of bronze coins for local use within Judaea are made in passing. These coins depict a *lituus* (a priest's wand) and a *patera* (a sacrificial bowl) on their obverse and reverse respectively. Both of these items were symbols of the Imperial power and cult and thus would have been offensive to many Jews of the day. Stauffer suggests that the decision to use these emblems on coins may indicate thinly veiled hostility against the Jews on the part of Pilate in retaliation for the incident involving the legionary shields in the temple precinct.

Theissen, G., *The Gospels in Context: Social and Political History in the Synoptic Tradition* (Edinburgh: T. & T. Clark, 1992), pp. 26-42: Discusses the reference to the 'shaken reed' in Mt. 11.7, and suggests that the reed was an emblem taken up by Herod Antipas and used as a motif on coinage issued in connection with the foundation of Herod's capital city of Tiberias in Galilee in c. 19 CE. Thus, the remark by Jesus in Mt. 11.7 is taken to be a veiled reference to Herod Antipas. The discussion here includes line drawings of three relevant coins.

Woodward, A.N., 'The Cistophoric Series and its Place in the Roman Coinage', in R.A.G. Carson and C.H.V. Sutherland (eds.), *Essays in Roman Coinage Presented to Harold Mattingly* (Oxford: Oxford University Press, 1956), pp. 149-73 and plates VII-VIII: Discusses the production of silver cistophori within the context of Roman history, particularly in the province of Asia Minor. The second-century BCE coins from Pergamum and Ephesus are discussed, as are those depicting Mark Antony from the first century BCE. The Ephesian and Pergamene cistophori of Augustus, Claudius, the Flavians, Nerva, Trajan and Hadrian are all discussed, as are the cistophori from Bithynia issued during Hadrian's reign. Of special interest to students of the New Testament are the coins depicting the Temple of Diana in Ephesus on their reverse. Photographs of 22 of the coins are contained in the plates.

II. *Additional Studies on Jewish Coinage and Roman Imperial Issues Associated with Judaea*

Barag, D.P., 'The Palestinian "Judaea Capta" Coins of Vespasian and Titus and the Era of the Coins of Agrippa II Minted under the Flavians', *NC* 18 (1978), pp. 14-23 + 3 plates (Plates 3-5).

—'Some Notes on a Silver Coin of Johanan the High Priest', *BA* 48 (1985), pp. 166-68.

—'A Silver Coin of Yohanan the High Priest and the Coinage of Judea in the Fourth Century BC', *INJ* 9 (1986–87), pp. 4-21 + 1 plate.

Barnett, R.D., *Illustrations of Old Testament History* (London: British Museum Publications, 1977, 2nd edn).

Betylon, J.W., 'Numismatics and Archeology', *BA* 48 (1985), pp. 162-65.

—'The Provincial Government of Persian Period Judea and the Yehud Coins', *JBL* 105 (1986), pp. 633-42.

—'Coinage', *ABD*, I, pp. 1076-89.

Brin, H.B., *A Catalogue of Judaea Capta Coinage* (Minneapolis: Emmett Publishing, 1986).

Hachlili, R. and A. Killebrew, 'Was the Coin-on-Eye Custom a Jewish Burial Practice in the Second Temple Period?', *BA* 46 (1983), pp. 147-53.

—'The Coin-in-Skull Affair: A Rejoiner', *BA* 49 (1986), pp. 59-60.

Hanson, R.S., 'Paleo-Hebrew Scripts in the Hasmonean Age', *BASOR* 175 (1964), pp. 26-42.

—'Toward a Chronology of the Hasmonean Coins', *BASOR* 216 (1974), pp. 21-23.

Hunkin, J.W., 'From the Fall of Ninevah to Titus', in T.H. Robinson, J.W. Hunkin and F.C. Burkitt, *Palestine in General History* (The Schweich Lectures, 1926; London: The British Academy, 1929), pp. 45-84 + 12 plates.

Jeselsohn, D., 'A New Coin Type with Hebrew Inscription', *IEJ* 24 (1974), pp. 77-78.

Kadman, L., *The Coins of Aelia Capitolina* (Corpus Nummorum Palaestinensium, 1; Jerusalem: Israeli Numismatic Society, 1956).

—'A Coin Find at Masada', *IEJ* 7 (1957), pp. 61-65.

Kanael, B., 'The Beginning of Maccabean Coinage', *IEJ* 1 (1951), pp. 170-75.

—'The Coins of King Herod of the Third Year', *JQR* 62 (1951–52), pp. 261-64.

—'The Greek Letters and Monograms on the Coins of Johanan the High Priest', *IEJ* 2 (1952), pp. 190-94.

—'The Historical Background of the Coins "Year Four…of the Redemption of Zion"', *BASOR* 129 (1953), pp. 18-20.

—'Ancient Jewish Coins and Their Historical Importance', *BA* 26 (1963), pp. 38-62.

Kaufman, S., 'A Note on Artistic Representations of the Second Temple of Jerusalem', *BA* 47 (1984), pp. 253-54.

Kindler, A., 'The Jaffa Hoard of Alexander Jannaeus', *IEJ* 4 (1954), pp. 170-85.

—'Epigraphic Table of the Hasmonean Coinage', *IEJ* 4 (1954), Plate 14.

—'More Dates on the Coins of the Procurators', *IEJ* 6 (1956), pp. 54-57 + Plate 8.

—'Addendum to the Dated Coins of Alexander Janneus', *IEJ* 18 (1968), pp. 188-91.

—'A Coin of Herod Philip—The Earliest Portrait of a Herodian Ruler', *IEJ* 21 (1971), pp. 161-63.

—'Coins and Coinage', *EncJud*, V, pp. 696-722.

—'Silver Coins Bearing the Name of Judaea from the Early Hellenistic Period', *IEJ* 24 (1974), pp. 73-76.

Kraay, C.M., 'The *Judaea Capta* Sestertii of Vespasian', *INJ* 3 (1963), pp. 45-46.

Madden, F.W., *History of Jewish Coinage and of Money in the Old and New Testament* (London: Bernard Quaritch, 1864).

Meacham, W., 'On the Archeological Evidence for a Coin-on-Eye Jewish Burial Custom in the First Century AD', *BA* 49 (1986), pp. 57-59.

Meshorer, Y., 'A New Type of YHD Coin', *IEJ* 16 (1966), pp. 217-19 + Plate 25.

—*Jewish Coins of the Second Temple Period* (Tel-Aviv: Am Hassefer & Massada, 1967).

—'Jewish Numismatics', in R.A. Kraft and G.W.E. Nickelsburg (eds), *Early Judaism and its Modern Interpreters* (Philadelphia: Fortress Press, 1986), pp. 211-20.

Meyshan, J., 'The Coinage of Agrippa the First', *IEJ* 4 (1954), pp. 186-200.

—'The Legion which Reconquered Jerusalem in the War of Bar Kochba (AD 132–135)', *PEQ* (January–June 1958), pp. 19-26 + 1 plate.

—'Two Notes on the Coins of Agrippa II', *BIES* 25 (1961), pp. 256-57.

Mildenberg, L., 'Yehud: A Preliminary Study of the Provincial Coinage of Judaea', in O. Mørkholm and N.M. Waggoner (eds.), *Greek Numismatics and Archaeology: Essays in Honor of Margaret Thompson* (Wetteren: Editions NR, 1979), pp. 183-96 + Plates 21-22.

—'Bar Kokhba Coins and Documents', *HSCP* 84 (1980), pp. 311-35.

—*The Coinage of the Bar Kokhba War* (Monographien zur antiken Numismatik, 6; Arrau, Switzerland: Sauerländer, 1984).

Minc, H., 'Ancient Jewish Coins in Correspondence between John Locke and Nicolas Toinard', *BA* 48 (1985), pp. 108-121.

Naveh, J., 'Dated Coins of Alexander Janneus', *IEJ* 18 (1968), pp. 20-26.

Perkin, H.W., 'Coins', in W.A. Elwell (ed.), *Encyclopedia of the Bible*, I (2 vols.; London: Marshall Pickering, 1988), pp. 485-94.

Rahmani, L.Y., 'Silver Coins of the Fourth Century BC from Tel Gamma', *IEJ* 21 (1971), pp. 158-60.

—' "Whose Likeness and Inscription is This?" (Mark 12.16)', *BA* 49 (1986), pp. 60-61.

Rappaport, U., 'The First Judean Coinage', *JJS* 32 (1981), pp. 1-17.

Reifenberg, A., *Ancient Jewish Coins* (Jerusalem: Da'ath Press, 1965).

Reinach, T., 'Numismatics', in I. Singer (ed.), *The Jewish Encyclopedia*, IX (12 vols.; New York: Funk & Wagnalls, 1905), pp. 350-56.

Romanoff, P., 'Jewish Symbols on Ancient Coins', *JQR* 33 (1942–43), pp. 1-15 and 435-44; *JQR* 34 (1943–44), pp. 161-77, 299-312, 425-40.

Ronen, Y., 'The First Hasmonean Coins', *BA* 50 (1987), pp. 105-107.

—'The Year-Reckoning of the Coins of the First Revolt', *NC* 2 (1962), pp. 91-100.

Schürer, E., *The History of the Jewish People in the Age of Jesus Christ (175 BC–AD 135)*, I (3 vols.; rev. and ed. G. Vermes, F. Millar and M. Black; Edinburgh: T. & T. Clark, 1973), pp. 602-606.

Spaer, A., 'Some More Yehud Coins', *IEJ* 27 (1977), pp. 200-203.

—'A Coin of Jeroboam?', *IEJ* 29 (1979), p. 218.

Sperber, D., 'A Note on a Coin of Antigonus Mattathias', *JQR* 54 (1963–64), pp. 250-57.

—'Palestinian Currency Systems During the Second Commonwealth', *JQR* 56 (1966), pp. 273-301.

Sukenik, E.L., 'Paralipomena Palaestinensia: I. The Oldest Coins of Judea', *JPOS* 14 (1934), pp. 178-84 + Plates 1-2.

—'More About the Oldest Coins of Judea', *JPOS* 15 (1935), pp. 341-43.

—'A Hoard of Coins of John Hyrcanus', *JQR* 37 (1946–47), pp. 281-84.

—'Some Unpublished Coins of Aelia Capitolina', *JQR* 37 (1946–47), pp. 281-84.

Sutherland, C.H.V., 'The Pattern of Monetary Development in Phoenicia and Palestine During the Early Empire', in *Proceedings of the International Numismatic Convention, Jerusalem 1963* (Tel Aviv, Jerusalem, 1967).

Thompson, H.O., 'A Tyrian Coin in Jordan', *BA* 50 (1987), pp. 101-104.

Wheaton, D.H. (and D.J. Wiseman), 'Money', *IBD* II, pp. 1018-21.

Yeoman, R.S., *Moneys of the Bible* (Racine, WI: Whitman, 1961).

Appendix

THE 'TRAVEL SESTERTIA' OF HADRIAN

Province or Region	Province Type	Restitutor Type	Adventus Type	Exercitus Type
1) Achaia		X		
2) Aegyptos	X			
3) Nilus	X			
4) Alexandria	X		X	
5) Africa	X	X	X	
6) Arabia		X	X	
7) Asia		X	X	
8) Bithynia		X	X	
9) Nicomedia		X		
10) Britannia	X		X	X
11) Cappadocia	X			X
12) Cilicia			X	
13) Dacia	X			X
14) Gallia		X	X	
15) Germania				X
16) Hispania	X	X	X	X
17) Italia		X	X	
18) Judaea	X		X	
19) Libya		X		
20) Macedonia		X	X	
21) Mauretania	X		X	X
22) Moesia			X	X
23) Noricum			X	X
24) Pannonia	X			
25) Phrygia		X	X	
26) Raetia				X
27) Sicilia	X	X	X	
28) Syria				X
29) Thracia			X	
TOTAL	12	13	18	10

BIBLIOGRAPHY

1. *Texts and Translations*

Classical translations used that are not listed here are from LCL. Pseudepigraphic works are from *OTP*.

The Gospel according to Thomas (trans. A. Guillaumont, H.-CH. Puech, G. Quispel, W. Till and Y. 'Abd Al Masih; San Francisco: Harper & Row, 1959).

Horace, *The Complete Odes and Epodes* (trans. W.G. Shepherd; Harmondsworth: Penguin, 1983).

Ovid, *The Erotic Poems* (trans. P. Green; Harmondsworth: Penguin, 1982).

Propertius, *The Poems* (trans. W.G. Shepherd; Harmondsworth: Penguin, 1985).

Tacitus, *The Annals of Imperial Rome* (trans. M. Grant; Harmondsworth: Penguin, 1956).

Virgil, *The Aeneid* (trans. W.F.J. Knight; Harmondsworth: Penguin, 1956).

—*The Georgics* (trans. L.P. Wilkinson; Harmondsworth: Penguin, 1982).

2. *Dictionaries, Encyclopedias and Multi-Volume Coin Catalogues*

British Museum Catalogue of Greek Coins (29 vols.; London: The British Museum, 1874–1927).

Cohen, H., *Description historique des monnaies frappées sous l'Empire Romain* (8 vols.; Paris: Chez M.M. Rollin & Feuardent, 1880–1892).

Coins of the Roman Empire in the British Museum (ed. H. Mattingly, E.A. Sydenham *et al.*; 5 vols.; London: Trustees of the British Museum, 1923–).

Crawford, M., *Roman Republican Coinage* (2 vols.; Cambridge: Cambridge University Press, 1974).

The Illustrated Bible Dictionary (ed. F.F. Bruce *et al.*; 3 vols.; Leicester: Inter-Varsity Press, 1980).

Roman Imperial Coinage (ed. H. Mattingly *et al.*; 10 vols.; London: Spink & Son, 1923–).

3. *Books and Periodical Articles*

Alderlink, L.J., 'The Eleusian Mysteries in Roman Imperial Times', *ANRW*, II.18.2, pp. 1426-56.

Alexander, P.J., 'Letters and Speeches of the Emperor Hadrian', *HSCP* 49 (1938), pp. 156-58.

Alexander, W., 'The Communique to the Senate on Agrippina's Death', *CP* 49 (1954), pp. 94-97.

Applebaum, S., 'Notes on the Jewish Revolt under Trajan', *JSJ* 2 (1950), pp. 26-30.

—'The Jewish Revolt in Cyrene in 115–117 and the Subsequent Recolonization', *JJS* 2 (1951), pp. 177-86.

—'Cyrenensia Judaica', *JRS* 12 (1962), pp. 31-43.

Askew, G., *A Catalogue of Roman Coins* (London: Seaby, 1948).

Altman, M., 'Ruler Cult in Seneca', *CP* 33 (1938), pp. 198-204.

Asimov, I., *The Left Hand of the Electron* (New York: Dell, 1974).

Askew, G., *The Coinage of Roman Britain* (London: Seaby, 1967).

Bailey, C., *Phases in the Religion of Ancient Rome* (London: Oxford University Press, 1932).

Baldwin, B., 'Nero and his Mother's Corpse', *Mnemosyne* 32 (1979), pp. 380-81.

Balsdon, J.P.V.D., *The Emperor Gaius (Caligula)* (Oxford: Clarendon Press, 1934).

—'Gaius and the Grand Cameo of Paris', *JRS* 26 (1936), pp. 152-60 + Plate 10.

—'The "Divinity" of Alexander', *Historia* 1 (1950), pp. 363-88.

Barnard, L.W., 'Clement of Rome and the Persecution of Domitian', *NTS* 10 (1963–64), pp. 251-60.

—'Justin Martyr's Eschatology', *VC* 19 (1965), pp. 86-98.

—'Hadrian and Judaism', *JRS* 5 (1968–69), pp. 285-98.

Barnes, T.D., 'The Victories of Augustus', *JRS* 64 (1974), pp. 21-26.

—'The Date of the Octavia', *Museum Helveticum* 39 (1982), pp. 215-17.

Barrett, A.A., *Caligula: The Corruption of Power* (London: Guild Publishing, 1989).

Barrett, C.K., *The New Testament Background: Selected Documents* (London: SPCK, 1956).

Bastomsky, S.J., 'The Emperor Nero in Talmudic Legend', *JQR* 59 (1969), pp. 321-25.

Beasley-Murray, G.R., *Jesus and the Future: An Examination of the Criticism of the Eschatological Discourse, Mark 13, with Special Reference to the Little Apocalypse Theory* (London: Macmillan, 1954).

—*A Commentary on Mark Thirteen* (London: Macmillan, 1957).

—*Jesus and the Kingdom of God* (Exeter: Paternoster Press, 1986).

Bell, A.A., 'The Date of John's Apocalypse: The Evidence of Some Roman Historians Reconsidered', *NTS* 25 (1978–79), pp. 93-102.

Bell, H.I., 'Antinoopolis: A Hadrianic Foundation in Egypt', *JRS* 30 (1940), pp. 133-47.

Benario, H.W., 'The Date of the *Feriale Duranum*', *Historia* 11 (1962), pp. 192-96.

—'The "Carmen de Bello Actiaco" and Early Imperial Epic', *ANRW*, II.30.3, pp. 1656-62.

Betylon, J.W., 'Numismatics and Archeology', *BA* 48 (1985), pp. 162-65.

Bickermann, E.J., *Religions and Politics in the Hellenistic and Roman Periods* (repr.; Como: Edizioni New Press, 1985).

Bilde, P., 'The Roman Emperor Gaius (Caligula)'s Attempt to Erect his Statue in the Temple of Jerusalem', *ST* 32 (1978), pp. 67-93

Bishop, J., *Nero: The Man and the Legend* (London: Robert Hale, 1964).

Blair, J. and K.T. Erim, 'Ancient Aphrodisias and its Marble Treasures', *National Geographic* 132 (August 1967), pp. 280-94.

—'Aphrodisias: Awakened City of Ancient Art', *National Geographic* 141 (June 1972), pp. 766-91.

Boer, W. den, 'Religion and Literature in Hadrian's Policy', *Mnemosyne* 8 (1955), pp. 123-44.

Bowersock, G.W., 'A Report on Arabia Provincia', *JRS* 61 (1971), pp. 219-42.

—'A Roman Perspective on the Bar Kochba War', in W.S. Green (ed), *Approaches to Ancient Judaism*, III (3 vols.; BJS, 9; Chico, CA: Scholars Press, 1980), pp. 131-14.

—'Augustus and the East: The Problem of the Succession', in F. Millar and E. Segal (eds.), *Caesar Augustus: Seven Aspects* (Oxford: Clarendon Press, 1984), pp. 169-88.

Bradley, K.R., 'The Chronology of Nero's Visit to Greece AD 66/67', *Latomus* 37 (1978), pp. 61-72.

Bradley, T.A., 'A Head of Sarapis from Corinth', *HSCP* 51 (1940), pp. 61-69.

Braumann, G., 'Die lukanische Interpretation der Zerstörung Jerusalems', *NovT* 6 (1963), pp. 120-27.

—'παρουσία', *NIDNTT*, II, pp. 898-901.

Braund, D.C., *Augustus to Nero: A Sourcebook on Roman History (31 BC–AD 68)* (London: Croom Helm, 1985).

Breglia, L., *Roman Imperial Coins: Their Art and Technique* (London: Thames & Hudson, 1968).

Brendel, O., 'The Great Augustus Cameo at Vienna', *AJA* 43 (1939), pp. 308-309.

Bruce, I.A.F., 'Nerva and the Fiscus Iudaicus', *PEQ* 96 (1964), pp. 34-35.

Bruce, F.F., 'Christianity under Claudius', *BJRL* 44 (1961–62), pp. 309-326.

Brun, L., 'Die romischen Kaiser in der Apokalypse', *ZNW* 26 (1927), pp. 128-51.

Brunt, P.A., 'The Revolt of Vindex and the Fall of Nero', *Latomus* 18 (1959), pp. 531-59.

—'The Administrators of Roman Egypt', *JRS* 65 (1975), pp. 124-47.

Brunt, P.A. and J.M. Moore) *Res Gestae Divi Augusti* (Oxford: Oxford University Press, 1967).

Bunge, J.G., '"Theos Epiphanes"', *Historia* 23 (1974), pp. 57-85.

Butcher, K., *Roman Provincial Coins: An Introduction to the Greek Imperials* (London: Seaby, 1988).

Buttrey, T.V., 'Vespasian as Moneyer', *NC* 12 (1972), pp. 89-109 + Plates 12-13.

—'Vespasian's Consecration and the Numismatic Evidence', *Historia* 25 (1976), pp. 449-57.

Cadoux, T.J., 'Marcus Crassus: A Revaluation', *Greece and Rome* 3 (1956), pp. 153-61.

Cahoon, L., 'The Bed as Battlefield: Erotic Conquest and Military Metaphor in Ovid's *Amores*', *TPAPA* 118 (1988), pp. 93-107.

Campbell, B., 'War and Diplomacy: Rome and Parthia, 31 BC–AD 235', in J. Rich and G. Shipley (eds.), *War and Society in the Roman World* (London: Routledge & Kegan Paul, 1993), pp. 213-40.

Campbell, J.B., *The Emperor and the Roman Army (31 BC–AD 235)* (Oxford: Clarendon Press, 1984).

Carbone, M., 'The *Octavia*: Structure, Date, and Authenticity', *Phoenix* 31 (1977), pp. 48-67.

Carlebach, A., 'Rabbinic References to Fiscus Judaicus', *JQR* 66 (1975–76), pp. 57-61.

Carradice, I., *Ancient Greek Portrait Coins* (London: British Museum Publications, 1978).

—'The Roman Empire and Provinces', in M.J. Price (ed), *Coins: An Illustrated Survey 650 BC to the Present Day* (London: Hamlyn, 1980), pp. 86-101.

Carson, D.A., 'Matthew', in F.E. Gabelein (ed.), *The Expositor's Bible Commentary*, VIII (Grand Rapids, MI: Zondervan, 1984), pp. 1-599.

Carter, G.F. and W.E. Metcalf, 'The Dating of the M. Agrippa Asses', *NC* 148 (1988), pp. 145-48.

Carter, J.M., *The Battle of Actium* (London: Hamish Hamilton, 1970).

Case, S.J., 'Josephus' Anticipation of a Domitianic Persecution', *JBL* 44 (1925), pp. 10-20.

Castriota, D., *The Ara Pacis Augustae and the Imagery of Abundance in Later Greek and Early Roman Imperial Art* (Princeton, NJ: Princeton University Press, 1995).

Catchpole, D., *The Quest for Q* (Edinburgh: T. & T. Clark, 1993).

Charles, R.H., *Revelation*, II (ICC; repr.; Edinburgh: T. & T. Clark, 1976 [1920]).

Charlesworth, M.P., 'Deus Noster Caesar', *CR* 39 (1925), pp. 113-15.

—'Some Observations on Ruler-Cult', *HTR* 28 (1935), pp. 5-44.

—*Documents Illustrating the Reigns of Claudius and Nero* (Cambridge: Cambridge University Press, 1939).

—'Nero: Some Aspects', *JRS* 40 (1950), pp. 69-76.

Chaumont, M.-L., 'L' Arménie entre Rom et l'Iran: I. De l'avènement d'Auguste à l'avènement de Dioclétian', *ANRW*, II.9.1, pp. 71-194.

Chilver, G.E.F., 'The Army in Politics, AD 68–70', *JRS* 47 (1957), pp. 29-35.

Chowen, R.H., 'The Problem of Hadrian's Visits to North Africa', *CJ* 65 (1969–70), pp. 323-24.

Clarke, G.W., 'The Date of the Consecration of Vespasian', *Historia* 15 (1966), pp. 318-27.

Clinton, K., 'The Eleusian Mysteries: Roman Initiates and Benefactors, Second Century BC to AD 267', *ANRW*, II.18.2, pp. 1499-1539.

Collange, J.-F., *The Epistle of Saint Paul to the Phillippians* (London: Epworth Press, 1979).

Collins, A.Y., 'Myth and History in the Book of Revelation: The Problem of its Date', in B. Halpern and J.D. Levenson (eds.), *Traditions in Transformation: Turning Points in Biblical Faith* (Winona Lake, IN: Eisenbrauns, 1982), pp. 377-403.

—'Numerical Symbolism in Jewish and early Christian Apocalyptic Literature', *ANRW*, II.21.2, pp. 1221-87.

Collins, J.J., *The Sibylline Oracles of Egyptian Judaism* (SBLDS, 13; Missoula, MT: Scholars Press, 1974).

—'The Provenance of the Third Sibylline Oracle', *BIJS* 2 (1974), pp. 1-18.

—'Pseudonymity, Historical Reviews and the Genre of the Revelation of John', *CBQ* 39 (1977), pp. 329-43.

Commager, S., 'Horace, Carmina I.37', *Phoenix* 12 (1958), pp. 47-57.

Court, J.M., *Myth and History in the Book of Revelation* (Atlanta: John Knox, 1979).

Crawford, M., 'Numismatics', in *idem* (ed.), *Sources for Ancient History* (Cambridge: Cambridge University Press, 1983), pp. 185-233.

Daly, L., 'Verginius at Vesontio: The Incongruity of the Bellum Neronis', *Historia* 24 (1975), pp. 75-100.

Daube, D., *The New Testament and Rabbinic Judaism* (New York: Arno Press, 1973).

Davies, M., *Matthew* (Readings; Sheffield: JSOT Press, 1993).

Davis, A.T., 'Cleopatra Rediviva', *Greece and Rome* 16 (1969), pp. 91-94.

Debevoise, N.C., *A Political History of Parthia* (Chicago: University of Chicago Press, 1938).

Deissmann, A., *Light from the Ancient East* (New York: Harper & Brothers, 4th edn, 1922).

Dodd, C.H., 'The Fall of Jerusalem and the "Abomination of Desolation"', *JRS* 37 (1947), pp. 47-54.

Dow, S., 'The Egyptian Cults in Athens', *HTR* 30 (1937), pp. 183-232.

Drury, J., *Luke* (JBPC; London: Collins, 1973).

Dunn, J.D.G., *Christology in the Making* (London: SCM Press, 1980).

Duruy, V., *History of Rome and the Roman People from Its Origin to the Establishment of the Christian Empire* (London: Kegan Paul, Trench & Co., 1885).

Earl, D., *The Age of Augustus* (London: Ferndale Editions, 1980).

Eden, S., *Military Blunders* (New York: Friedman, 1995).

Egan, R.B., 'Lexical Evidence on Two Pauline Passages', *NovT* 19 (1977), pp. 34-62.

Ellis, E.E., *The Gospel of Luke* (NCB; London: Marshall, Morgan & Scott, 1974).

Elsner, J., 'Cult and Sculpture: Sacrifice in the Ara Pacis Augustae', *JRS* 81 (1991), pp. 50-61 + Plates 1-7.

Erim, K.T., *Aphrodisias* (Istanbul: Net Turistik Yayinlar, 1989).

Fantham, E., H.P. Foley, N.B. Kampen, S.B. Pomeroy and H.A. Shapiro, *Women in the Classical World* (Oxford: Oxford University Press, 1994).

Farrar, F.W., *The Life and Work of St. Paul* (London: Cassell, Petter, Galpin & Co., 1919).

Fears, J.R., 'The Cult of Jupiter and Roman Imperial Ideology', ANRW, II.17.1, pp. 3-141.

—'The Theology of Victory at Rome: Approaches and Problems', *ANRW*, II.17.2, pp. 736-826.

—'The Cult of Virtus and Roman Imperial Ideology', *ANRW*, II.17.2, pp. 827-948.

Ferguson, J., *The Religions of the Roman Empire* (New York: Cornell University Press, 1970).

Ferrill, A., *Caligula: Emperor of Rome* (London: Thames & Hudson, 1991).

Fink, R.O., A.S. Hoey and W.S. Snyder, 'The Feriale Duranum', *YCS* 7 (1940), pp. 1-222.

Fishwick, D., 'Genius and Numen', *HTR* 62 (1969), pp. 356-67.

—'The Development of Provincial Ruler Worship in the Western Roman Empire', *ANRW*, II.16.2, pp. 1201-1253;

—*The Imperial Cult in the Latin West: Studies in the Ruler Cult of the Western Provinces of the Roman Empire* (2 vols.; Leiden: Brill, 1987, 1991).

Fitzmyer, J.A., *The Gospel according to Luke I–IX* (AB, 28A; New York: Doubleday, 1985).

—*The Gospel according to Luke X–XXIV* (AB, 28B; New York: Doubleday, 1985).

Flory, M.B., 'Honorific Statues for Women in Rome', *TPAPA* 123 (1993), pp. 287-308.

Ford, D., *The Abomination of Desolation in Biblical Eschatology* (Washington, DC: University Press of America, 1979).

Francis, F.O., 'Eschatology and History in Luke–Acts', *JAAR* 37 (1969), pp. 49-63.

Fraser, P.M., 'Hadrian and Cyrene', *JRS* 40 (1950), pp. 77-90.

Freyne, S., *Galilee from Alexander the Great to Hadrian, 323 BCE–135 CE: A Study of Second Temple Judaism* (Wilmington, DE: Michael Glazier, 1980).

Friesen, S.J., *Twice Neokoros: Ephesus, Asia and the Cult of the Flavian Imperial Family* (Leiden: Brill, 1993).

Fuchs, S., 'Deutung, Sinn und Zeitstellung des Wiener Cameo mit den Fruchthornbüsten', *RM* 51 (1936), pp. 233-36.

Fuks, A., 'Aspects of the Jewish Revolt in AD 115–117', *JRS* 51 (1961), pp. 98-104.

Funk, R.W., R.W. Hoover and the Jesus Seminar, *The Five Gospels: The Search for the Authentic Words of Jesus* (New York: Macmillan, 1993).

Gallivan, P., 'Nero's Liberation of Greece', *Hermes* 101 (1973), pp. 230-34.

—'The False Neros: A Reexamination', *Historia* 22 (1973), pp. 364-65.

—'Suetonius and Chronology in the "de vita Neronis"', *Historia* 23 (1974), pp. 297-314.

Gapp, K.S., 'The Universal Famine under Claudius', *HTR* 28 (1935), pp. 258-65.

Garson, R.W., 'The Pseudo-Senecan Octavia: A Plea for Nero?', *Latomus* 34 (1975), pp. 754-56.

Garzetti, A., *From Tiberius to the Antonines* (London: Methuen, 1974).

Gaston, L., *No Stone on Another: Studies in the Significance of the Fall of Jerusalem in the Synoptic Gospels* (Leiden: Brill, 1970).

Geldenhuys, N., *Commentary on the Gospel of Luke* (NICNT; Grand Rapids, MI: Eerdmans, 1979).

Gichon, M., 'New Insight into the Bar Kokhba War and a Reappraisal of Dio Cassius 69.12-13', *JQR* 77 (1986–87), pp. 15-43.

Gillam, J.F., 'The Roman Military Feriale', *HTR* 47 (1954), pp. 183-96

Ginsburg, M.S., 'Fiscus Judaicus', *JQR* 21 (1930–31), pp. 281-91.

Golan, D., 'Hadrian's Decision to Supplant "Jerusalem" by "Aelia Capitolina"', *Historia* 35 (1986), pp. 226-39.

Goodman, M., 'Nerva, the Fiscus Judaicus and Jewish Identity', *JRS* 79 (1989), pp. 40-44.

Grant, M., *Roman History from Coins* (Cambridge: Cambridge University Press, 1968).

—*The Army of the Caesars* (London: Weidenfeld & Nicolson, 1974).

—*From Alexander to Cleopatra* (London: Weidenfeld and Nicolson, 1982).

Greenhalgh, P.A.L., *The Year of the Four Emperors* (London: Weidenfeld & Nicolson, 1974).

Grether, G., 'Livia and the Roman Imperial Cult', *AJP* 67 (1946), pp. 222-52.

Griffin, M.T., *Nero: The End of a Dynasty* (London: B.T. Batsford, 1984).

Guenther, H.O., 'When "Eagles" Draw Together', *Foundations and Facets Forum* 5 (1989), pp. 140-50.

Gundry, R.H., *Matthew: A Commentary on his Handbook for a Mixed Church under Persecution* (Grand Rapids, MI: Eerdmans, 2nd edn, 1994).

Hafemann, S.J., *Suffering and the Spirit: An Exegetical Study of 2 Cor. 2.14–3.3 within the Context of the Corinthian Correspondence* (WUNT, 19; Tübingen: Mohr [Paul Siebeck], 1986).

Hainsworth, J.B., 'Verginius and Vindex', *Historia* 11 (1962), pp. 86-96.

Handler, S., 'Architecture on the Roman Coins of Egypt', *AJA* 75 (1971), pp. 57-74 + Plates 11-12.

Hannestad, N., *Roman Art and Imperial Policy* (Aarhus: Aarhus University Press, 1986).

Hanson, A.T., *The Paradox of the Cross in the Thought of St Paul* (JSNTSup, 17; Sheffield: JSOT Press, 1987).

Harris, R., 'Hadrian's Decree of Expulsion of the Jews from Jerusalem', *HTR* 19 (1926), pp. 199-206.

Hart, H.St.J., 'Judaea and Rome: The Official Commentary', *JTS* 3 (1952), pp. 172-98.

Hartman, L., *Prophecy Interpreted: The Formulation of Some Jewish Apocalyptic Texts and of the Eschatological Discourse Mar 13 Par* (Uppsala: Gleerup, 1966).

Hays, R.B., 'The Corrected Jesus', *First Things* 43 (1994), pp. 43-48.

Helgeland, J., 'Roman Army Religion', *ANRW*, II.16.2 , pp. 1470-1505.

Hemer, C.J., 'The Edfu Ostraka and the Jewish Tax', *PEQ* 105 (1973), pp. 6-12.

—*The Letters to the Seven Churches of Asia in their Local Setting* (JSNTSup, 11; Sheffield: JSOT Press, 1986).

Henderson, B.W., *The Life and Principate of the Emperor Hadrian* (London: Methuen, 1923).

Hengel, M., *The Son of God* (London: SCM Press, 1976).

Herington, C.J., 'Octavia Praetexta: A Survey', *CQ* 11 (1961), pp. 18-30.

Herz, P., 'Diva Drusilla', *Historia* 30 (1981), pp. 324-36.

Hewitt, K.V., 'The Coinage of L. Clodius Macer', *NC* 143 (1983), pp. 64-80 + Plates 10-13.

Hill, D., *The Gospel of Matthew* (NCB; London: Marshall, Morgan & Scott, 1972).

Hill, G.F., *Historical Roman Coins* (London: Constable and Co., 1909).

Hoey, A.S., 'Official Policy Towards Oriental Cults in the Roman Army', *TPAPA* 70 (1939), pp. 456-81.

Huzar, E.G., *Mark Antony* (London: Croom Helm, 1986).

—'Alexandria and Aegyptos in the Julio-Claudian Age', *ANRW*, II.10.1, pp. 619-68.

Isaac, B. and A. Oppenheimer, 'The Revolt of Bar Kokhba: Ideology and Modern Scholarship', *JJS* 36 (1985), pp. 33-60.

Isaac, B. and I. Roll, 'Judaea in the Early Years of Hadrian's Reign', *Latomus* 38 (1979), pp. 54-66.

—'Legio II Traiana in Judaea', *ZPE* 33 (1979), pp. 149-56.

—'Legio II Traiana in Judaea—A Reply', *ZPE* 47 (1982), pp. 131-32.

Jameson, S., 'The Date of the Asses of M. Agrippa', *NC* 6 (1966), pp. 95-124 + Plates 6-10.

Jenks, C.G., *The Origins and Early Development of The Antichrist Myth* (BZNW, 59; Berlin: de Gruyter, 1991).

Jeremias, J., *The Parables of Jesus* (London: SCM Press, 1972, 2nd edn).

Jewett, R., *Dating Paul's Life* (London: SCM Press, 1979).

Johnson, L., *The Gospel of Luke* (Sacra Pagina, 3; Collegeville, MN: Liturgical Press, 1991).

Jones, A.H.M., 'Numismatics and History', in R.A.G. Carson and C.H.V. Sutherland (eds.), *Essays in Roman Coinage Presented to Harold Mattingly* (Oxford: Oxford University Press, 1956), pp. 13-33.

Jones, B.W., *The Emperor Titus* (Beckenham: Croom Helm, 1984).

—*The Emperor Domitian* (London: Routledge & Kegan Paul, 1992).

Jones, D.L., 'Christianity and the Roman Imperial Cult', *ANRW*, II.23.2, pp. 1023-1054.

Kadman, L., *The Coins of Aelia Capitolina* (Corpus Nummorum Palaestinensium, 1; Jerusalem: Israeli Numismatic Society, 1956).

Kasher, A., 'Some Comments on the Jewish Uprising in Egypt in the Time of Trajan', *JJS* 27 (1976), pp. 147-58.

Katzoff, R., 'Where Was Agrippina Murdered?', *Historia* 22 (1973), pp. 72-78.

Kearsley, R.A., 'The Asiarchs', in D.W.J. Gill and C. Gempf (eds.), *The Book of Acts in*

Its First Century Setting. II. *Graeco-Roman Setting* (Grand Rapids, MI: Eerdmans, 1994), pp. 363-76.

Kee, H.C., 'A Century of Quests for the Culturally Compatible Jesus', *TTod* 51 (1995), pp. 17-28.

Keppie, L.J.F., 'The Legionary Garrison of Judaea under Hadrian', *Latomus* 32 (1973), pp. 859-64.

—*Understanding Roman Inscriptions* (London: B.T. Batsford, 1991).

Keresztes, P., 'The Jews, the Christians, and the Emperor Domitian', *VC* 27 (1973), pp. 1-23.

Klein, S., 'The Hadrianic Persecution and the Rabbinic Law of Sale', *JQR* 23 (1932–33), pp. 211-31.

Kleiner, F.S., 'An Arch of Domitian in Rome on the Coins of Alexandria', *NC* 149 (1989), pp. 68-81 + Plates 20-21.

Kloppenborg, J.S., *The Formation of Q* (SAC; Philadelphia: Fortress Press, 1987).

Kocsis, E., 'Ost-West Gegensatz in den Judischen Sibyllinen', *NovT* 5 (1962), pp. 105-110.

Kokkinos, N., *Antonia Augusta: Portrait of a Great Roman Lady* (London: Routledge & Kegan Paul, 1992).

Kraay, C.M., 'The Bronze Coinage of Vespasian: Classification and Attribution', in R.A.G. Carson and C.M. Kraay (eds.), *Scripta Nummaria Romana: Essays Presented to Humphrey Sutherland* (London: Spink & Son Ltd, 1978), pp. 47-57.

Kraeling, C.H., 'The Episode of the Roman Standards at Jerusalem', *HTR* 35 (1942), pp. 263-89.

Kreitzer, L.J., *Jesus and God in Paul's Eschatology* (JSNTSup, 19; Sheffield: JSOT Press, 1987).

Kuttner, A.L., *Dynasty and Empire in the Age of Augustus: The Case of the Boscoreale Cups* (Berkeley, CA: University of California Press, 1995).

Lambert, R., *Beloved and God* (London: Weidenfeld & Nicolson, 1984).

Lawrence, J., 'Nero Redivivus', *Fides et Historia* 11 (1978), pp. 54-66.

Leaney, A.R.C., *The Gospel according to St. Luke* (London: A. & C. Black, 1958).

LiDonnici, L.R., 'The Images of Artemis Ephesia and Greco-Roman Worship: A Reconsideration', *HTR* 85 (1992), pp. 389-415.

Lifschitz, B., 'Sur la Date du transfert de la legion VI Ferrata en Palestine', *Latomus* 19 (1960), pp. 109-111.

Lightfoot, J.B., *Saint Paul's Epistle to the Philippians* (London: Macmillan, 1885).

Lincoln, A.T., *Ephesians* (WBC, 42; Dallas, TX: Word Books, 1990).

Lindsay, H., 'Suetonius as *Ab Epistulis* to Hadrian and the Early History of the Imperial Correspondence', *Historia* 43 (1994), pp. 454-68

Lindsay, J., *Cleopatra* (London: Constable & Company Ltd, 1971).

Lohse, E., *The New Testament Environment* (London: SCM Press, 1976).

Longden, R.P., 'Notes on the Parthian Campaign of Trajan', *JRS* 21 (1931), pp. 1-35.

Luce, J.V., 'Cleopatra as Fatale Monstrum (Hor., Carm. I.37.21)', *CQ* 57 (1963), pp. 251-57.

MacCormack, S., 'Change and Continuity in Late Antiquity: The Ceremony of Adventus', *Historia* 21 (1972), pp. 721-52.

MacDonald, D.R., 'A Conjectural Emendation of 1 Cor. 15.31-32: Or the Case of the Misplaced Lion Fight', *HTR* 73 (1980), pp. 265-76.

MacDowall, D.W., 'The Organisation of the Julio-Claudian Mint at Rome', in R.A.G

Striking New Images

Carson and C.M. Kraay (eds.), *Scripta Nummaria Romana: Essays Presented to Humphrey Sutherland* (London: Spink & Son Ltd, 1978), pp. 32-46.

Maclaren, A., *Expositions of Holy Scripture: The Gospel according to St Matthew (Chapters XVIII–XXVIII)* (London: Hodder & Stoughton, 1906).

Madden, F.W., *History of Jewish Coinage and of Money in the Old and New Testament* (London: Bernard Quaritch, 1864).

Magie, D., 'The Mission of Agrippa to the Orient in 23 BC', *CP* 3 (1908), pp. 145-52.

—*Roman Rule in Asia Minor to the End of the Third Century after Christ* (Princeton, NJ: Princeton University Press, 1950).

—'Egytian Deities in Asia Minor in Inscriptions and on Coins', *AJA* 57 (1953), pp. 163-87.

Maier, P.L., 'The Episode of the Golden Roman Shields at Jerusalem', *HTR* 62 (1969), pp. 109-121.

Malherbe, A.J., 'The Beasts at Ephesus', *JBL* 87 (1968), pp. 71-80.

Mandell, S., 'Who Paid the Temple Tax When the Jews Were under Roman Rule?', *HTR* 77 (1984), pp. 223-32.

Manning, C.E., 'Acting and Nero's Conception of the Principate', *Greece and Rome* 22 (1975), pp. 164-75.

Mantel, H., 'The Causes of the Bar Kokba Revolt', *JQR* 58 (1967–68), pp. 224-42 and 274-96.

Marshall, B.A., 'Crassus' Ovation in 71 BC', *Historia* 21 (1972), pp. 669-73.

—*Crassus: A Political Biography* (Amsterdam: A.M. Hakkert, 1976).

Marshall, I.H., *Commentary on the Gospel of Luke* (NICNT; Grand Rapids, MI: Eerdmanns, 1979).

Martin, C., 'The Gods of the Imperial Roman Army', *History Today* 19 (1969), pp. 255-63.

Maxfield, V.A., *The Military Decorations of the Roman Army* (London: B.T. Batsford, 1981).

McDonald, S.M., 'Phoenix Redivivus', *Phoenix* 14 (1960), pp. 187-206.

Meiklejohn, K.W., 'Alexander Helios and Caesarion', *JRS* 24 (1934), pp. 191-95.

Meshorer, Y., *Jewish Coins of the Second Temple Period* (Tel Aviv: Am Hassefer and Massada, 1967).

Metcalf, W.E., 'Hadrian, IOVIS OLYMPIVS', *Mnemosyne* 27 (1974), pp. 59-66.

Meyer, H.D., *Die Aussenpolitik des Augustus und die Augusteische Dichtung* (Kölner Historische Abhandlungen, 5; Böhlau Verlag: Köln, 1961).

Meyshan, J., 'The Legion which Reconquered Jerusalem in the War of Bar Kochba (AD 132–135)', *PEQ* (January–June, 1958), pp. 19-26.

Mildenberg, L., 'Bar Kochba Coins and Documents', *HSCP* 84 (1980), pp. 311-35.

Millar, F., *The Roman Near East (31 BC–AD 337)* (Cambridge, MA: Harvard University Press, 1993).

Momigliano, A., 'Nero', *CAH*, X, pp. 702-80.

Mor, M., 'The Bar-Kokhba Revolt and Non-Jewish Participants', *JJS* 36 (1985), pp. 200-209.

Moretti. G., *The Ara Pacis Augustae* (Rome: Instituto Poligrafico Dello State, 1961).

Mørkholm, Ø., *Studies in the Coinage of Antiochus IV of Syria* (Copenhagen, 1963).

Moule, C.F.D., *The Epistles to the Colossians and to Philemon* (Cambridge: Cambridge University Press, 1957).

Newell, E.T., *Royal Greek Portrait Coins* (Racine, WI: Whitman, 1937).

—*Standard Ptolemaic Silver* (New York: Sanford J. Durst, 1981).

Newman, B., 'The Fallacy of the Domitian Hypothesis', *NTS* 10 (1963–64), pp. 133-39.

Nock, A.D., 'Notes on the Ruler-Cult, I-IV', *JHS* 48 (1924), pp. 21-43.

—'ΣΥΝΝΑΟΣ ΘΕΟΣ', *HSCP* 41 (1930), pp. 1-62.

—'Religious Developments from the Close of the Republic to the Death of Nero', *CAH*, X, pp. 465-511.

—'The Emperor's Divine Comes', *JRS* 37 (1947), pp. 102-116.

—'The Roman Army and the Roman Religious Year', *HTR* 45 (1952), pp. 187-252.

O'Brien, P.T., *Colossians, Philemon* (WBC, 44; Waco, TX: Word Books, 1982).

Oepke, A., 'παρουσία', *TDNT*, V, pp. 858-71.

Ogilvie, R.M., *The Romans and their Gods in the Age of Augustus* (New York: W.W. Norton & Co., 1969).

Oliver, J.H., 'Documents concerning the Emperor Hadrian', *Hesperia* 10 (1941), pp. 361-70.

—'The Divi of the Hadrianic Period', *HTR* 42 (1949), pp. 35-40.

Osborne, R.E., 'Paul and the Wild Beasts', *JBL* 85 (1966), pp. 225-30.

Oster, R., 'Numismatic Windows into the Social World of Early Christianity: A Methodological Inquiry', *JBL* 101 (1982), pp. 195-223.

Oster, R.E., 'The Ephesian Artemis as an Opponent of Early Christianity', *JAC* 19 (1976), pp. 23-45.

—'Ephesus as a Religious Center under the Principate I: Paganism before Constantine', *ANRW*, II.18.3, pp. 1661-1728.

Parker, H.M.D., *The Roman Legions* (Cambridge: Heffer & Sons Ltd, 1958).

Parrish, E.J., 'Crassus, New Friends and Pompey's Return', *Phoenix* 27 (1973), pp. 357-80.

Payne, R., *Rome Triumphant: How the Empire Celebrated Its Victories* (New York: Barnes and Noble, 1993).

Pearson, B.A., 'The Gospel according to the Jesus Seminar', *Religion* 25 (1995), pp. 317-38.

Perowne, S., *Hadrian* (Beckenham, Kent: Croom Helm Ltd, 1960).

Pesch, R., *Naherwartungen: Tradition und Redaktion in Mk 13* (Düsseldorf: Patmos, 1968).

Pleket, H.W., 'An Aspect of the Imperial Cult: Imperial Mysteries', *HTR* 58 (1965), pp. 331-47.

Plummer, A., *The Gospel according to St Luke* (ICC; Edinurgh: T. & T. Clark, 5th edn, 1922).

Price, M.J., 'Foreword', in *idem* (ed.), *Coins: An Illustrated Survey—650 BC to the Present Day* (London: Hamlyn Publishing Group, 1980), p. 7.

Price, S.R.F., 'Between Man and God: Sacrifice in the Roman Imperial Cult', *JRS* 70 (1980), pp. 28-43.

—'Gods and Emperors: The Greek Language of the Roman Imperial Cult', *JHS* 104 (1984), pp, 79-95.

—*Rituals and Powers: The Roman Imperial Cult in Asia Minor* (Cambridge: Cambridge University Press, 1984).

Rabello, A.M., 'The Legal Condition of the Jews of the Roman Empire', *ANRW*, II.13, pp. 662-762.

Ramage, E.S., 'Denigration of Predecessor under Claudius, Galba, and Vespasian', *Historia* 32 (1983), pp. 201-14.

Raubitschek, A.E., 'Octavia's Deification in Athens', *TPAPA* 77 (1946), pp. 146-50.

Rea, J.R., 'The Legio II Traiana in Judaea?', *ZPE* 38 (1980), pp. 220-22.

Reece, B., 'The Date of Nero's Death', *AJP* 90 (1969), pp. 72-74.

Reece, R., *Coinage in Roman Britain* (London: Seaby, 1987).

Reicke, B., 'Synoptic Prophecies on the Destruction of Jerusalem', in D.A. Aune (ed.), *Studies in New Testament and Early Christian Literature: Essays in Honor of Allen F. Wikgren* (NovTSup, 33; Leiden: Brill, 1972), pp. 121-34.

Reynolds, J.M., 'New Evidence for the Imperial Cult in Julio-Claudian Aphrodisias', *ZPE* 43 (1981), pp. 317-27.

Richardson, G.W., 'Actium', *JRS* 27 (1937), pp. 153-64.

Richmond, I.A., 'The Roman Army and Roman Religion', *BJRL* 45 (1962–63), pp. 185-97.

Rigaux, B., 'βδέλυγμα τῆς ἐρημώσεως: Mc 13,14; Mt 24,15', *Biblica* 40 (1959), pp. 675-83.

Roberts, A., *Mark Antony: His Life and Times* (Upton-upon-Severn: Malvern Publishing, 1988).

Roberts, C.H., *The Antinoopolis Papyri* (London: Egypt Exploration Society, 1950), pp. 39-40.

Robertson, A.S., 'Romano-British Coin Hoards: Their Numismatic, Archaeological and Historical Significance', in J. Casey and R. Reece (eds.), *Coins and the Archaeologist* (London: Seaby, 2nd edn, 1988), pp. 13-38.

—'The Circulation of Roman Coins in North Britain: The Evidence of Hoards and Site-Finds from Scotland', in R.A.G. Carson and C.M. Kraay (eds.), *Scripta Nummaria Romana: Essays Presented to Humphrey Sutherland* (London: Spink & Son Ltd, 1978), pp. 186-216.

Romer, F.E., 'A Numismatic Date for the Departure of C. Caesar?', *TPAPA* 108 (1978), pp. 187-202.

—'Gaius Caesar's Military Diplomacy in the East', *TPAPA* 109 (1979), pp. 199-214.

Rosenau, H., *Vision of the Temple: The Image of the Temple of Jerusalem in Judaism and Christianity* (London: Oresko Books, 1979).

Rossi, L., *Trajan's Column and the Dacian Wars* (London: Thames and Hudson, 1971).

Roth, C., 'An Ordinance against Images in Jerusalem, AD 66', *HTR* 49 (1956), pp. 169-77.

Roxan, M., 'The Auxilia of Mauretania Tingitana', *Latomus* 32 (1973), pp. 838-55.

Sadek, M., 'On the Billon Output of the Alexandrian Mint under Nero', *Phoenix* 20 (1966), pp. 131-47.

Sandford, E.M., 'Nero and the East', *HSCP* 48 (1937), pp. 75-103.

Schäfer, P., 'Hadrian's Policy in Judaea and the Bar Kokhba Revolt: A Reassessment', in P.R. Davies and R.T. White (eds.), *A Tribute to Geza Vermes: Essays on Jewish and Christian Literature and History* (JSOTSup, 100; Sheffield: JSOT Press, 1990), pp. 281-303.

Schnackenburg, R., 'Der eschatologische Abschnitt Lk 17.20-37', in A. Descamps and A. de Halleux (eds.), *Mélanges Bibliques: En Hommage au R.P. Béda Rigaux* (Gembloux: Duculot, 1970), pp. 213-34.

Schotter, D.C.A., 'The Principate of Nerva: Some Observations on the Coin Evidence', *Historia* 32 (1983), pp. 215-26.

Schulz, S., *Q: Die Spruchquelle der Evangelisten* (Zürich: Theologische Verlag, 1972).

Schürer, E., *The History of the Jewish People in the Age of Jesus Christ*, I (3 vols.; rev. and ed. G. Vermes, F. Millar and M. Black; Edinburgh: T. & T. Clark, 1973).

Scott, J.M., 'The Triumph of God in 2 Cor 2.14: Additional Evidence on Merkabah Mysticism in Paul', *NTS* 42 (forthcoming).

Scott, K., 'The Identification of Augustus with Romulus-Quirinus', *TPAPA* 56 (1925), pp. 82-105.

—'Plutarch and the Ruler Cult', *TPAPA* 60 (1929), pp. 117-35.

—'Emperor Worship in Ovid', *TPAPA* 61 (1930), pp. 43-49.

—'The Significance of Statues in Precious Metals in Emperor Worship', *TPAPA* 62 (1931), pp. 101-123.

—'Tiberius' Refusal of the Title "Augustus"', *CP* 27 (1932), pp. 43-50.

—'The Elder and Younger Pliny on Emperor Worship', *TPAPA* 63 (1932), pp. 156-65.

—'The Sidus Julium and the Apotheosis of Caesar', *CP* 36 (1941), pp. 257-72.

Scott, R.D., 'The Death of Nero's Mother (Tacitus, Annals, XIV, 1-13)', *Latomus* 33 (1974), pp. 105-15.

Scramuzza, V.M., *The Emperor Claudius* (Cambridge, MA: Harvard University Press, 1940).

Sear, D.R., *Roman Coins and their Values* (London: Seaby, 2nd rev. edn, 1974).

—*Greek Imperial Coins and their Values: The Local Coinages of the Roman Empire* (London: Seaby, 1982).

Seltman, C., 'The Wardrobe of Artemis', *NC* 12 (1952), pp. 33-51 + Plates 5-6.

Sherrer, S.J., 'Signs and Wonders in the Imperial Cult: A New Look at a Roman Religious Institution in the Light of Rev. 13.13-15', *JBL* 103 (1984), pp. 599-610.

Sherwin-White, A.N., 'Early Persecutions and Roman Law Again', *JTS* 3 (1952), pp. 199-213.

—*Roman Society and Roman Law in the New Testament* (Oxford: Oxford University Press, 1963).

—'Why Were the Early Christians Persecuted?—An Amendment', *PP* 27 (1964), pp. 23-27.

—*Fifty Letters of Pliny* (Oxford: Oxford University Press, 2nd edn, 1969).

—*Roman Foreign Policy in the East (168 BC to AD 1)* (London: Gerald Duckworth, 1984).

Shotter, D.C.A., 'A Time-Table for the *Bellum Neronis*', *Historia* 24 (1975), pp. 59-74.

Sijpesteijn, P.J., 'A New Document concerning Hadrian's Visit to Egypt', *Historia* 18 (1969), pp. 109-18.

Simonetta, B., 'On Some Tetradrachms of Orodes II and the Probable Issues of Pacorus I', *NC* 18 (1978) pp. 7-13.

Simpson, C.J., 'The Date of the Dedication of the Temple of Mars Ultor', *JRS* 67 (1977), pp. 91-94.

—'The Cult of the Emperor Gaius', *Latomus* 40 (1981), pp. 489-511.

Skeat, T.C., 'The Last Days of Cleopatra', *JRS* 43 (1953), pp. 98-100.

Slingerland, D., 'Suetonius *Claudius* 25.4, Acts 18, and Paulus Orosius' *Historiarum Adversum Paganos Libri VII*: Dating the Claudian Expulsion(s) of Roman Jews', *JQR* 83 (1992–93), pp. 127-44.

Smallwood, E.M., 'The Hadrianic Inscription from the Caesareum at Cyrene', *JRS* 42 (1952), pp. 37-38.

—'Domitian's Attitude towards the Jews and Judaism', *CP* 51 (1956), pp. 1-13.

—'The Chronology of Gaius's Attempt to Desecrate the Temple', *Latomus* 16 (1957), pp. 3-17.

—'The Legislation of Hadrian and Antonius Pius against Circumcision', *Latomus* 18 (1959), pp. 334-47.

—'Addendum', *Latomus* 20 (1961), pp. 93-96.

—'Palestine c. AD 115–118', *Historia* 11 (1962), pp. 500-10.

Smith, D.E., 'The Egyptian Cults at Corinth', *HTR* 70 (1977), pp. 201-31.

Smith, M.S., 'Greek Precedents for Claudius's Actions in AD 48 and Later', *CQ* 57 (1963), pp. 139-44.

Smith, R.R.R., 'The Imperial Reliefs from the Sebasteion at Aphrodisias', *JRS* 77 (1987), pp. 88-138 + Plates 3-26.

Solon, G., *The Three Legions* (London: Constable, 1957).

Spawforth, A.J.S., 'The Achaean Federal Cult Part I: Pseudo-Julian, Letters 198', *TB* 46 (1995), pp. 151-68.

Spicq, C., *Theological Lexicon of the New Testament* (3 vols.; Peabody, MA: Hendrickson, 1994).

Ste Croix, G.E.M. de, 'Why Were the Early Christians Persecuted?', *PP* 26 (1963), pp. 6-38.

—'Why Were the Early Christians Persecuted?—A Rejoiner', *PP* 27 (1964), pp. 28-33.

Stiehl, R., 'The Origin of the Cult of Sarapis', *HR* 3 (1963–64), pp. 21-33.

Stinespring, W.F., 'Hadrian in Palestine, 129–130 AD', *JAOS* 59 (1939), pp. 360-65.

Stone, M.E., *Fourth Ezra* (Hermeneia; Minneapolis, MN: Fortress Press, 1990).

Stoops, R.F., 'Riot and Assembly: The Social Context of Acts 19.23-41', *JBL* 108 (1989), pp. 73-91.

Strobel, A., 'Abfassung und Geschichtstheologie der Apokalypse nach Kap. XVII. 9-12', *NTS* 10 (1963–64), pp. 433-45.

Strong, E., 'The Art of the Augustan Age', *CAH*, X, pp. 545-82.

Sutherland, C.H.V., *Coinage in Roman Imperial Policy* (London: Methuen, 1951).

—*Ancient Numismatics: A Brief Introduction* (New York: American Numismatic Society, 1958).

—*The Cistophori of Augustus* (London: Royal Numismatic Society, 1970).

—*The Emperor and the Coinage: Julio-Claudine Studies* (London: Spink & Son Ltd, 1976).

—*Roman Imperial Coinage: Volume 1 (31 BC–AD 69)* (London: Spink & Son Ltd, 1984, rev. edn).

—*Roman History and Coinage (44 BC–AD 69)* (Oxford: Clarendon Press, 1987).

Sweet, L.M., *Roman Emperor Worship* (Boston: Gorham Press, 1919).

Swete, H.B., *The Apocalypse of St John* (London: Macmillan, 1909).

Sydenham, E.A., *The Coinage of Nero* (London: Spink & Son Ltd, 1920).

—*Coinage of the Roman Republic* (London: Spink & Son Ltd, 1952).

Syme, R., 'The Imperial Finances under Domitian, Nerva and Trajan', *JRS* 20 (1930), pp. 55-70.

—'The Wrong Marcius Turbo', *JRS* 52 (1962), pp. 87-96.

—'Hadrian and Italica', *JRS* 54 (1964), pp. 142-49.

—'Guard Prefects in Trajan and Hadrian', *JRS* (1980), pp. 64-80.

—*Fictional History Old and New: Hadrian* (Oxford: Somerville College, 1984).

—'The Journeys of Hadrian', *ZPE* 73 (1988), pp. 159-70.

Talbert, C.H., 'Political Correctness Invades Jesus Research: A Review Essay', *PRS* 21 (1994), pp. 245-52.

Tarn, W.W., 'The Battle of Actium', *JRS* 21 (1931), pp. 173-99.

—'Anthony's Legions', *CQ* 26 (1932), pp. 75-81.

—'Alexander Helios and the Golden Age', *JRS* 22 (1932), pp. 135-60.

—'Actium: A Note', *JRS* 28 (1938), pp. 165-68.

Taylor, L.R., 'The Worship of Augustus in Italy during his Lifetime', *TPAPA* 51 (1920), pp. 116-33.

—'Tiberius' Refusals of Divine Honours', *TPAPA* 60 (1929), pp. 87-101.

—*The Divinity of the Roman Emperor* (Middletown, CT: American Philological Association, 1931).

—'Note XXII. The Asiarchs', in F.J. Foakes-Jackson and K. Lake (eds.), *The Beginnings of Christianity*, V (5 vols.; London: Macmillan, 1933), pp. 256-62.

—'M. Titius and the Syrian Command', *JRS* 26 (1936), pp. 161-73.

Taylor, V., 'A Cry from the Siege: A Suggestion Regarding a Non-Marcan Oracle Embedded in Lk. XXI 20-36', *JTS* 26 (1925), pp. 136-43.

Tcherikover, V., 'The Decline of the Jewish Diaspora in Egypt in the Roman Period', *JJS* 14 (1963), pp. 1-32.

Tcherikover, V. and A. Fuchs (eds.), *Corpus Papyrorum Judaicarum*, II (London: Harvard University Press, 1960).

Thompson, L.A., 'Domitian and the Jewish Tax', *Historia* 31 (1982), pp. 329-42.

Thornton, M.A.K., 'Nero's New Deal', *TPAPA* 102 (1971), pp. 621-29.

—'Hadrian and His Reign', *ANRW*, II.2, pp. 433-76.

—'Nero's Quinquennium: The Ostian Connection', *Historia* 38 (1989), pp. 117-19.

Tinh, T.T., 'Sarapis and Isis', in B.F. Meyer and E.P. Sanders (eds.), *Jewish and Christian Self-Definition. III. Self-Definition in the Graeco-Roman World* (London: SCM Press, 1982), pp. 101-17.

Tödt, H.E., *The Son of Man in the Synoptic Tradition* (London: SCM Press, 1965).

Townsend, G.B., 'A Clue to Caesar's Unfulfilled Intentions', *Latomus* 42 (1983) pp. 601-606.

Toynbee, J.M.C., *The Hadrianic School* (Cambridge: Cambridge University Press, 1934).

—'The Ara Pacis Reconsidered', *PBA* 39 (1953), pp. 67-96.

—'The "Ara Pacis Augustae"', *JRS* 51 (1961), pp. 153-56.

Trebilco, P., 'Asia', in D.W.J. Gill and C. Gempf (eds.), *The Book of Acts in Its First Century Setting. II. Graeco-Roman Setting* (Grand Rapids, MI: Eerdmans, 1994), pp. 302-57.

Trell, B.L., *The Temple of Artemis at Ephesos* (New York: American Numismatic Society, 1945).

Versnel, H.S., *Triumphus: An Inquiry into the Origin, Development and Meaning of the Roman Triumph* (Leiden: Brill, 1970).

Walker, S. and A. Burnett, *The Image of Augustus* (London: British Museum Publications, 1981).

Wallace-Hadrill, A., 'The Emperor and his Virtues', *Historia* 30 (1981), pp. 298-323.

Wardman, A., *Religion and Statecraft among the Romans* (London: Granada, 1982).

Waters, K.H., 'The Character of Domitian', *Phoenix* 18 (1964), pp. 49-81.

Weber, W., 'Hadrian', *CAH*, IX, pp. 294-324.

Webster, G., *The Roman Invasion of Britain* (London: Book Club Associates, 1980).

Weinstock, S., 'Victor and Invictus', *HTR* 50 (1957), pp. 211-47.

—'Pax and the Ara Pacis Augustae', *JRS* 50 (1960), pp. 44-58.

—*Divus Julius* (London: Oxford University Press, 1971).

Wellesley, K., *The Long Year AD 69* (London: Paul Elek, 1975).

Wenham, D., *The Rediscovery of Jesus' Eschatological Discourse* (Gospel Perspectives, 4; Sheffield: JSOT Press, 1984).

Wigtil, D.N., 'The Ideology of the Greek "Res Gestae"', *ANRW*, II.30.1, pp. 624-38.

Williams, M.H., 'Domitian, the Jews and the "Judaizers"—A Simple Matter of Cupiditas and Maiestas?', *Historia* 39 (1990), pp. 196-211.

Williamson, L., 'Led in Triumph: Paul's Use of Thriambeuo', *Int* 22 (1968), pp. 317-32.

Winter, B.W., 'The Imperial Cult', in D.W.J. Gill and C. Gempf (eds.), *The Book of Acts in Its First Century Setting.* II. *Graeco-Roman Setting* (Grand Rapids, MI: Eerdmans, 1994), pp. 93-103.

—'The Achaean Federal Cult II: The Corinthian Church', *TB* 46 (1995), pp. 169-78.

Wood, S., '*Memoriae Agrippinae*: Agrippina the Elder in Julio-Claudine Art and Propaganda', *AJA* 92 (1988), pp. 409-426.

Woodward, A.M., 'Notes on the Augustan Cistophori', *NC* 12 (1952), pp. 19-32.

Wright, F.A., *Marcus Agrippa: Organizer of Victory* (London: George Routledge & Sons, 1937).

Wright, N.T., *The New Testament and the People of God* (London: SPCK, 1992).

Wyke, M., 'Augustan Cleopatras: Female Power and Poetic Authority', in A. Powell (ed.), *Roman Poetry and Propaganda in the Age of Augustus* (London: Bristol Classical Press, 1992), pp. 98-140.

Yadin, Y., *Bar-Kokhba* (New York: Random House, 1971).

Yourcenar, M., *Memoirs of Hadrian* (London: Secker and Warburg, 1955).

Youtie, H.C., 'The *Kline* of Sarapis', *HTR* 41 (1948), pp. 9-29.

Zahrnt, M., 'Antinoopolis in Agypten: Die hadrianische Gründung und ihre Priviligien in der neueren Forschung', *ANRW*, II.10.1, pp. 669-706.

Zanker, P., *The Power of Images in the Age of Augustus* (Ann Arbor, MI: University of Michigan Press, 1988).

Ze'ev, M.P. ben, 'Greek Attacks against Alexandrian Jews during Emperor Trajan's Reign', *JSJ* 20 (1989), pp. 31-48.

Ziegler, K.-H., *Die Beziehungen zwischen Rom und dem Partherreich* (Wiesbaden: Franz Steiner Verlag, 1964).

INDEXES

INDEX OF REFERENCES

OLD TESTAMENT

NEW TESTAMENT

INDEX OF AUTHORS

JOURNAL FOR THE STUDY OF THE NEW TESTAMENT
SUPPLEMENT SERIES